15.00

Cambridge Studies in Social Anthropology

NO. 5

THE MAJANGIR:
ECOLOGY AND SOCIETY OF A SOUTHWEST
ETHIOPIAN PEOPLE

Cambridge Studies in Social Anthropology

General Editors

M. FORTES, E. R. LEACH, J. R. GOODY, S. J. TAMBIAH

THE MAJANGIR

ECOLOGY AND SOCIETY OF A SOUTHWEST ETHIOPIAN PEOPLE

JACK STAUDER

Department of Social Relations
Harvard University
Cambridge, Massachusetts

CAMBRIDGE

AT THE UNIVERSITY PRESS

1971

Published by the Syndics of the Cambridge University Press
Bentley House, 200 Euston Road, London N.W.1
American Branch: 32 East 57th Street, New York, N.Y.10022

Library of Congress Catalogue Card Number: 78–155578

ISBN: 0 521 08094 0

Printed in Great Britain
at the University Printing House, Cambridge
(Brooke Crutchley, University Printer)

CONTENTS

ILLUSTRATIONS

TABLES

FIGURES

MAPS

Illustrations

PLATES

Between pages 72 and 73

1 (*a*) Young man with beer on his lips
 (*b*) *Shonggwidike*: young people making music following a beer party

2 (*a*) Two women drinking together from a pot during a ritual drink
    for a *waldi* spirit
 (*b*) Young girl digging holes to plant taro in a recently cut and
    burned *gedi* field

3 (*a*) Man dancing in the clearing around a *wai* and a *pan* hut
 (*b*) Man smoking 'Galla' tobacco from a waterpipe

4 (*a*) *Tapat* (on right, with bracelets) and others holding the spear
    in sacrificing a goat
 (*b*) Girls and children grouped around a hut during a ritual
    beer drink

To Riwai, age 5, who died of malaria
And to Bangwili who died in childbirth

PREFACE

This book is based on fieldwork which my wife and I conducted from November 1964 to September 1966 among the Majangir of southwest Ethiopia.

In Majangirland there are no roads, but narrow and difficult trails through thick forest, passable only by foot. Even animal transport is made impossible by the presence of tse-tse fly. From the town of Gambela, outside of Majangirland and served by air from Addis Ababa, my wife and I journeyed in November 1964 to the Majang settlement I call Til-Emyekai, on the Shiri River, two-and-a-half days' walk from Gambela (see Map 1, chapter 1). Til-Emyekai became our home and base for fieldwork during the following year.

Very little had previously been known about the Majang language; in fact my wife and I are presumably the first Westerners to have learned to speak it. As no Majangir speak English, we at first communicated with them through the Galla language which a few of them speak. As our own knowledge of Galla was as rudimentary as that possessed by most Majangir, we quickly abandoned it as we learned Majang. We acquired the language of the Majangir necessarily through close attention and use, without formal aids or instruction but with the advantage of having no one to speak to but Majangir, and no real alternative to speaking their language. Therefore virtually all our data were obtained directly, and through the native language, without any use of interpreters or intermediary languages.

In the spring and summer of 1965 we journeyed by foot to other areas of Majangirland, including the 'Sale' area north of the Bongga River (see Maps 1 and 3), and the areas south to the Mi'i, Godare and Facha'a Rivers. In September 1965 we moved our home and camp to the Majang settlement of 'Gilishi-Gabwi' at the confluence of the Facha'a and Bakko Rivers, a day's walk from the Ethiopian town of Teppi (see Maps 1 and 4), which is served by air from Addis Ababa. From Gilishi I later visited Majang settlements in the Alanga or 'Dawar' River area. The only regions of Majangirland I did not visit were those south of Gurrafarda, east of Teppi and north of the Baro (see Map 1).

In September 1966 we left Majangirland to return to Cambridge University, after having spent almost 24 months in Ethiopia, about 20 of these months in the field.

My field research, and a subsequent nine months in writing the dissertation on which the present work is based, were supported by a generous

Preface

Fellowship grant from the Foreign Area Fellowship Program. Following this support, I received a grant from the Wenner-Gren Foundation. I wish to acknowledge the financial assistance of these two bodies which made this work possible.

In Addis Ababa I was given practical advice, supervision and hospitality by Dr William Shack and Dorothy Shack, by Professor Jean Comhaire, and by Mr Georges Savard, to all of whom I owe much thanks. I wish to acknowledge also the essential help I received through the offices of Dr Richard Pankhurst and the Institute for Ethiopian Studies, particularly in gaining governmental permission for my research.

In the provinces we were given assistance and hospitality by many persons. Our greatest debt is to Alex Kydoniatis, and later his wife, for the help and kindness they showed to us in Gambela. In Teppi we received similar help and hospitality from Mr Kochera and from our close friend Tsege Kebede. We are grateful also for the friendly attention shown us in Meti by Ato Getachew.

In both Gambela and Teppi we benefited from the friendly and efficient services of the Ethiopian Airlines and of the Imperial Posts. We want to thank their several employees who personally helped us in so many ways, and extended as well their hospitality on many occasions. Especially we are grateful to Zerihoun Alemayhou of Ethiopian Airlines for the interest he showed in our work.

There had been no Christian missionary activity in Majangirland at the time of our arrival there, but in early 1965 the American (Presbyterian) Mission began its project of building an airfield, church, school and dispensary on the Godare River. We were able to visit for a short time the site of this project, and while there we were the guests of Mr and Mrs Harvey Hoekstra of the Mission. They were very helpful and kind to us during our stay.

Among the people in whose lands we travelled and lived during our time in the field – the Galla, Anuak, and of course Majangir – we received sympathy and hospitality from so many persons that it would be impossible to cite all of them individually. As it would seem unlikely that any of them might ever read this, such acknowledgments are perhaps unnecessary. Nevertheless, I would like to recognize those whom we remember especially: our first friend and good informant, Pendangke; our good neighbours Lapita, Tondeshiro, Yemyengkai and Kwedejop; our protectors Pajau and Yodn; our helper Sheshakan; our friends Iwiak and Shoshokek; our comrades, the youths Ngingkani, Yanggan, Podengat and Jilkit; and the old man Lempeshe.

I would like to thank several persons who helped me in England. Pro-

Preface

fessor Meyer Fortes gave me timely advice and encouragement, both before and after I went to the field. My fellow student Elizabeth Kennedy read and offered very valuable criticism of several chapters of this work. Dr Godfrey Lienhardt and Dr Paul Baxter, the readers of my Ph.D. dissertation, offered a number of useful criticisms. Dr Jack Goody supervised my research and the writing of my dissertation from beginning to end, and I owe him a great debt of gratitude for the innumerable ways in which he helped and encouraged me.

I revised my dissertation for publication while at Harvard University. I was encouraged in this project by Professor Evon Z. Vogt, who also helped me to obtain a small University grant to complete my work. I should thank Professor Vogt too as the teacher who originally interested me in the field of anthropology.

Finally, I should acknowledge the contribution of my wife Wunderley. Although not trained in anthropology, she provided constant and valuable assistance in my field research, and of course she was my co-worker in the various practical problems of everyday life in Ethiopia. Since our return, she has also helped me in various ways to prepare the data we collected.

J. S.

June 1970
Cambridge, Massachusetts

1

INTRODUCTION: THE MAJANG TRIBE

The 'Majangir', as they call themselves – 'Majang' in the singular or adjectival – are known to their neighbours by the various names 'Masango', 'Masongo', 'Messengo', 'Ujang' and 'Tama'. The Majangir are a small tribe with a population I estimate to be less than 20,000 people. They are sparsely settled throughout a rather large area, roughly 4,000 square miles, of thick forests on the southwestern edge of the Ethiopian Plateau. Their present extent of settlement runs from north of the Baro River near Dembidollo, southwards to the Gurrafarda Range, the Erbu (Arbuca) River and other tributaries of the Akobo. From east to west their extent of settlement is narrower, almost entirely restricted to forested areas lying at altitudes between 2,000 and 5,000 feet (see Map 1).

The Majangir are sandwiched between 'Nilotic' peoples such as the Anuak and Nuer to their west on the savannah of the Sudan–Ethiopia borderlands; and 'Cushitic' peoples such as the Galla, Mocha and Shakko-Gimirra, to their east on the highland plateau of Ethiopia. The Majangir are radically distinguished from the Nilotes and Cushites, their immediate neighbours, by language, culture and physical appearance. The Majangir are nearest in these respects to other little-known black peoples (Suri, Mekan, Zilmamu, Tirma, Tid, etc.) to their south, in Ethiopia and the Bom Plateau region of the southern Sudan. These peoples speak, like Majangir, languages of the Murle–Didinga group (Tucker and Bryan 1956: 87–91) which can be classed tentatively as belonging to a wider grouping called East Sudanic (Greenberg 1963: 168; H. C. Fleming, personal communication, 1966).

The affinities of Majangir with tribes to their south correlate with Majang traditions of having come from the south in the indefinite past. Genealogies and life histories indicate that Majang settlement in recent times has continued to shift northward. Northernmost areas of Majang settlement have been pioneered within living memory. But most of Majangirland, the area south of the Chiru (Shiri) River, has been settled for more generations than Majangir recall – at least three or four.

Unfortunately, Majangir have little interest in the past and retain few notions of their 'history' beyond the memories of living men. Nor are there written records mentioning the Majangir before this century, and what has since been written about them is scanty and often misleading (see Bibliography).

The areas that Majangir now occupy, or into which they are expanding, may be described as an 'ecological niche' in the sense that these areas are well suited to the modes of livelihood of the Majangir but not to those of their main neighbours, the Galla and Anuak. The Anuak are a riverain people, relying greatly on the slow, big rivers of the savannah for fishing and transportation. They do not try to settle in the thickly forested country rising to their east, where watercourses are numerous but small and shallow and swift, preventing canoeing or good fishing. The Galla are a semi-pastoral people, relying greatly on large stock which, below a certain altitude in this region, are exposed to bites by tse-tse fly pathogenic to cattle, horses and mules, but not to humans (cf. Evans-Pritchard 1940: 68). It is below this altitude, from about 5,000 feet down, that most Majangir are settled in the tse-tse fly zone where Galla and other highland pastoralists will not usually settle. Neither stock-raising nor canoeing nor fishing is a necessary or important element in Majang culture. Their culture is well adapted, instead, to the particular environment of Majangirland, and not well adapted to the environmental conditions of Galla or Anuak territory, in ways which I will describe in detail in the next two chapters.

If Majangir have indeed migrated recently into their present lands, there is no evidence that in doing so they displaced any previous inhabitants. Apparently they moved into a vacuum of virgin territory which only they were willing to exploit. Large tracts of unsettled territory still exist on the borders of Majang settlement, and beyond. Not only Majangirland but this entire region of Ethiopia appears greatly underpopulated in relation to the population that could, by their present modes of livelihood, support themselves in the region.

The general absence of population pressures in the area, and the absence specifically of foreign territorial pressures against the Majangir, have been an important condition for their society. Majangir have not been threatened over their lands; and they have never organized to defend their territories. The implications of these factors will be drawn out in subsequent chapters of this study.

Since the 1950s, with the introduction of coffee as a large-scale cash crop near Teppi, some Majangir in this area have been dispossessed of their lands by Amhara, Galla and other highland peoples operating behind the authority of the Ethiopian government. But this displacement of Majangir in one as yet small area has not affected the general situation of the tribe in regard to its natural resources.

That Majangir have not usually been in competition with other tribes

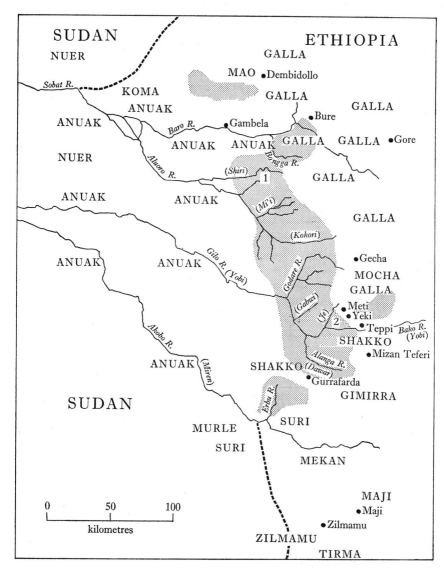

Map 1. Majangirland and surrounding region of southwest Ethiopia.

Key: Shading indicates lands used and settled by Majangir (in a few areas inter-spersed with members of other tribes). Names of towns are written in small letters. Names of ethnic groups are written in capital letters, and indicate approximate locations. In addition, Amhara and Galla are settled in all towns. Names of rivers in parentheses are Majang names only. Other names are in general use. ' 1 ' – Base area from which fieldwork was first done, 1964–5 (Til-Emyekai). ' 2 ' – Base area from which fieldwork was later done, 1965–6 (Gilishi-Gabwi, *dok Yodntung*).

Sources: East African Metre Grid Map, published by the War Office (Great Britain), Fourth Edition, 1947: G.S.G.S. 4355, Sheet NB 36/3. E. Cerulli 1956: map and *passim*. (Note: the locations of the Majangir (' Masongo ') in both of these sources are inaccurate. Distribution of the Majangir in Map 1 is based entirely on information collected in my own fieldwork.)

for territory does not mean that they have had only peaceful relations with them. Majang culture, as will be apparent, holds little or nothing of material value which would encourage plundering – except the Majangir themselves, as humans and potential slaves. Slave raiding and trading were rife in southwest Ethiopia around the turn of this century (see Montandon 1913: *passim*), and the Majangir were not spared. Frequently up until the 1930s and even in some instances afterwards, the Majangir were raided for women and children by bands of Galla, Amhara, Anuak, Shakko-Gimirra and (rarely) Sudanese Arabs.

The Majang reaction to these raids was invariably to flee, or hide. Little or no organized defence was attempted. Majangir say it was a hopeless situation, as raiders from other tribes were much superior to them in numbers of rifles and bullets. Even if they had been better armed, however, it is doubtful whether Majangir in most areas could have organized themselves quickly and effectively for war or defence. They not only lack the probably necessary political institutions (see below), but their mobilization would also have been made difficult by the dispersed nature of their settlements (see chapter 8).

On the other hand, the fact that the Majangir live in dispersed homesteads and not in villages no doubt allowed them to escape more easily from raiders, as large groups of Majangir could never be surrounded. At the alarms and shots of the first homesteads being attacked, Majangir of nearby homesteads could flee into the forest or towards other settlements. As the news spread throughout a whole area, persons could abandon their homesteads, taking their most precious possessions (iron tools, beads, chickens, etc.) with them. Such is the description Majangir give of their reaction to raids in the past. Individuals with rifles sometimes returned fire, but the general response to attack was to evacuate an area, to flee not fight. The primitive and difficult trails through the forests, and the danger to horses and mules of tse-tse in Majang territory, made it impossible for raiding parties to pursue Majangir more quickly than they could escape. And the thick cover of forest made it virtually impossible to find them when they hid.

While not able to resist their stronger enemies, Majangir were at least able to avoid the enslavement of most of their number, and thus to reconstitute their communities. If their food stores were not destroyed by the raiders, the Majangir could return to their settlements after the raiders had left. If the raiders did raze habitations and stores, the population would be forced to disperse to other Majang communities to seek food and shelter, and to make new farms. The effect of raids on Majang settlement and mobility will be discussed in a subsequent chapter (chapter 10). The important fact here to note is that because their mode of settlement and their environment protected them from total enslavement, and because ecological conditions prevented their territories from being occupied by neighbouring peoples, the Majang tribe has emerged relatively intact and independent from an era in which many groups in this region suffered either dismemberment, decimation, or reduction to virtual serfdom (Montandon 1913: *passim*; Corfield 1938: 123 ff.; Lyth 1947: 106 ff.).

This era ended when first the Italian occupation, and after it the post-war Ethiopian government, finally imposed 'peace' in the region, and definitely ended warfare and raiding. Otherwise, the Italian administration did not effectively penetrate Majangirland, and the subsequent Ethiopian administration, while attempting to collect taxes and discourage fighting, has so far had little effect on the constitution of Majang society. The limited effects it has had will be described below where pertinent. But it is important to realize that, except for the coffee-growing areas around Teppi where highland Ethiopians have settled among the Majangir, the national government has not established administrative or police posts within Majangirland. Majang society continues to function largely independently of interference from outside authority.

The relations of the Majangir with neighbouring tribes have not, of course, been confined only to warfare. Much borrowing of items of culture and some intermixing of blood have occurred. But despite intercourse with their neighbours, Majangir self-consciously share a distinct culture and language which set them apart from other peoples in their vicinity. The Majangir are a 'tribe' in this cultural sense, though as a tribe they are not united by political organization. Although trails are primitive and a man would need at least two weeks to travel from the northernmost to southern-most settlements of Majangirland, a great deal of communication is, in fact, maintained between different communities and areas. Variations in dialect and custom are very few between 'northern' and 'southern' Majangir. Generalizations made in this monograph, unless otherwise qualified, may be taken to apply to the Majang tribe as a whole.

Majang society may be described as virtually homogeneous in character. If regional differences are minimal, so are differences within given com-munities. All Majangir share the same, materially simple, culture. They all gain their livelihood in the same manner. They all possess more or less the same skills and same kinds of property. Their homes, their ways of dressing, are always similar. Their conversations, their ideas and views of the world, tend also to be similar, to conform to the same pattern. So does their behaviour.

Despite a conformity or homogeneity in these phenomena which should facilitate generalization, it is surprisingly difficult to characterize Majang society in simple, positive terms. It is much easier to characterize their society in a negative form, to say what it is not, what Majangir do not 'have', what is absent. For example, there is an absence of formal political or legal administration. There are no rulers or 'chiefs' or even councils of elders. There are no lineage heads. There are no lineages. No age-set system exists. Villages do not exist. Organized, corporate local groups are absent, etc. The list could be extended. Majang society lacks many, or most, of those familiar institutions by which societies of Africa and elsewhere are conventionally labelled and categorized in thumbnail descriptions of 'social structure'. It has been suggested to me that the Majang social system is 'fluid', 'not highly structured', 'lacking in formal, explicit organization'. The validity of these generalizations would depend on what was meant by such concepts as 'fluidity', 'structure', and 'formal'. I do not intend at the outset to discuss such generalities. Here it is enough to state the salient fact that Majang society totally lacks any organized, corporate groups having continuity in time beyond the life of an individual or family.

I have said that the Majangir lack corporate lineage groups; they do, however, have clans (*komwoyir*). Majang clans are 'corporate' groups in that members ideally share collective responsibility in cases of fighting and homicide. Majangir also conceptualize other kinds of activity in terms of clans. But clans or their local segments are not organized: they have no leaders, no representatives, no meetings, no joint activities. Collective action of any kind is never organized solely or even primarily on the basis of clanship. In practice, clanship among the Majangir has little to do with group action or group relations. It has more to do with dyadic relations, as an extension of kinship. A clan is a category of people.

Clan membership is inherited patrilineally. In other respects, such as kin terms, Majang kinship has a patrilineal bias. In practice, however, Majang kinship takes on a 'bilateral' aspect. Actual groups formed *ad hoc* for collective tasks are never based on kinship alone, but kin who do cooperate together may fall into any kinship category. In behaviour towards kin, little distinction is made between matrilateral and patrilateral relatives.

The important distinction in Majang society is between kin (*tekanir*) and non-kin (*gatiat*), or kin and affines. Affines are ideally, though actually not necessarily, non-kin; non-kin are potential if not actual affines.

Marriage is regulated by relatively high bridewealth payments and by initially antagonistic relations between affines. While a wide range of relatives is involved in minor ways, the marriage transaction is mainly a matter between two small groups: on the one hand, the prospective husband, his parents and brothers and half-brothers; and, on the other, the parents and brothers and half-brothers of the prospective bride. Polygamy is the ideal and is actually achieved by a large proportion of men during their lifetime.

Marriages often break down and the partners separate. Broken marriages, re-marriages, suspicions of adultery, arguments over bridewealth and, in general, arguments over women are a major source of disputes between men. Other major sources of disputes are debts, theft – particularly of honey – and drunken quarrels arising from apparently trivial reasons.

Whatever their source, disputes are not settled through the adjudication of impartial authorities. Public opinion, particularly the opinions of older men, may be brought to bear in informal discussions to persuade the principals to compromise or back down. But outsiders to a dispute will never intervene with force or the threat of force. These are the resort only of the parties directly in dispute. They may settle their differences by negotiations; or, more likely, they may adjust to a *modus vivendi* based on the incapacity or unwillingness of one or both parties to use force. But the sanction of self-help is recognized as legitimate, and is frequently employed by aggrieved parties either to seize property as recompense, or to retaliate bodily against an offender.

Disputes may lead to fighting, and fighting to homicide. Rarely can cases of homicide be 'settled' peacefully. Nor can vengeance and counter-vengeance usually be limited or regulated. Homicide tends to result in virtual war, on a small scale, between the kin and friends of the killer, and the kin and friends of the killed. The only solution is the removal, by extermination or flight, of one of the two groups (see chapter 10).

Such groups which form to exercise or resist force are always *ad hoc* and temporary. They are not based on territory. The persons occupying any given territory are never organized on a territorial basis as 'political communities' having exclusive interests, unity of action or recognized leaders (cf. Schapera 1956: 8, 16). Communal cooperation, as well as conflict, operates through groups which are *ad hoc* and temporary, and recruited on the basis not of a single principle but of a mixture of several: kinship, friendship, neighbourhood, affinity, social and economic reciprocity, ritual following, etc.

While no permanent political leaders ('chiefs') exist, because of the non-existence of permanent political groups, there are of course men who in different situations tend to exercise a sort of informal leadership based on relative age, experience, skill, personal influence and social relationships. Persons having these qualifications, and who are also ritual experts of the kind called *tapa* (sing. *tapat*), sometimes become exceptional leaders with chief-like functions. That is, they may organize and coordinate communal activities, attract followers and tribute, offer ritual protection from violence, mediate disputes, etc., as well as exercise the general mystical powers of *tapa* to divine the future, cure illness and manipulate the elements. Ritual prohibitions disallow *tapa*, even if they otherwise were able, from exercising physical coercion to enforce their will – though their moral influence and mystical sanctions are not inconsiderable.

Although *tapa* are distributed throughout Majangirland, only a handful at any one time will have attained the exceptional influence described; and most Majangir will live outside their zones of influence. The extent of a *tapat*'s powers is personal, and at his (or her) death no one will immediately succeed to his influence, though a child of his may, if otherwise well qualified, eventually do so. But in any case, while the ritual role of the *tapat* is well defined, the secular or 'political' extension of this role is not, and neither is the geographical area of its extent.

The subjects on which I have touched in the preceding pages are not a prelude to a fuller description in this monograph of the same things. They have been sketched out to provide the very general outlines of Majang society. But the focus of this book is on other matters which I have not yet mentioned. These matters are, roughly, shifting cultivation, domestic organization, settlement patterns and local groups.

If any justification for my approach were needed, it has been given by E. R. Leach in *Pul Eliya*:

Every anthropologist needs to start out by considering just how much of the culture with which he is faced can most readily be understood as a direct adaptation to the environmental context, including that part of the context which is man-made. Only when he has exhausted the possibility of explanation by way of normality should it be necessary to resort to metaphysical solutions whereby the peculiarities of custom are explained in terms of normative morality. (Leach 1961: 306)

This monograph deals first, then, with Majang ecology, or 'adaptation to the environmental context'. It goes on to deal with aspects of the Majang economy, and of Majang demography. But none of these words, and no simple phrase I know, adequately summarizes the unity of the content of this study. Yet shifting cultivation, domestic organization, settlement patterns and local grouping in Majangirland are very much interrelated phenomena – and they can be treated naturally as a whole.

The subject of this book is how Majangir are attached to the earth, and how they are related to each other in respect to this attachment. In other words, I am dealing with the social aspects of land use; or the spatial aspects of Majang society (cf. Bohannon 1963: 110 f.). This study is a partial analysis of Majang social organization: the organization of those social groupings which are also spatial groupings in that they can be defined only by the areas of ground they occupy.

An analysis of this dimension of Majang social organization gives by no means a complete picture of the total organization. Kinship (including the family), marriage, friendship, age relations, social control and political relations – these and other important aspects of the Majang social system enter into this study where they are pertinent factors influencing the social organization of space, of land. But they are not fully described or explained here within the description and explanation of the phenomena I have undertaken to write about. A more complete ethnography of the Majangir remains to be written.

I will turn now to the first part of my subject: how Majangir are attached to the earth by their means of taking a living from it.

2

SUBSISTENCE: SECONDARY SOURCES

I ENVIRONMENT

The section of southwest Ethiopia inhabited by Majangir, and which I call Majangirland, lies within the latitudes 6° 30′ to 8° 30′ north of the equator, and longitudes 34° 30′ to 35° 30′ east of Greenwich (see map, p. 3). Majangirland occupies the transitional zone between the southwestern highlands of the Ethiopian Plateau and the savannah lowlands of the Sudan–Ethiopia border. While the general characteristics of the geography of these regions are known (Last 1962: 94–101; FAO 1961: 42–6, 63–9), no scientific information is available of the specific geography of Majangirland. Therefore to describe the environment of the Majangir I must rely on a combination of my own untrained observations with extrapolations from geographical data about neighbouring areas.

Topographically, Majangirland is located on the escarpment of the Ethiopian Plateau, where within thirty or so miles the Plateau descends rapidly from altitudes of 5,000–6,000 ft. down to less than 2,000 ft., to where the land levels out on the plains. Majangir are settled at all altitudes between 2,000 and 5,000 ft., but most of the population lives at between 2,000 and 3,500 ft.

At the eastern borders of Majang settlement, the descending escarpment is dramatized in places by steep mountains. But in other places the descent is gradual though very noticeable. There is no flat land in Majang territory. The general tendency is for high land to be to the east, and lower land to the west, and for all water to flow off in an ultimately westward direction towards the Nile. This natural tendency is so marked that Majangir equate, in linguistic usage and cosmological orientation, the two categories *dega*: 'west'/'sunset'/'sleep'; and *pani*: 'downhill'/'downriver'/'lowlands'. Conversely, they also equate the opposite categories of *rangk*: 'east'/'sunrise'/'rising'; and *eden*: 'uphill'/'upriver'/'highlands'.

Although the land slopes down from highlands, at first precipitously in places, the terrain through most of Majangirland is unbroken in its slope by more than a few hills, and its general aspect is not rugged. This regular appearance of the lay of the land is accentuated by the near absence, except on hill-tops, of outcroppings of rock. In most areas stones cannot be found except in the stream-beds.

The soil, to judge from performance, appears to be very fertile, and I assume it is typical of the 'Lava Plateau' soils of the southwestern highlands of Ethiopia, which are mixtures of clay and loam, without sand, with excellent structure and a good supply of mineral content and organic matter. The soils of the Lava Plateau are of recent geological origin, and being in their youth are still unleached. (See Last 1962: 101; FAO 1961: 44–6.)

The climate of Majangirland is tropical, characterized by warm temperatures, high relative humidity, and abundant precipitation. These features, however, show a marked seasonal character. Rainfall reaches its maximum, the 'rainy season', between June and September, and falls to a minimum, the 'dry season', between December and February. No rainfall measurements are available for Majangirland itself, but some idea may be gained from the official recordings at the towns of Gambela (alt. 1,476 ft.) and Gore (alt. 6,578 ft.) located west and east, respectively, of Majangirland (see map, p. 3). As rainfall in this part of Africa generally varies with altitude, and as Majangirland is intermediate in altitude as well as in geographical location between Gambela and Gore, the rainfall over Majangirland should fall somewhere between the readings at these two places, presented in Table 1.

Majangirland would then appear to experience yearly rainfall averaging between sixty and eighty inches, varying according to its different altitudes. This interpolation agrees with my rough impressions. Despite this relatively high rainfall, drainage is excellent owing to the slope of the land, which is crossed by numerous rivers and streams originating in the highlands and flowing swiftly westward until they reach the Baro-Akobo plains through which they continue more slowly towards the Nile. Many of these watercourses, though reduced in volume, flow throughout the year, nourished by the constant rainfall of the higher lands to the east of Majangirland.

Temperature and humidity also vary with the season, and with the altitude. Higher altitude, heavier rainfall, shorter dry season, lower temperature and more humidity here tend to go together; conversely, so do lower altitude, lighter rainfall, longer dry season, higher temperature and less humidity. During the rainy season between May and October, cloud amounts and humidity are high, and temperatures at night descend into the 50s (Fahrenheit). During the dry season between December and February the sky is usually cloudless, the days are dry, and the hottest temperatures reach into the 90s. The extremes of humidity and temperature in Majangirland are, however, quite moderate in comparison with most climates, including the quite chilly highlands or sultry Sudanic lowlands of Ethiopia itself. A European would find the climate of Majangirland quite temperate and pleasant, year-round.

11

TABLE I. *Average annual rainfall in millimetres*
(information from FAO 1961: 69)

	Gambela	Gore
January	3·9	16·9
February	15·3	38·2
March	28·3	147·0
April	75·2	139·0
May	166·4	256·0
June	182·1	334·9
July	237·4	296·1
August	311·2	313·4
September	216·4	312·2
October	108·6	173·0
November	44·3	87·9
December	16·0	64·7
Yearly totals	1405·1 mm.	2179·3 mm.
or	54·3 in.	85·9 in.

The vegetation of Majangirland is uniformly that of broadleafed tropical rain forest. This forest is characterized by large trees and moderately luxuriant undergrowth, lianas, creepers, mosses and ferns. With descending altitude (and less rainfall) trees are smaller and undergrowth less lush, until at the western border of Majangirland the tropical rain forest undergoes a gradual conversion into a radically different type of vegetation, savannah grasslands with scattered trees and shrubs, vegetation typical of much of southern Sudan.

Majangir do not inhabit the savannah, or quasi-savannah, which they call the *patoi*. Even if they wanted, their agricultural methods would not permit them to cultivate grasslands. These lands and the slow rivers which flow through them are the habitat of the Anuak who live in relatively permanent villages and cope with the grass by means of hoe cultivation. In opposition to this way of life the Majangir see themselves as, and are, inhabitants only of the forest, *duk*, which they can exploit with knives and axes and without hoes, as I will describe. Nevertheless, as I will also describe, the Majangir make much use of the savannah-lands at the western borders of their territory, seeking there honey and game to contribute to their subsistence.

2 LIVESTOCK

While the Majangir see themselves as ecologically different from their lowland neighbours to the west, the Anuak, in terms of habitat, forest *versus* savannah, they see themselves as different from their highland neighbours in terms of these peoples – Galla, Shakko, Mocha, Maji – raising livestock while Majangir do not.

As I mentioned in chapter 1, the tse-tse fly prevents the keeping of large stock in most Majang areas. But this is not the only factor involved in their non-pastoral way of life. Even in the few cases where Majangir live above the tse-tse fly zone and near tribes who keep stock, they have not begun stock-raising. Furthermore, other tribes such as the Anuak, Suri, Zilmamu, Tirma, etc., who are neighbours of the Majangir and who also live in the tse-tse zone, manage to raise some smaller stock, goats and sheep. But the Majangir do not raise these either. The only domestic animals kept by them are dogs and chickens.

The Majangir themselves do not realize, as the Galla do, that the tse-tse fly is an obstacle to cattle-raising in Majangirland. The Majangir see the obstacle instead to be the Galla themselves, and the Amhara and the Ethiopian government. The Majangir believe, with some justification from the experiences of other tribes in the area, that the government police or other groups of armed Amhara and Galla would try to steal, extort or tax away from them whatever livestock, large or small, they came to possess. Therefore, say the Majangir, why bother to raise animals?

The argument is partly valid. But neighbouring tribes in the same situation have continued to maintain some livestock despite depredations by the government police and other outsiders. And these depredations are of recent times, whereas Majangir appear never to have had livestock.

The fact is that the Majangir also seem uninterested in keeping livestock. This lack of interest is manifest in a number of ways: their poverty of vocabulary relating to livestock; their ignorance of animal husbandry, of even the simplest principles of caring for and raising stock; their opinion of stock animals as perhaps dangerous but surely troublesome, and bound to break into fields and stores of grain and destroy things – in short, as being more trouble than keeping them would be worth.

Majang lack of interest in livestock keeping does not mean that Majangir have no use, or even need, for livestock. Majangir appreciate any meat. But the reason Majangir do obtain animals occasionally is not to eat them but to sacrifice them. Chickens are sacrificed for most ritual purposes, but a sheep or goat (or rarely a cow) is demanded in some cases, and Majangir will then buy an animal from a neighbouring tribe. They never keep it for long or try to breed it, but kill it soon. They hate the bother of looking after it and the risk of losing it.

Whatever the reasons they have not taken up stockkeeping, Majangir accept that they are a stockless people with the explanation that it is simply their custom, 'in the nature of things' (*gore*), not to keep stock. They do not conceive of themselves as ever having stock in the past, or in the future; and there is no indication that they ever did, or will.

Majangir often explain that what are and are not their modes of livelihood were defined for them from the 'beginning', that is, in the mythical past. Once as I was sitting idly tying knots in a strip of sorghum leaf, I was reproached by a slightly distressed visitor:

Do not tie up sorghum leaf like that, or sorghum will go back to the land of its father, Ler. Do you know of Ler? Ler was the father of all men. He made the beehives of stone near here on the banks of the Bakko. Haven't you seen them?... He once a long time ago lived here, and showed men how to make beehives and how to hunt, and he gave them maize and sorghum and told them to plant it...He had a son who was a Majang, the ancestor of all the Majangir, but this child behaved badly and made Ler angry, so Ler took a stick and beat the child with it, and told him to go off into the forests and eat warthog and make hives and plant maize ...But Ler left here long ago, travelling to the north, taking his cattle with him... He went to your home, have you seen him? He was white like you.

This is a variation of the myth of Ler, culture hero of the Majangir. This myth always sets down the principle that it is the lot of the Majangir to cultivate, hunt and keep bees; but not to keep cattle or goats or sheep. In this version of the myth, Ler takes his livestock away with him; in other versions, he gives livestock to the Galla, etc., as their lot.

Majangir do not necessarily think they have been given the inferior lot. 'Cattle?' they will say, 'Our cattle are buffalo', referring to the large and dangerous wild buffalo (*Syncerus caffer aequinoctialis*) they like most to hunt.

The Majangir are indeed what they imagine themselves to be: cultivators, hunters and bee-keepers. It is these three kinds of subsistence activities which I will now describe, each in turn.

3 HUNTING AND FISHING

Majangir obtain some animal protein from the occasional sheep and goat they buy to sacrifice; and from chickens, of which the average household keeps about half a dozen; and from chickens' eggs. But largely the Majangir look to hunting and fishing to provide them with the animal protein they want.

With the exception of a few kinds of creatures (frogs, mongooses, dogs, humans, insects) any animal is regarded as edible by Majangir, though many species are eaten only by children or by persons in certain ritual stages. Majangir will try to kill any animal they encounter, if they have the means. But of the many species of wildlife in their territory, Majangir deliberately hunt only some. These are the species they think most worth the effort of the hunt.

Some animals are killed for more than their meat. Elephant tusks and leopard skins are very valuable trading commodities (see below). Elephant and buffalo are very prestigious to kill (also lion, though this is rarely achieved) for reasons having to do with attaining manhood and ritual well-being. Deer and antelope skins are especially liked to make leather articles for home use. Monkeys, warthogs, baboons and various birds are dangerous pests to crops; several species of wild-cats are dangerous to chickens.

Animals most frequently hunted for meat (*tar*) are those which are plentiful or relatively easy to find and to shoot or trap, and whose meat is generally desirable. These animals include elephant, buffalo, many varieties of deer and antelope, giant forest hogs, warthogs, bush-pigs, groundhogs, large bush rats, francolin, guinea fowl and a few other varieties of small birds. All kinds of fish (*oltir*) are sought, though men devote much less time and energy to fishing than they do to hunting.

Majang hunting techniques are varied, but can be divided into two sets according to the two different types of environment in which they are employed: savannah (*patoi*) and forest (*duk*).

The savannah is covered by tall grasses which the Anuak and Majangir, sharing a savannah no-man's land between them, burn off as much as possible each dry season. Burning the grass is desired because it makes travelling easier, but mainly because it aids hunting greatly by improving visibility and allowing easy chase.

Majangir do not live on the savannah, which they cannot exploit agriculturally, but most Majangir live within an hour's to a day's walk from it. Men go frequently to the savannah for two purposes: to collect honey there from their hives, and to hunt. These activities are usually combined on the same trip, honey gathering by night and hunting by day, with the second activity regarded as less important than the first. The number of men who go to a locality is usually limited to two or three adults, for reasons having to do with honey-collecting. Majangir do not usually hunt in larger groups.

Even when a group of a half-dozen or so men hunt together, they do not use collective techniques such as driving or surrounding game. Majangir hunt on the savannah in the same way regardless of the numbers in their parties. They simply walk about looking for animals. They will not usually follow tracks, saying that these do not tell them the distance away of an animal. They do not follow animals for long. They always intend to return to their campsite (and hives) by nightfall. Although they have ideas of where to look for animals, they do not spend time lying in wait to ambush game. In short, they hope to surprise an animal fortuitously and kill it before it can flee. But by the standards of tribes which depend on hunting, or even by those of European sportsmen, the Majangir show a disconcerting lack of patience, silence and stealth in hunting. They walk boldly along, talking and laughing occasionally and not keeping to cover, at least until they sight an animal.

Undoubtedly, these unsophisticated techniques explain why so few deer and antelope are killed on the savannah by Majangir. These animals are easily frightened while buffalo are not, and buffalo are the favourite savannah game of the Majangir. The buffalo will often stand its ground or attack on provocation. This trait makes them vulnerable, though also dangerous. Elephant are as dangerous, but more difficult to kill, and less frequently encountered.

In the past Majangir could hunt only with spears – they do not have bows and arrows except miniature ones children use to shoot mice – and they confess that with spears they could kill few of the fast and skittish animals such as deer and antelope. But buffalo and elephant were approachable.

Nowadays Majangir hunt on the savannah with rifles. They have possessed occasional rifles since the turn of the century, but only since the 1940s have they acquired a large number of them, enough for every hunting party to carry one, even if by borrowing. Majangir will not now hunt on the savannah with only spears, which they consider futile weapons compared to rifles. Majangir still hunt mostly buffalo, but hunting groups may be smaller now than they were in the past when larger parties of spearmen might have been safer for hunting buffalo. However, Majangir do not recall this as a factor.

Rifles are limited in use, for almost all of them require expensive 8 mm. shells selling to them in 1966 at about Eth. $3 (45p, U.K.) apiece – the price, in fact, of about four pounds of beef at the Galla markets near Majangirland. So Majangir will not waste bullets on game that is small or not normally desirable meat. Rifles are also of limited usefulness in the forests where visibility is limited, as it is on the savannah when the grass is high. In the forest movement also is limited. Occasionally an individual or a small party with dogs will track warthog in the forest. Like the buffalo, the warthog will stand or charge and can be relatively easily killed with rifle or spear.

Most forest hunting, however, and the hunting of small animals on the savannah, is not by searching, chasing and shooting, but rather by trapping. This is the hunting technique by which Majangir most succeed. They construct a wide variety of traps: snares, springes, deadfalls of all sizes, and traps triggered with loaded rifles. Traps can be made to catch most forest game animals. The animals most commonly trapped are warthogs, giant forest hogs, bush-pigs, groundhogs, bush-buck, duiker, birds of all sorts, monkeys, leopards and small cats.

The forest surrounding a Majang settlement will be almost cluttered by various traps. Majangir are restricted to laying their devices near to home, or camp, because they must check constantly to see if they have caught an animal, before it rots or is eaten by vermin. Traps are built and checked easily by one or two individuals, and require no collective enterprise.

Majangir fish as they hunt, by many techniques: poles, lines and baited hooks; basket-traps; spearing; poisoning. Fishing is usually done by individuals, who do not go far from home or camp to fish. Majangir are not as adept or interested in fishing as the Anuak down-stream, for whom fish is an important staple of diet as it is not for Majangir. The latter explain this difference as due to the swift, shallow streams of Majangirland which they say do not afford the opportunities provided by the deep slow rivers of Anuakland.

When fish or game is obtained, it is consumed within a few days. Majangir have no methods for preserving and storing meat and fish. These products are widely, as well as immediately, shared out (see chapters 4, 6 and 7), many persons getting a little each, and few getting much.

Even with wide distribution of meat and fish, no Majang eats them regularly. Majangir say that if a person should manage to eat a little meat or fish only about once a week, the person would feel fortunate, become fat, and never suffer from what Majangir call *kide*, a physiological craving they sometimes feel for meat, fish or salt. Individuals commonly complain that they have not tasted meat or fish for weeks or months. From my observations, these complaints are entirely believable. Throughout my entire stay among the Majangir I saw the meat or carcasses of only five warthogs, one leopard, one bush-buck, one bush-rat, one groundhog, one hartebeest, one buffalo, several dozen birds and a few monkeys killed by Majangir. Partly these observations reflect a certain amount of secrecy surrounding consumption of meat and fish to prevent them being too widely shared. Nevertheless, it remains apparent that Majangir do not catch much game. A man can usually count on the fingers of one hand the numbers of large animals he has ever killed on the savannah.

The horns of buffalo are always brought back to settlement and placed at a *tapat*'s shrine (*shalo*). By counting pairs of horns at a shrine, and dividing the number by the years in existence of the shrine and the male adults in its 'congregation', one can calculate the success of the Majangir of the area in hunting buffalo. My calculations indicate that only about one man in twenty kills a buffalo in any particular year. Yet buffalo is the most commonly sought and killed animal on the savannah.

Majangir are somewhat more successful in trapping warthogs and smaller animals in the forest: they do not usually recollect the numbers they have trapped, which indicates numbers of more than five, the highest Majangir usually try to recollect. But even trapping obtains meat for Majangir only occasionally.

It is impossible to estimate how much time Majangir spend in hunting and fishing, for this time is usually part of the time spent on honey-gathering expeditions (see below), or it is spare time from domestic and agricultural activities around the homestead. Hunting and fishing never override or interfere with agricultural activities, which are regarded by Majangir as their primary and only dependable source of food. Majangir look on hunting and fishing as ancillary pursuits. Though meat and fish are the most desirable of relishes to Majangir, they are regarded as luxuries, not necessities. They are valued because of their scarcity, not because Majangir rely on them. Majangir do not think that health or life depends on eating animal protein: health and life depend on eating something, and Majangir have no confidence that they could eat regularly or live decently without their cultivations.

Majangir can conceive of the possibility of subsisting entirely by hunting and gathering, which they imagine is sometimes the fate of outcast criminals and of half-crazed bachelors with no women to cook or work for them. Majangir say such men may occasionally be found in the forests, but my informants could cite no specific cases. Such a way of life is represented by Majangir as profoundly anti-social, not to mention uncomfortable. The Majang way of life, in ideal and practice, is to live in settled homesteads and make fields on which to depend for sustenance, and to supplement this living from time to time with the expectedly scarce and irregular products of hunting and fishing.

4 HONEY AND TRADE

The interest and effort Majangir give to hunting and fishing is greatly surpassed by that they give to honey (*etet*). Honey is very highly valued by Majangir, but its value does not lie in its nutritive aspect. Majangir eat little of the honey they collect, and, except for the children, they are not particularly fond of it as food.

The value of honey lies instead in its intoxicating power when it is mixed with water and yeast and converted into an alcoholic drink which Majangir call *ogol*, and love to drink. Besides honeywine Majangir also brew a grain beer, *tajan*. Drinking is a very important social activity in Majang society. The distribution and sharing of drink are charged with social significance, and the drinking party is an essential institution in the organization of work, ritual and other social activities (see chapter 9).

Honey is valuable in providing drink for these activities. It is also valuable in another way. Neighbours of the Majangir, like most peoples of Ethiopia, make honeywine also. Near the Majangir, many Amhara and Galla, in particular, buy honey on a commercial basis to sell its wine and wax (for candles). The Majangir can sell leopard skins and ivory to traders, but they only rarely come by these items. Red peppers, sesame seeds, chickens, etc., can also be sold to traders, but only at low prices. The only product Majangir can sell regularly in large amounts for high prices to the outside world is honey. Majangir largely depend on trading honey for the articles they want from the outside.

Majang culture, both now and in the known past, has never been self-sufficient in that it could function independently of contacts and trade with other cultures. For their livelihood Majangir need several iron tools: the large knife (*jamai*) and axe (*kabi*) to cut the vegetation to make their fields; and the spear (*biya*) and, more recently, the rifle (*kawe*) to hunt animals and to protect themselves from attack. The Majangir cannot make iron, and have necessarily depended on outside sources. Historically these sources have been both the highland peoples, Galla, Shakko, etc., who can smelt and forge iron; and the lowland peoples who obtained iron from Arab traders in the Sudan.

From their various neighbours, therefore, the Majangir obtained all the knives, axes and spears they needed, and occasionally bracelets and beads, by the sporadic barter of various items including honey and ivory, or through exercising links of kinship and friendship crossing tribal boundaries. In the past this volume of trade was low, both because of endemic warfare and because Majangir do not need many tools. A Majang man requires only one knife, one spear and one axe to exploit his environment satisfactorily, and the durability of these items meant only a trickle of trade was necessary to replace broken, lost or worn ones.

Since the 1940s with the final suppression of slave-raiding and warfare by the Ethiopian government, the Majangir have been able to trade freely with their neighbours, especially with the Galla and Amhara who came to colonize and garrison areas near Majang settlement. These people, with their markets and towns and commercial demand for honeywine and beeswax church candles, are able to provide in exchange for Majang honey a number of goods, often of European origin, which Majangir previously were rarely able to obtain, but for which, once available, they have readily developed wants. Such goods at present include rifles and bullets, steel machetes and axes and files, cloth and clothing, fish-hooks, salt, beads, razor blades, processed 'Galla' tobacco, mousetraps, perfume, and a host of other small items. Also Majangir continue to buy iron tools, and occasional goats and sheep for sacrificing.

All of these trade goods have entered the internal exchange networks of the Majangir, and now have become socially and ritually necessary to obtain. For example, the bridewealth now demanded by a girl's family is, in addition to other items, a rifle and bullets, in place of the spears and axes acceptable in the past. Sweethearts and wives now demand cloth and beads from their lovers and husbands. Mothers ask salt from their sons. Men borrow clothing and beg Galla tobacco from their friends. Kin ask kin for anything; as do affines. Spirits require animal sacrifices and gifts of beads, coins, tools, etc.

Although commercial trade goods have entered Majang culture, commercial principles have not much affected Majang social relations themselves. Majangir do not often buy and sell or barter with each other, or use money in their dealings with other Majangir. These modes of exchange Majangir adopt usually only in their dealings with members of other tribes. No markets exist in Majangirland. Sometimes Majangir sell or barter their honey to itinerant Galla or Anuak traders who come to buy it. But more often they take their honey to one of the major market centres near Majangirland: Gambela, Bongga on the Baro, Dembidollo, Bure, Gore, Gecha, Meti, Yeki, Teppi, Gurrafarda, Mizan Teferi, or Maji (see map, p. 3). Most Majangir must walk at least a day from home to reach one of these centres, and from some areas up to four days to reach the nearest market.

The price of honey may vary between Eth. $0.50 and Eth. $1.50 per kilo (Eth. $7 = £1 sterling; Eth. $ 2.50 = US $ 1.00 in 1966) depending on where it is sold, the sophistication of the seller, the seasonal supply and demand, etc. Of the honey Majangir produce, they drink some and sell some. I estimate, on the basis of my records of *ogol* drinks and sales of honey, that a Majang, on the average, takes from all his hives more than 200 kilos (440 lb.) of honey per year. But some men may collect 600 kilos or more in a good year.

Most Majangir sell less than half their yearly production. Those living convenient to market may sell more. The only large expenditures a Majang ever faces are (1) when he wants to buy a rifle, commonly a used, pre-World War I make costing Eth. $100 to Eth. $200; or (2) when he must pay bridewealth, which usually consists of goods costing from Eth. $150 to Eth. $250. When a Majang is in such a situation he sells as much of his honey as possible, while still keeping enough for drink to meet social obligations and economic necessities. With an average number of hives, he would be able to sell 100 or more kilos of honey a year, for as many dollars.

My data show that the average man, however, without the above motives, will sell only about fifty to sixty kilos of honey a year for an income of about Eth. $50 to Eth. $75. This annual income is quite sufficient to provide a man and his family with all the necessities and many cheap luxuries which they can consume, keep or give away. Iron tools, for example, cost only Eth. $1 each, a kilo of salt costs Eth. $0.40, a yard of cloth or a yard of beads Eth. $1, etc. A Majang can buy a great number of such articles and yet be able to reserve much or most of his honey for drinking parties.

The importance of honey in Majang economy is therefore twofold: (1) to exchange for the trade goods necessary to maintain the present Majang standard of living both socially and technologically (tools and weapons); and (2) to brew into drink to mobilize groups for cooperative activities (see chapters 4 and 9), especially agricultural work.

Majangir acquire large amounts of honey by apiculture. They gather very little honey from wild bees' nests, but depend instead on honey produced in hives (*dane*, sing.) which they make, place in trees, care for, and visit regularly to remove honey. The hives are made from hollowed-out logs, about five feet long and a foot in diameter, taken from certain softwood trees, especially *Cordia africana*. The finished hive is pulled up to the high branches of a tree. Majangir believe that bees like height, and that it also makes the theft of honey more visible and difficult.

As most hives are higher than fifty feet, climbing to them is risky. Despite the dangers of falling, Majangir show no fear. A man visits each of his hives several times a year, not only to remove honey but to renew the ropes fastening the hive to the tree, the leaves stopping the entrance, the charred wood on the interior of the hive, etc. A hive that is not tended will eventually lose its bees, or it will fall to the ground and be destroyed by termites.

Hives are not difficult to make, and a male begins to put up his own when he is a boy, and continues to add to their number as he grows older. Majangir do not count their hives, which are scattered, but from my own observations it appears that a young man around twenty years old will normally have about twenty to thirty hives, while a man of around forty will often have sixty to one hundred or even more hives, although the men with the most hives are helped by their sons. The number of hives a man maintains is limited not by the labour needed to make them, but rather by the labour needed to tend them.

Neither does the number of hives kept by a man determine the amounts of honey he obtains. Honey production depends on a complex of ecological factors, apart from which many hives at any given time are empty, having not attracted or having lost their bee colonies. In these cases a man will deposit a little honey or something sweet inside the hive to try to lure a new colony. He may try for years before succeeding.

Given bees in a hive, the amounts of honey they produce is always dependent firstly on the number of bees, which is affected by swarming, their honey resources, periods between collections, etc.; and secondly on environmental factors such as wind, rain and the spatial and temporal distribution of the flowering plants from which the bees draw nectar.

Majangir recognize more than forty species of trees, bushes and grasses which are important sources of nectar for bees. Different species flower at different times of the year, and prefer different locales, particularly in regard to altitude. As the weather may cause some flowerings to fail, and as Majangir want to obtain as much honey as possible and also to obtain it regularly throughout the year, there is a recognized advantage for a man to own hives in several different locations, particularly at different altitudes. A Majang maximizes this advantage not by dispersing his hives singly in very many places, for these would require too much labour and inconvenience to visit and keep up. Rather he maintains a large group of hives at each of usually less than a half-dozen sites.

Therefore most men at any one time are each keeping hives at two, three, or four or so sites, including at least one site on the savannah and at least one in the higher forest. These will necessarily be widely separated, and some of a man's sites will usually be as far as half a day's or a day's walk from his home, though Majangir do not like them further and prefer them nearer. Most hive sites are apart from settlement, or as Majangir say, *jang*, 'in the bush'. A man almost invariably puts up some hives very near his homestead so that he may have honeywine within hours if he wants it. But as Majang settlements are constantly moving, these hives are eventually left behind, either abandoned or maintained as an additional *jang* site.

Apart from former residence and ecological advantages, various social factors, such as kinship, friendship and inheritance, enter into where a man owns and maintains *jang* sites (see chapter 11).

Just as a man continues to add new hives and hive sites as time passes, he may also abandon others because they do not produce honey or because he cannot tend them due to distance, illness, age, etc. A man who moves too far, more than a day's walk, from his former hive sites, is disadvantaged for several years before he has made new hives at new sites near him.

Apart from such temporary conditions, and apart from the vicissitudes of nature, the honey a man collects in a year depends largely on the time and energy he devotes to apiculture. In these a Majang is limited by the competing demands of agriculture. Agriculture is the more essential pursuit in that Majangir depend on their crops and not their honey for their immediate subsistence needs. In addition to agriculture, there are also the social demands and attractions of settlement life, especially drinking parties, which limit the time a man can devote to apiculture.

A man 'tries' each of his hives at least twice a year, and more often if he wants. Majangir take honey from a hive usually at night when, they say, bees do not sting so badly. Since Majangir do not like to walk far at night in the forest, they will stay overnight at a *jang* site more than a few miles from home. A man will visit several hives a night, and may be helped by friends or relatives. But a man can deal with only so much honey at once, and will not usually try all his hives at one site in one trip.

Only males pursue apiculture, and normally only males camp at a *jang* site. They bring the food they need from home. For safety, in case of injury by falling or of attack by animal or human enemies, as well as for conviviality, men like to go in small parties to overnight sites. Often they combine honey-gathering at night with making hives or hunting or fishing by day. But men do not like to stay very long in the wild, away from settlement. They complain of the discomforts of *jang* life: rude shelters, poor food, and the absence of drinking parties and the other social activities of settlement life.

For several reasons, therefore, Majangir prefer to make frequent trips, rather than extended ones, to their *jang* sites. Most trips are for only one or two nights. Apicultural work and honey collection are spread over the year. Of the men whose activities I recorded, almost every one of them spent more than ten nights a year at their *jang* sites, and some of them spent up to forty and fifty nights there. The average was about twenty nights. These figures do not of course include the instances men collected honey from hives near enough to home to return there the same night. If we add to this the time men spend in making hives, brewing and drinking honeywine, and taking honey to distant markets to trade, it becomes apparent how important in Majang life are activities related to honey.

5 GATHERING

I have described how Majangir depend on the forest and savannah – together, the *jang* – for game, fish and honey. The Majangir are of course directly dependent on their environment for many more things – in fact, for almost all the items which go to make up their material culture. Aside from the few trade goods mentioned in the previous section, Majangir can find what they need and want in nature, in the localities where they live.

From the wood of trees and vines growing in their forests, Majangir make their shelters, fires, baskets, stools, bee-hives, ropes, wooden tools, etc. From the earth they take clay to make pots, jars, and pipes; laterite to make red cosmetics; rocks to make hearths and grinding stones. Grass is taken to roof huts. Leaves are used as wrappings and coverings; saps as medicines; flowers and seeds as decorations. Majangir can make a kind of stiff cloth from bark. If necessary, Majangir can also make a poor kind of salt from a wood ash.

It is unnecessary here to list all the items composing Majang material culture, or their means of manufacture. One negative point, however, may be made. Though they are very knowledgeable, as might be expected, about the wild plants of their environment and about various material uses that can be made of these, the Majangir do not use more than a very few wild vegetable products for food. It is impossible, however, for me to say whether or not this is because their environment offers few potentially edible products.

The Majangir make almost no use of forest fruits and nuts. One kind of nut, from the *gamiak* tree, and one kind of fruit called *aime*, a sort of custard-apple, are eaten occasionally by children and rarely by adults. Neither are highly regarded foods. Mushrooms, on the other hand, are prized as 'tasting like meat', and are found in limited quantities and picked during the rainy season.

More important in the Majang diet are a number of spinach-like greens, especially the one called *jongge* (*Bidens pilosa*), which grow as weeds in the fields. They are plentiful in rainy season, and in lieu of something better, Majangir often use them as relish for starchy main foods. Majangir think little of their taste or nutritive value, but probably these greens do contribute to the Majang diet certain elements, such as Vitamin C, without which it would otherwise be deficient.

Another edible wild vegetable which is important, though for other reasons, is a tuber of the yam family (*Dioscurea* sp.) called *kawun* by Majangir. It occurs at lower altitudes and on the savannah, and is particularly useful to men hunting or honey-collecting in these areas, away from home and out of food. Also it is sought in times of famine. Majangir think little, however, of its bitter taste and small size, compared to the domesticated yams they plant. The wild *kawun* is not a normal part of Majang diet.

Coffee, *Coffea arabica*, grows wild over large areas of southwest Ethiopia, including many parts of Majangirland. Majangir make a drink not from the beans, but rather from an infusion of the scorched leaves and branches of the coffee bush. Majangir are fond of this drink, *kari* (see chapter 7), and they will travel many miles to find wild coffee bushes. Galla and Amhara in the Teppi area have recently begun growing crops of domesticated strains of coffee for sale on the world market, and Majangir living near them can buy coffee bush prunings from them. Majangir do not themselves cultivate coffee, probably because it would not fit into their present system of agriculture. Coffee requires several years' growth before it begins to produce, and being perennial it requires a permanence of cultivation and settlement which would be incompatible with Majang patterns of shifting cultivation and shifting settlement, as I shall describe. In any case, coffee is marginal to Majang subsistence, as are other wild vegetable products Majangir gather to eat.

Majangir say that were their agriculture to fail totally, even for a season, most of them would probably die rather than be able to subsist on the combined products of their hunting, fishing, gathering, livestock and bee-keeping. Majang crops have never failed totally, at least not within memory. But Majangir are correct in their opinion that they are primarily dependent on cultivation for their food.

3

SUBSISTENCE: SHIFTING AGRICULTURE

The staple, starch foods of the Majangir are maize, sorghum, taro, yams (several species of *Dioscurea*) and pumpkins (*Cucurbito* sp.). Majangir complement these staples in their meals with 'relishes' (*malan*) such as sesame seeds (*Sesamum indicum*) and a dozen varieties of beans, peas and pulses; also pumpkin and taro leaves, wild greens and mushrooms, and meat and fish when available. Majangir grow small amounts of spices, herbs and peppers mainly to flavour coffee, not food – which they prefer plain. In only some areas of Majangirland do they grow small amounts of recently introduced foods such as sweet potatoes (*Ipomoea batatas*), sweet cassava, ensete, banana (rarely), and sugarcane; but these foods are not an important part of the Majang diet.

Majangir grow their crops by a system of shifting field cultivation. The general features of this type of agriculture, as it occurs world-wide, have been described by Conklin (1957a, 1961), Watters (1960), Pelzer (1963), and others. In this chapter I will describe the particular technical features of the Majang system of shifting cultivation, first, as it operates through a yearly cycle of agricultural activities; and second, as it operates over a 'swidden cycle' of an indeterminate number of years. In subsequent chapters I will describe the social units and settlement patterns involved in Majang shifting cultivation.

I   THE YEARLY CYCLE: FIELD TYPES

The annual sequence of agricultural activities of the Majangir can best be seen as they themselves see it: as geared primarily to the cultivation of their two staple grain crops, maize (*makale*) and sorghum (*ngiding*), and, to a lesser extent, to the cultivation of sesame (*nyumwe*). These crops are grown in five distinct types of fields, or 'field types' (for this concept, see de Schlippe 1956: 117 f.), which in their order of being made succeed each other seasonally through the annual cycle of agricultural activity. Furthermore, with one exception, these field types succeed each other in the same order through the 'swidden cycle', the stages of agricultural use and fallow through which a given piece of land passes over a number of years (for this concept, see Conklin 1957a: 30–2).

26

Subsistence: Shifting Agriculture

Listed in their order in the annual and swidden cycles, the names of these field types are: *gedi*, 'new field'; *bori*, 'old field'; *kate*, 'mulched field'; and *nyumwe*, 'sesame field'. A fifth type which stands outside this order in the swidden cycle, but not in the yearly one, is the *gol*, 'riverside field'. During each year each Majang domestic group normally cultivates on its homestead a complement of every type of field: *gedi, bori, kate, nyumwe* – but *gol* only where possible.

To clarify what is meant by the sequence proposed, I will begin by describing the field type which chronologically and logically comes first, the *gedi* or 'new field'.

Annually each Majang domestic group normally makes a *gedi*: it brings into cultivation an area of forested land, by 'clearing' off the forest. Majangir, in some areas at least, probably clear 'significant portions of climax vegetation' every year, and so may be rated as 'pioneer' shifting cultivators (Conklin 1957*a*: 3). But, seemingly, it makes no difference to Majangir whether the forest vegetation they clear is primary, 'virgin', climax growth; or whether it is secondary growth on land that was previously cleared in the distant past, was abandoned, and has regenerated into forest again. For their 'new fields' Majangir simply look for 'forest' (*duk*) of whatever kind.

Majangir say that they clear *gedi* from forest each year because *gedi* give better results than fields cleared from unforested, immature secondary growth. *Gedi* burn off better, have fewer weeds and thus produce much higher yields of maize. *Gedi* land, Majangir say, is also necessary to grow successfully large crops of taro, yams and tobacco. While these arguments are confirmed by my observations, Majangir do not articulate a more important point: that they must continually be making new fields from the forest to replace their old fields which they must continually be abandoning to bush. I will discuss this point later.

A man selects the site for his new *gedi* according to a number of criteria, some ecological and some social. Of the ecological criteria, some restrict site selection by excluding certain kinds of land as agriculturally unsuitable for *gedi*. Excluded is land which is too rocky, or impossibly steep, or without forest vegetation. Of land which is suitable, Majangir prefer sites covered by well-developed forest growth rather than those where the trees are small and undergrowth sparse. Majangir pay little attention to soil itself, but vegetation serves them as an index of the fertility of a site. They estimate that the lusher the forest vegetation of an area, the more years it can be kept under cultivation, and the larger its yields. On the other hand Majangir prefer to avoid clearing patches of forest which include too many huge hardwood trees which would require too great an amount of labour to cut down.

Subsistence: Shifting Agriculture

Majangir choose *gedi* sites according to their location as well as their vegetation. Land on a river's banks, if they are not steep or rocky, is the best *gedi* site because in subsequent years the site can be recultivated as a *gol*, planted with a dry season crop sustained by moisture from the river (see below, p. 34). Also, since the location of a homestead's residence follows the *gedi*, Majangir prefer to cultivate as close to water as possible for its convenient use in cooking, drinking, bathing, etc. Enough land is available in most areas to permit most Majangir to live less than twenty minutes' walk from water.

Another important factor in site selection is that a domestic group usually prefers to clear its *gedi* adjacent to its older fields, *bori*, which are still being cultivated. This allows a homestead to maintain its spatial continuity and to cultivate and guard both fields conveniently, as a single unit. Guarding is crucial, as I will explain.

When a homestead's old fields have become choked by spreading grasses, however, it is advantageous for it to make its new fields at a new location discontinuous with the old, rather than allow the grass to spread easily into the new fields, thereby shortening their useful lifetimes.

All the various ecological factors I have mentioned combine with other, purely social factors, to guide the decisions Majangir make of where to clear new fields and live. Owing to the constant nature of some of the factors, general tendencies emerge which produce what can be called 'settlement patterns'. I will describe this phenomenon and the operation of the social and ecological factors involved in chapter 8.

Wherever Majangir choose to make their *gedi*, the way they make it is the same. The first stage is to cut the forest undergrowth, an activity called *purike* or *ragade*. To fell the trees first would make this impossible. So men begin at the onset of the dry season in November to cut down only the smaller undergrowth they can fell with their big knives (*jamai*, sing.) or machetes. This work continues throughout the dry season.

After the forest undergrowth has been cut, the trees can be felled on top of it (called *o'orike* or *ketdike*). The men use axes for this work. They do not fell the very large hardwood trees which would require too much labour; and they do not cut down some species which can be killed by the subsequent burning of the *gedi*. It is only necessary to fell most of the trees to open the ground to the sun. No pollarding is done.

The work of felling trees is done during the latter half of the dry season, from January to March. It must be finished before the end of the season because the cuttings and vegetable debris on the ground require at least a week's exposure to the sun, with no rain, in order to become dried and inflammable enough for the field to be burned properly.

28

Subsistence: Shifting Agriculture

During the last two months of the dry season the Majangir also begin work on another type of field, the *bori* or 'old field'. This field is cleared not from the forest but from secondary growth in its earliest and most herbaceous stages. It is usually land, called *butan*, that was *gedi* the year before. As a household, with its limited personnel, wants to guard its *gedi* and *bori* most conveniently, the two fields are usually made adjacent to each other. Planted with the same crops, they form in practice one large field.

As there are no trees on its land, making the *bori* requires only *purike*, cutting the growth with big knives. Once cut, *bori* vegetation needs only a week of drying to be burned well. It is burned together with the *gedi*.

Burning the fields (*motdike*, v.) is an important activity, for the subsequent crop depends on the proper burning of a field to kill its weeds for a season, to fertilize its soil with ash, and to reduce its woody debris for easier planting. The timing of the burn is crucial, for it should be left until late in the dry season to allow a man to cut as large a field as possible, and for the cut fields to dry out as much as possible. But also the firing must be done before the arrival of the heavy rains which would make burning impossible.

Majangir have no calendar except that based on their own seasonal cycle of activities based in turn on the behaviour of the natural environment (see Figure 2 towards the end of this chapter). They do not know exactly when the rainy season will arrive – if indeed, which is doubtful, it arrives at precisely the same time each year. Majangir do know approximately how many moons the dry season should last, and therefore approximately when its end is approaching. The signal for burning fields is the first small rains heralding the imminence of the rainy season, usually in March.

The onset of the rains is gradual, and it is almost always possible to burn the fields after the first rain but before it has begun to rain daily. Majangir pick a hot day when there has been no rain for several days, and if possible when the wind is blowing. When Majangir think that conditions are right, or gamble that they will be no better, persons start the fires using torches to ignite many spots around a field. Persons of different homesteads but with adjoining fields must cooperate in burning together. The aim is to start many fires simultaneously all about the swidden site, which hopefully will be totally burnt over, each fire being helped by the heat generated by all the fires, some of which eventually converge into a single large intense fire destroying even matter not completely dried, and also any weed seeds lying in the ground.

Aside from the cooperation of owners of adjacent swiddens, there is no common action by different households. Different ones may burn their fields on different days. Nor is there any need for common protection against fire spreading, for it will not spread into uncut forest or secondary growth; these always retain enough moisture to prevent the fire from escaping the cut fields it was planned to burn. Care only must be taken by each household to protect its habitations.

Occasionally Majangir do not succeed in burning their fields properly. If the fields do not burn at all, perhaps because of early, unexpected heavy rains, they can be planted anyway but with great loss of yields through unchecked weeds. If this occurs over a whole region, there is a threat of famine. But even when natural conditions are normal, many fields are not burned off completely, either because they had been fired at the wrong time or in the wrong way, or because the wind changed or the dried matter was not sufficiently uniformly distributed, etc. In these cases Majangir often try to re-burn parts of the fields as they are, although they will rarely trouble to pile and burn all unburned debris. They will go ahead and plant what is not burned together with what was.

In any case, it is advantageous to Majangir not to burn their *gedi* fields completely, at least not to reduce to ashes all the medium-sized tree trunks and branches, those approximately six to fifteen inches in diameter. This size of log is needed by them for domestic fires, not so much for cooking as for the slow-burning logs they need at night to sleep by (see chapter 6). The *gedi* becomes the source of most of their firewood, large and small. Therefore Majangir are not concerned to cut and pile branches to burn them efficiently, or to fell large trees earlier so they might dry out. Even after a good burn, a field is left with many large trunks and branches incompletely burned. Majangir plant the field around these and gradually the right-sized wood is taken for fires. After several years only the very largest, unwieldy trunks will remain, and the household will be obtaining wood from its more recent *gedi*.

The time to plant is signalled by the first rains after the burning. Planting (*waidike*) may extend from March into May. Except for certain areas reserved for root crops and tobacco (see below), the entire field area is planted with maize. Near a woman's cooking hut, pumpkins are planted among the maize.

Immediately after planting, the fields must be guarded against monkeys and birds unearthing the seeds. After it has germinated and emerged from the ground, the maize needs no watching for a month or so. Then the young stalks become vulnerable to baboons and monkeys who like to chew them for sugar. As the maize slowly develops ears, these too become targets for animal pests. During the last two months before harvesting, fields must be guarded constantly by day against the major pests: monkeys, baboons and various birds. Warthogs and jackals may attack the fields at night, but only occasionally.

All fields lose some of the crop to pests, and Majangir expect this. But if the fields were constantly left unguarded, the whole crop would be lost. To protect their fields, Majangir cannot build fences, which would be useless against monkeys, baboons and birds. Traps are tried, but are insufficient. The Majangir must rely primarily on a human presence in their fields to frighten off pests. Majangir live among their fields, but if their previous habitations are not strategically enough located to guard their new fields, either they are moved to fit the new situation or new special shelters (called *tebungk*, sing.) are built for watching the fields (*tebike*, v.). The requirements for guarding the fields are therefore an important factor affecting the lay-out of a homestead's habitations (chapter 6).

Other than guarding, *gedi* maize requires little attention between planting and harvesting. Weeds are usually insignificant. A good firing destroys them and their seeds, and in any case the *gedi* occupies a very recently forested environment, the plants of which were species adapted to the deep shade and so unable subsequently to compete in the open sun with maize.

The *bori*, however, will be more infested by weeds. Not only is the *bori* usually not burned over as completely and intensely as the *gedi*, but also the *bori* occupies a site cleared from, and probably directly adjoining, secondary growth which does include weeds that can compete in the open with maize. Given a head start by the burning and planting, maize normally shoots ahead in growth and succeeds in shading out most of the competing weeds. When the burn is bad, and weeds threaten to stunt and ruin the maize, Majangir sometimes resort to weeding (*momonake*). They do not weed as a matter of course, to improve any yield; but only when necessary to save a crop. Their agriculture is extensive, not intensive, and they would rather devote their labour to making more and bigger fields (at this time, the *kate*: see below) rather than to improving the yields of smaller and fewer fields.

The little weeding Majangir do is mostly by knife and hand. Although both their highland and lowland neighbours, the Anuak, Galla and Shakko, commonly use hoes, the Majangir own very few and use them rarely for weeding. They prefer their own system of agriculture to any other involving intensive hoeing and weeding, which they view as undesirable, hard work. A hindrance to hoe cultivation in their forest environment is the presence of many roots and lianas which make hoeing difficult.

Harvesting (*dotadike*) is done gradually. Some maize is taken from the stalk and eaten as soon as it is ripe. The rest is left in the field to dry out on the stalk. Early maturing varieties ripen in three months, later maturing varieties with larger ears ripen in four months. The eating of maize begins then in June, but the harvesting of drying maize does not begin until July, and is carried out gradually through August and sometimes into September for the fields planted late. The harvested ears are stripped, dried in the sun, and put into storage.

Because maize is stored on the cob, and in irregular spaces, and because much of it is daily picked and eaten before the final harvest, it was impossible to measure accurately the yields of this crop. The same is true of other crops. The Majangir themselves do not measure their harvests except to judge them in general terms.

Maize is stored, with other goods, on a platform (*pali*) built under the roof and over the fire of most huts. Majangir do not build separate granaries, they say, for the reason that when the maize is harvested the rainy season has reached its peak, and the moisture in the air will cause grain to germinate if it is not kept dry. The only way to keep it dry is to keep a fire burning more or less continuously beneath it, and this is accomplished most efficiently by storing grain above the constantly smouldering fires in the cooking and sleeping huts. The smoke and heat of these fires also protects maize and sorghum from being attacked by *dubi*, small insects that eat out the cores of grains to lay their eggs. Small, occasional fires could not protect Majang grain: this is another reason why the Majangir depend on the large slow-burning logs they produce yearly in the making of their *gedi*.

The harvest of *gedi* and *bori* maize stored by Majangir is meant to last almost a year, until the ripening of next year's crop. However, it would not normally last by itself if it were not supplemented by another, possibly two, crops more. At the height of the rainy season, when the first crop is being harvested from the *gedi* and *bori*, Majangir begin work to grow a second crop in the type of field they call *kate*, 'mulch sorghum field'.

The *kate* site does not have to be adjacent to the *gedi* or *bori*, though Majangir tend to choose *kate* sites near their habitations, again for convenience in guarding. The *kate* site may be any land with secondary growth vegetation which has not yet grown to mature forest (*duk*). It may, like *bori*, be land which was *gedi* the year before (*butan*); it may be land which has been cultivated for several years (*shompai*); or it may be land which has been left uncultivated for several years to regenerate into immature forest (*aime*) containing young trees. *Kate* made on this last kind of land, *aime*, Majangir recognize as providing the best yields; but such land is usually at an unacceptable distance from a household's habitations.

Majangir choose *kate* sites with regard to the vegetation. They prefer lush secondary growth. They avoid sites with much grass, and also sites dominated by certain species of weeds, especially *Bidens pilosa*. These are the weeds which cause trouble to crops. Probably also, though Majangir do not see them in such terms, these weeds indicate loss of soil fertility. With grass, they begin to dominate land that has been cropped with maize or sorghum three or four or more years consecutively. Majangir regard these weeds and grass as a sign to stop cultivating a piece of land.

The abandoning of land, as well as the relationship between *kate*, *gedi*, *bori* and other field types, will be discussed in the second section of this chapter.

The making of *kate* begins in July and extends through August, September and even into October depending on the rain. At the selected sites, men broadcast (*shoudike*) sorghum and perhaps a little maize, scattering it over the vegetation which they then cut (*purike*) to fall over the seeds. As it is the middle of the rainy season, to burn the fields is impossible, so 'slash–mulch' cultivation is necessary. Majangir do not clear the felled vegetation, but leave it to shelter the germinating seeds from the sun. The broadcast seed sprouts from the top of the ground into thick stands of sorghum interspersed with maize. Maize, as well as being sometimes broadcast, is also often planted after the vegetation has been cut down.

The grain is usually hardy and quick-growing enough to push out most of the weeds competing with it. Majangir rarely weed *kate*, if indeed weeding would much help the yields of sorghum – there is evidence that it does not (de Schlippe 1956: 53). In any case, Majangir regard weeding as unnecessary.

Kate must be guarded, just as *gedi* and *bori*, during the last two months of its maturation. Sorghum has a variable period of maturation depending, among other things, on moisture conditions. Maize will suffer in conditions of drought whereas sorghum simply matures faster. Drought resistance, together with the better response of smaller sorghum seeds to slash–mulch methods, is why sorghum, and not maize, is suited to be the bulk of the year's second crop, which must often mature during the early part of the dry season. The harvesting of *kate* begins in November and continues through January. The grain is brought in from the fields, tied into bundles and stored similarly to the first crop, on platforms above the fire in the huts.

After a man has finished cutting fields for his *kate*, during August to October, he usually makes another, much smaller type of field known as *nyumwe*, 'sesame', from the name of its crop. The preferred site for the sesame field is usually land which would not be used for *kate* or *bori*: that is, land which has been cultivated many times previously and has been in-filtrated by grass. Sesame does well on such land. The field also need not be located near the household's habitations, because sesame is not bothered by pests, so requires no guarding.

Nyumwe is made, as *kate*, by broadcasting seed and cutting down the vegetation over it. Several days after it has been cut, the field must be swept up (*garike*) and cleared of its fallen weeds. The field may then be left without attention until the crop is ready to harvest, around December or January. Sesame yields are not much hurt by an early arrival of the dry season; like sorghum, sesame simply matures faster under conditions of drought. Extended rains, however, can rot maturing sesame on the stalk; therefore *nyumwe* is planted late.

The final Majang field type to describe is the *gol*, 'riverside field'. It requires a site on flat land by a river which flows during the dry season. The moisture from this water sustains the *gol* crops, which are planted late in the rainy season, to grow and mature during the dry season. Otherwise, the *gol* may resemble either *bori* or *kate*: that is, a *gol* may grow either maize or sorghum or both; it may either be burned and planted, or broadcast and mulched. Which procedure is followed depends on the nearness of the dry season. Made in October, the *gol* follows the *kate* pattern; but in November and later, the *bori* pattern.

Suitable sites for *gol* are limited in most locations, absent in many. However, the minority of Majang homesteads which in any year do have riverside fields are able to add a third crop to their food production. This crop matures towards the end of the dry season, helpfully just at the time food stores from the other crops may be getting low. Therefore *gol* sites are much prized, and are re-worked year after year until grass or other conditions render them unusable.

It remains to describe the cultivation of non-grain crops. Special fields are not made for these, but they are planted either at certain locations around the homestead's habitations, or within the *gedi* and *bori*. The greatest part of a *gedi* will be planted only in maize, but root crops will be planted in smaller enclaves suited to them. Majangir do not interplant most of their crops in 'associations'; instead, most crops are grown with each crop in its own segregated location.

An exception is pumpkins (*kolde*), which are planted with maize in the *gedi* nearest a household's cooking huts, so the leaves and the flowers of the pumpkins will be at hand to cook for relish. The pumpkins themselves will be picked and eaten as wanted during the latter part of the rainy season.

Also immediately around the cooking hut will be planted many varieties of greens, cucurbits, and spices. The spacing of such crops is not organized, except that each kind is usually grown in a separate cluster.

Plants like bananas (*muji*), ensete (*uti*) and sugar cane (*kadi*) are only infrequently grown, a few plants at some households. They are located usually near the household's habitations.

Tobacco (*tabai*) is planted both around habitations, and also in special patches in the *gedi*. As tobacco is perennial, old stands continue to produce

34

at scattered locations about a homestead. Tobacco is given much attention when it is young and delicate, but once established it is hardy. Majangir take leaves from the plants as they want them to smoke, and only in the dry season do they sometimes harvest, cure and store tobacco.

Root crops are planted each species in its own separate patch. Sometimes they are replanted in the patches they occupied the previous year; but usually these are abandoned and new sites are found in the *gedi*. Of root crops, taro (*shakwe*) is the one grown most in quantity. Majangir plant large patches of it, favouring for sites any depressions or gulleys because of the relatively high ground moisture there. Sweet potato (*bambi*) and sweet cassava (*anshote*) may be planted anywhere. All varieties of yams (*bade*, *wokwoi*, *kawun*) send out climbing runners which require support, so they are either planted beside stumps, or poles are stuck beside them to use for climbing.

The *kawun* yam (a variety of the wild yam of the same name) is planted at the end of the rainy season to be dug up for food the next rainy season. But the other tubers are planted early in the rainy season, in May or June. None of the root crops requires guarding. They may want weeding, but do not always receive it; they will in any case survive. Tubers are dug up in small quantities when desired, for immediate consumption, particularly in the dry season. Seed tubers are reserved for planting by being left in the earth, or stored in a shady dry spot.

Taken together, the tuber crops contribute importantly to the Majang diet. But their cultivation, like the cultivation of less important plants, does not determine the structure of Majang agriculture which is determined rather by the grain crops. The cultivation of non-grain crops is fitted into a system of shifting cultivation geared primarily to the production of maize and sorghum.

Crops which are 'long-term' perennial producers with delayed returns will either not be grown (coffee) or will be grown only rarely (bananas, ensete), because their serious cultivation would require a permanence of settlement which, it will be obvious, is totally incompatible with the present Majang system of shifting field cultivation. The tuber crops Majangir grow are not incompatible with the present system, but neither do they provide its dynamic, either in determining the field types and the cycle of activities surrounding them, or in determining the swidden cycle. It is the latter to which we turn now.

2 THE SWIDDEN CYCLE

Once a piece of land has been brought into cultivation by the Majangir, it normally passes through a sequence of agricultural use, abandonment to fallow and regeneration to forest. This sequence, following Conklin (1957a: 30–2), may be called 'the swidden cycle'. This cycle can be described succinctly and precisely only by using the vernacular terms for types of fields and vegetation. On the other hand, the heavy use of such terms may be confusing and stultifying. To remedy this situation, the reader is invited to familiarize himself with the terminology and diagrammatic representation of the swidden system presented in Figure 1.

Land during the first year it has been cleared of forest is called *gedi* and is used to make the field of the same name. After harvest, the field is allowed to become overrun with a thick, incipient secondary growth of non-cultigens or 'weeds'. This land is now called *butan*, or land which has been cropped only once.

In the next agricultural year, *butan* is generally used to make *bori* adjacent to the new *gedi*. Failing this, *butan* is usually used for *kate*. *Butan* is not often left unused, as it is considered, next to *gedi*, to produce the best crops. It will not yet usually contain significant amounts of grass, *Bidens pilosa* or other troublesome weeds.

Majangir sometimes will crop a piece of land twice in the same year, first as *gedi* or *bori*, followed immediately by *kate*. But this is done usually only when a homestead is short of otherwise suitable land for *kate*.

After a piece of land has been cropped two or more times, it is called *shompai* by Majangir. 'Newer' *shompai*, which is only two or three years from its use as *gedi*, is generally similar to *butan* in vegetation. But every consecutive year it is cultivated, more grass and *Bidens pilosa* appear, and vegetation of the *shompai* becomes less lush. 'Newer' *shompai* may be used either for *bori* or *kate*. The 'older' a *shompai* becomes, the more times it has been cultivated, the less favourable its vegetation, the further it is (usually) from the latest *gedi* of a homestead – then the less likely it will be used for *bori* and the more likely for *kate* or, finally, *nyumwe*. A piece of *shompai* may be used several successive years for *kate*; or it may be used once for *kate*, left fallow for a year or two, and used again for *kate*.

There are two possible courses of development for *shompai*. If it is left fallow for more than two years, undesirable vegetation such as grass and *Bidens pilosa* are normally gradually eliminated by forest species including young trees. Land occupied by this immature forest growth is called *aime*. *Aime* is either left to grow to mature forest, or it may be cleared for *kate* (only mature forest is cleared for *gedi*). Although *aime* will usually be distant from the homestead's habitations – these having been moved to keep up with recent *gedi* and *bori* – and therefore more difficult to guard if it is re-cleared for a field, *aime* is recognized as giving better yields than *shompai*. After it has been cropped, and loses its young forest growth, *aime* reverts once more to *shompai*.

The other course of development for older *shompai* is not to leave it fallow, but to use it year after year as *kate* until the land is interspersed with grass, and then to use it for *nyumwe*. *Nyumwe* requires only a small field, however, so most grass-invaded *shompai* is abandoned at this point to

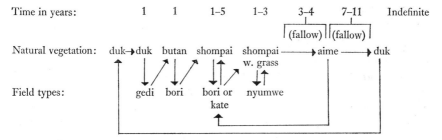

Meanings of terms:

Types of natural vegetation: *duk*: land uncropped for many years, mature or nearly mature ligneous growth with leafy cover (forest). *butan*: land cropped once, herbaceous growth (weeds). *shompai*: land cropped more than once, herbaceous growth (weeds). *aime*: land uncropped for several years, ligneous mixed with herbaceous growth (young forest).

Field types:

gedi: field on land recently taken from forest and being cropped for the first time. *bori*: field of planted maize on land previously, recently cropped. *kate*: field over which sorghum is broadcast and slash-and-mulch techniques are used. *nyumwe*: field of sesame.

Fig. 1. Swidden cycle.

fallow to turn to *aime*, either to be cropped again as *kate* in the sequence described above, or to return gradually to the mature forest, *duk*, with which the land was covered at the beginning of the swidden cycle, before it was converted to *gedi*.

While a piece of land moves through the cycle *duk–gedi–bori–kate–nyumwe*-fallow–*duk*, this same sequence may be seen in static form on the ground at any given time. A homestead tends to move, or shift, in one direction; after a number of years, its linear progress results in a pattern of fields and fallow which tends to resemble, on a map, the diagram in Figure 1. Forest, *duk*, is at the advancing edge of the homestead, the side (the left side of the diagram) to which the homestead shifts, year by year, by taking *gedi* from the forest. The homestead's most recent *gedi* will be located at this edge. Behind the *gedi* will be the homestead's *bori*, and behind the *bori* the site for *kate*. Even further back will be the *nyumwe* site. Behind the homestead's fields will be *shompai*, its past fields abandoned to fallow. The further back, the longer the land has been left to fallow, the more its vegetation will resemble forest, *duk*. In practice, of course, homesteads will not always advance on straight lines, though they tend to do so. Figure 1 is an idealized abstraction of actual patterns. (Maps of actual homesteads are found in chapter 6, pp. 95–104).

Majang shifting field cultivation should be understood, not as an annual moving of cultivation from one spot to another, but rather as the shifting of a series of field types in a fixed sequence over space. In one year, at each homestead, a piece of forest is taken to become a *gedi*, the previous year's *gedi* turned *butan* becomes *bori*, previous *bori* turned *shompai* becomes *kate*, older *shompai* becomes *aime*, older *aime* becomes *duk*. Every year the different types of fields, and the types of uncontrolled vegetation which follow, shift forward, one type shifting into the location of another. The shifts may be either abrupt due to man's action on nature ('clearing' for a field), or gradual due to natural regeneration.

The cropping of fields by Majangir results in changes in the kinds of uncontrolled secondary vegetation (weeds) which succeed the crops. In turn, these changes make necessary the continual shifting of crops and fields. This process is the internal dynamic of the Majang system of shifting field cultivation; I will clarify the factors involved in it.

The cropping of land results gradually but inevitably in an overall deterioration of its agricultural potential. This deterioration is generally proportional to the number of years, particularly consecutive years, a site has been cropped. Majangir express this deterioration not so much in terms of loss of fertility, but rather in terms of the spread of undesirable kinds of uncontrolled vegetation. In fact, these kinds of weeds probably spread partly as a result of declining soil fertility. As Majangir do not usually weed, their fields invariably develop a healthy undergrowth of weeds which after harvest overrun the fields. Majangir do not attempt to control this secondary growth until they want to use the land for another crop. Most kinds of vegetation can be temporarily destroyed or dominated by Majang methods of cultivation – slashing, burning, infrequent and superficial weeding – to allow crops to be raised in place of the weeds.

However, with repeated cultivation, more intractable kinds of vegetation inevitably enter and spread over a field, eventually dominating it. These kinds of vegetation include all grasses, *Bidens pilosa* and other species which tend to stifle the growth of competing young crops, and drastically reduce crop yields; also, these grasses and weeds cannot be eradicated or checked by Majang techniques of slashing and weeding – nor, in the case of grasses, by fire.

Grass (*elti*) is the most serious menace to Majang agriculture. The rate at which it inevitably spreads into fields may vary, presumably dependent on such factors as the number of times a field is burned over and cropped, and with what; the position of the field in respect to sources of grass seed; directions of wind and differences in altitude which facilitate or impede the transportation of grass seed. Once grass has established itself, however, Majangir cannot fight it and must abandon the site, except perhaps for *nyumwe*.

Normally, Majang fields may be cultivated for at least four or five consecutive years before they must be abandoned. But when *gedi* is made near land already infested with grass, the new field may have to be abandoned to the rapid spread of grass after only two or three consecutive years of cropping.

The forced abandonment of older field sites renders it necessary that new land continually be brought into cultivation to replace the abandoned land. The yearly clearing of new fields, *gedi*, from the forest allows all field types to be continually shifted onto land permitting successful crops, while worn-out sites are left to fallow. A homestead adds *gedi* at one end as it abandons grassy *shompai* at its other end. The dynamic factor, therefore, in the Majang system of shifting cultivation – the reason why they must shift fields – lies in this necessity to abandon/replenish land.

Given their present resources and knowledge, it would probably be impossible for the Majangir to avoid this necessity, even if they wanted – which they do not – and even if they tried different farming techniques. Majangir do not envy their neighbours' great expenditures of labour in weeding. But even if Majangir were to emulate them, and learn to weed assiduously with hoes to hold back the grass, they would eventually have to find some means of restoring fertility to land after it is lost through crops like maize. Majangir do not recognize the value of livestock dung for this, and in any case they do not possess livestock. Nor do they know how, or have the right crops, to restore fertility to land by proper rotation or 'pseudo-rotation' of crops (cf. de Schlippe 1956: 210 ff.).

Majangir leave soil regeneration to nature. Used-up land is left to fallow for a period much longer than the period it was under cultivation. Ten years is about the minimum fallowing time Majangir observe before judging land acceptable again to clear for *gedi*. In practice, Majangir do not calculate fallow in terms of years, but rather they judge the agricultural potential of a plot, as always, by the state of its vegetation. Grass and other undesirable weeds must have virtually disappeared, and a lush thick cover of trees must have grown up on a site before it is regarded as *duk*, 'forest' fit for making into *gedi*. This growth takes from about ten to fifteen years' time.

In practice most land is fallowed for longer periods as enough land is available in relation to population in most parts of Majangirland so that it is unnecessary for the cycle to run at the minimum. In some areas, especially those into which Majangir have recently expanded (see chapter 1), primary 'virgin' forest is available.

Not all land, when cropped and abandoned, returns to forest. According to Majangir, some areas at lower altitudes bordering the savannah were once farmed by them but subsequently succeeded to grassland climax rather than to replacement forest. Perhaps this was the result of overcropping and repeated burning of grass for hunting purposes (cf. Conklin 1957a: 60–2). Whatever the exact causes and extent of this phenomenon, it appears likely that the Majang agricultural system can have the effect of permanently degrading forest to grassland, which Majangir cannot restore to cultivation. The land is then removed from the swidden cycle and from their agricultural system.

Despite such losses in the past and perhaps at present, the Majangir still retain ample land surplus to their needs, as I have commented. In the foreseeable future their low density of population, unaffected as yet by modern medicines, will permit their system of agriculture to continue existing and working as it does now.

One may calculate the population/land balance of Majangirland, using the formula devised by Conklin (1957b). One figures that (1) the minimum average area of land required for clearing, per year, per individual Majang, is about one-third of a hectare or 4,000 square yards; (2) the maximum cultivable land available in Majangirland is at least half their territory of 4,000 square miles; (3) the minimum average duration of a full agricultural cycle is fifteen years. Therefore, the critical population size of Majangirland would be 100,000 persons. That is, the maximum number of Majangir who could subsist on their present territory, using their present system of agriculture, would be more than five times the number of Majangir in fact at present living in this territory. But an even larger number could be supported if Majangir continue to occupy virgin territories bordering them in the north and east.

Even in the few areas of Majangirland where population comes to be concentrated, such concentration is rendered temporary by the system of shifting cultivation, rather than changes being rendered in the system by concentration. Majang settlement patterns are so related to their agriculture that when a shortage of *gedi* develops in a particular locality, the shortage is resolved by emigration from that area to another, more forested locality. The Majang system of shifting cultivation encourages residential mobility. These points will be taken up in chapters 8 and 10.

3 SEASONS, PLENTY AND HUNGER

I have described the various ways by which Majangir make their living. But it remains to describe this living as Majangir see it, within the seasonal cycle of a year.

Majangir recognize the natural cycle of a year (*eme*), but they do not conceive of it having any particular beginning point. For convenience, we may begin with the commencement of the rainy season, or rather seasons, as Majangir see it.

The arrival of the rains in March or April marks for Majangir the start of the season they call *banggi*. Fields are burned and planted with maize. Honey is plentiful and much honeywine is drunk. Wild greens are also plentiful. But generally this is the hungriest season, for it has been a number of months since the harvesting of the previous year's fields, and the grain stores of most homesteads are low. Whatever dry maize or sorghum remains is eaten cracked (toasted), boiled, or as stiff porridge, rather than as beer which must be more widely shared than other foods outside the household (see chapter 9). The absence of beer drinks is a symptom of scarcity of food. By *banggi* root crops have also been depleted, and the remainder are dug up to eat or to use for new plantings. Hunting and fishing are impeded by the rains.

Banggi continues during the growing of the *gedi* and *bori* maize, from March to June. It ends with the maturity of maize and its gradual harvesting during June and July. This season when sweet maize (*tawakir*) is plentiful is known as *kere*. Sweet maize is eaten on the cob, or made into cakes (*shoe*).

Another season, *tota*, enters when the new crop of maize is sufficiently dried to make beer (*tajan*). During this season, around August to October, much beer is drunk, especially at working parties to make *kate*. Honey collections fall off except for hives near the *dampai* tree (*Cordia africana*), the flowering of which is also a sign of *tota*. Fresh maize becomes scarce, and the diet returns to dry maize, cracked, boiled or pounded into flour for stiff porridge (*kyu* or *ki*). Pumpkins are ripe to eat, but root crops are not yet large enough.

As the *kate* maize and sorghum ripens and becomes edible around November and December, a new season called *kuo* is marked. During *kuo* rainfall tapers off, and Majangir who have riverside fields (*gol*) begin to clear them. Also work begins cutting forest undergrowth for the next year's *gedi*. Falling streams and clearer water make fishing good. On the savannah rain has stopped, the grass can be burned and hunting is easier.

All these activities in *kuo* continue and reach their peak in the succeeding season, *matok*. This is the 'dry season' when rain ends in Majangirland and drought ensues in most parts from the end of December until early March. This is the season to travel and visit long distances. But also there is much work to do. Forest is cut and felled to make *gedi*, the savannah is hunted and rivers are fished. Honey yields rise, and there is both honeywine and grain beer to drink. Food is plentiful: dry grain, root crops, sesame, pumpkins. *Matok* is usually cited by Majangir as their favourite season.

The end of *matok* is the coming of *banggi* and the rains, beginning another yearly cycle. The subsistence activities and natural changes in this cycle are summarized in Figure 2.

Rainfall in Majangirland is heavy (see chapter 2, section 1), and is fairly regular and predictable. Majangir do not regard the possibility of drought as a serious general danger to their agriculture. Occasionally lowland settlements suffer from short spells of drought, but in most parts of Majangirland the rains have never been known to fail to provide moisture enough for two crops in a year.

A much more serious threat to crops, and to hunting and honey, is too much rain. If the dry season is too short, as sometimes happens in higher areas, or if the rains arrive in force unexpectedly early before *gedi* and *bori* have been cut and dried, then it is not possible to burn these fields which normally provide the bulk of Majang food. The loss will also occur at the time of year when food stores are lowest. In such cases, Majangir may still make *kate* on their *gedi* sites, and grow two crops of *kate* in the year. With weeding they can start their root crops. Production will be lower than normal, but hunger will be postponed until the next *banggi* when stores will be even lower than usual.

Majang fields may also be damaged by such phenomena as locust or grasshopper plagues, or hailstorms or heavy winds which break down maize and sorghum stalks. Various animal pests can wreck unguarded fields.

When food supplies fail in one household or in one locality, the persons affected can borrow or share the surpluses of relatives, neighbours, and friends. When a food shortage is more wide-spread Majangir may resort to eating wild yams and greens, grain chaff, honey, and other items of which they normally do not eat much.

But general famine seems historically rare. In 1966 the dry season failed

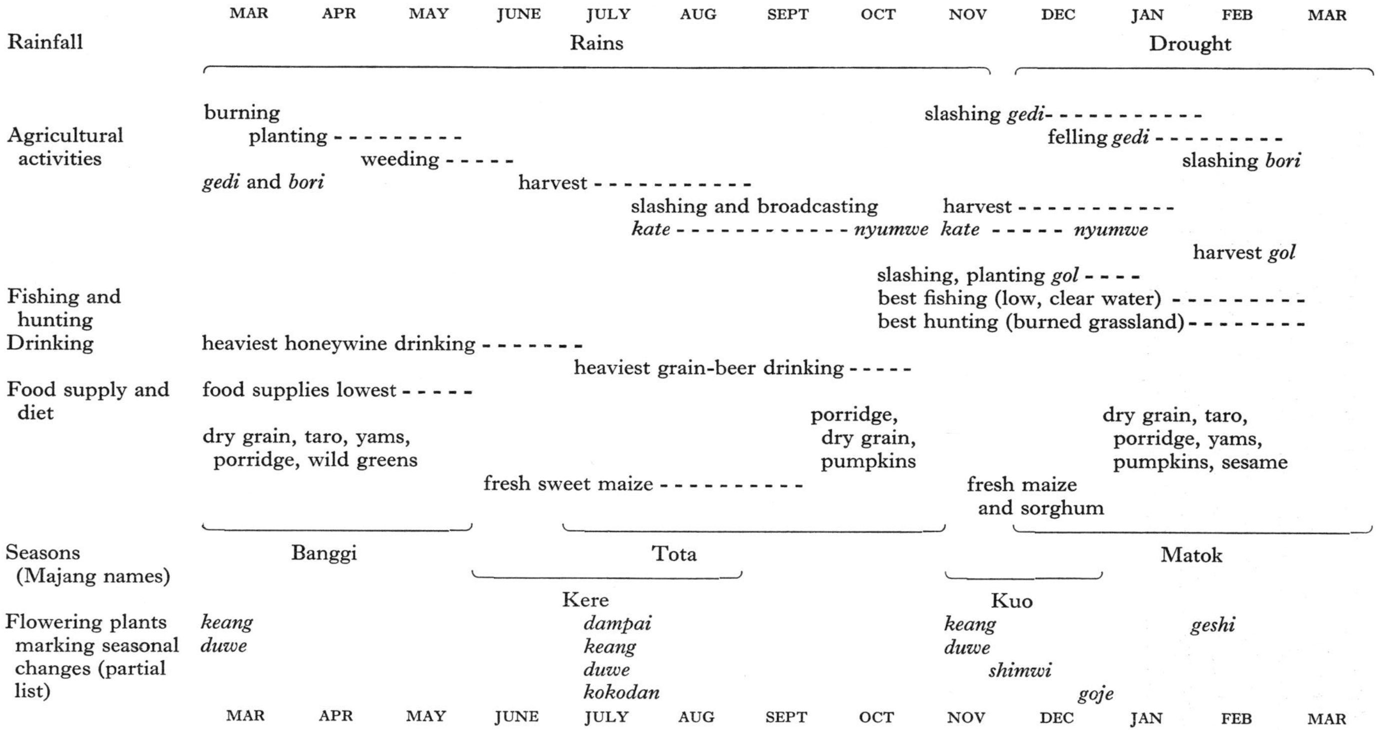

	MAR	APR	MAY	JUNE	JULY	AUG	SEPT	OCT	NOV	DEC	JAN	FEB	MAR
Rainfall	Rains									Drought			
Agricultural activities	burning; planting - - - - ; weeding - - - -; *gedi* and *bori*; harvest - - - - - - - - - -; slashing and broadcasting *kate* - - - - - - - - *nyumwe kate* - - - - - *nyumwe*								slashing *gedi* - - - - - - - -; felling *gedi* - - - - -; slashing *bori*; harvest *gol*				
Fishing and hunting					slashing, planting *gol* - - - -; best fishing (low, clear water) - - - - -; best hunting (burned grassland) - - - -								
Drinking	heaviest honeywine drinking - - - - - - - -; heaviest grain-beer drinking - - - - - -												
Food supply and diet	food supplies lowest - - - - -; dry grain, taro, yams, porridge, wild greens; fresh sweet maize - - - - - - - - -						porridge, dry grain, pumpkins		fresh maize and sorghum	dry grain, taro, porridge, yams, pumpkins, sesame			
Seasons (Majang names)	Banggi			Kere			Tota		Kuo		Matok		
Flowering plants marking seasonal changes (partial list)	*keang duwe*			*dampai keang duwe kokodan*					*keang duwe shimwi*	*goje*	*geshi*		
	MAR	APR	MAY	JUNE	JULY	AUG	SEPT	OCT	NOV	DEC	JAN	FEB	MAR

Fig. 2. Seasons and seasonal activities

43

south of the Godare River, and hunger was common over large areas. No one starved, but quite probably a number of persons died as a result of weakened resistance to disease. Majangir claimed this was the worst food shortage they could remember. Normally, however, Majangir have plenty of food to eat – though always a shortage of protein – and rather than have to conserve grain within the household, most domestic groups are able to convert their surpluses into beer for general consumption.

4

THE DOMESTIC GROUP:
LABOUR AND PROPERTY

Preceding chapters have described the subsistence activities of the Majangir. Succeeding chapters will describe the social organization of these activities. First, we shall consider Majang domestic organization.

All Majangir are organized by households or 'domestic groups'. (For a discussion of the 'domestic group' as a general concept, see Fortes: 1958.) The Majang domestic group is a distinct economic unit. The modal form of this group is the nuclear family. But many of Majang domestic groups do not include complete nuclear families and many others include persons extra to the nuclear family. The actual composition of domestic groups is best described numerically (see chapter 5). But before looking at the forms taken by the Majang domestic group, it is necessary first to describe the general conditions which govern its formation. These conditions have to do with the production and distribution of food and other necessities.

Virtually every Majang belongs to a domestic group, because a pooling of labour and skills is necessary if one is to obtain a normal livelihood by Majang standards. The necessity for collaboration in subsistence activities is essentially a function of the sexual division of labour as conceived and practised by Majangir. Males and females must depend on each other, for each sex is trained in certain skills the other sex is not. In addition, many tasks not requiring special skills are nevertheless conventionally assigned to one sex or the other as its particular responsibility.

The conventions of the sexual division of labour are in most cases not rigidly maintained. When necessary, a man or woman will often do some unskilled task normally and normatively done by the opposite sex. A person who breaks this convention is not usually embarrassed, but may often resent the necessity. Members of each sex expect members of the other to do certain jobs as their side of the general partnership between sexes, and reinforcing this partnership are the jobs which in fact only one sex is able by training to do well. In Table 2 are summarized the important aspects of the sexual division of labour.

A domestic group is formed when a man, or several men, undertake the male tasks listed in Table 2 for the sake of a woman, or several women, who in return undertake the female tasks for the sake of the male partner(s).

45

The Domestic Group: Labour and Property

TABLE 2. *Sexual division of labour*

Male tasks	Female tasks
Clear fields: slash, chop, burn	Cultivate fields: plant, weed, guard from pests, harvest
Hunt, trap and fish	
	Gather wild greens and mushrooms
Make hives, gather honey, brew honeywine	Pound grain to flour
Sell honey, buy trade goods	Cook meals requiring boiling or steaming
Build huts	Prepare and brew grain beer
Fight and defend against dangerous enemies, animal and human	Brew *kari* (coffee leaves)
	Fetch water from stream or spring
Fashion wood and iron implements	Care for small children
Weave basketry	Make pots

The partners in this group pool their labour and skills, and the resulting products of their joint effort are pooled also. The benefits of their undertakings are shared by both male and female partners, and also by any of their dependants not able to contribute labour to the partnership. The partners and their dependants constitute a domestic group. All Majangir are divided into these small groups, with very little overlap of membership (see chapter 5).

Although Table 2 presents the essential responsibilities of the male and female members of a domestic group, an adequate description requires an outline of how the group is seen to operate as such, in specific activities.

Fields and Crops. The domestic group is a crop-producing unit. The men of the group are responsible for clearing the yearly set of fields described in chapter 3, and the women of the group are responsible for most of the subsequent care of the fields, though men and children may help. Especially in the production of grains, the most important kind of crop, male and female responsibilities are complementary, and every grain field must be a joint enterprise of at least two persons, one of each sex. But less important kinds of crops are also usually produced as a joint enterprise.

All the working members of a domestic group normally cooperate to clear and care for a single set of fields (*gedi, bori, kate, nyumwe*: see chapter 3). A group containing several males and females may, however, in addition to

46

this set, make several separate fields – usually slash–mulch sorghum fields (*kate*) or sesame fields (*nyumwe*). In these cases, a male/female pair within a domestic group takes responsibility for a separate field. Such pairing off within the domestic group is inconsequential, however, for the harvested crops of the separate fields are pooled, together with what other crops have been produced in the same fields by the entire group. Also, assistance, when needed, is freely asked for and given within a domestic group regardless of separate field responsibilities. This is not normal between different domestic groups.

Neighbourhood or community working parties are often gathered to do the heavier agricultural tasks. A domestic group provides drink to attract and compensate the people who come to help. Any member of the domestic group may provide the ingredients for the drink – if grain beer, it is usually made from the group's pooled resources – and any member may provide the labour to make the drink. Who contributes what to the drink does not determine rights of ownership. The subsequent produce of the field belongs to the entire domestic group, and is pooled with their other stores.

Wild Products. The domestic group is a food-pooling unit. Its members do not necessarily cooperate in every productive activity – though males and females cooperate in producing grain crops – but what food its members do produce singly or collectively they largely produce for their domestic group, not for themselves as individuals. The members of the group pool the fruits of their production. This is true of crops and also of wild products such as meat, fish, greens and mushrooms.

Only women should gather and cook wild (or domestic) greens and mushrooms. In this case, men would be embarrassed to be seen, by women, cooking or gathering these items, though men will sometimes do so secretly for themselves when their female partners have neglected them. It is the responsibility of the women of the domestic group to gather and cook greens and mushrooms and to distribute the dish to all the members of their group to eat.

On the other hand, women never hunt or trap or skin game, and they rarely fish. But it is the responsibility of a man, when he obtains some game or fish, and after having perhaps eaten certain portions of it, to bring the remainder home to present to the women (or woman) of his domestic group. The women then cook it and distribute it to all the members of the group to eat, including to the man who provided it.

Food Stores and Meals. Majang eating habits are irregular. During the day individuals eat whatever food comes to hand, whenever it is offered, or cook

47

food for themselves if they are hungry. The staple food stores of a person's domestic group are normally always freely available to him, without his having to ask, at his home. The pooled grain crop of all the harvested fields of a domestic group is kept in one of the group's huts, or perhaps in two or three if the harvest was large. While fresh, maize may be taken directly from the field, and root crops are always pulled from the ground as wanted. Normally, a person takes freely what food he (she) wants to cook and eat himself from the crops jointly owned by all the members of his group. In a small minority of cases, which I shall explain in chapter 5, the crops are divided after harvest and some members of the group will be restricted from taking freely from one portion or another.

Except in these few instances, and except in times of scarcity when senior members of the group exercise a sort of rationing to conserve food stores, all members can and do help themselves to the uncooked food of their domestic unit, without asking permission. This right, together with the pooling of labour and produce, is the most distinctive feature of domestic group membership, for normally one would never take the food of another domestic group without asking and receiving permission; or, more typically, being invited to take.

Except for smaller children, every Majang is then able when at home to take freely raw food and cook a meal for himself (herself). All starch staples and some relishes may be cooked by toasting on a shard, baking in embers or roasting beside a fire – techniques at which Majangir, of whichever sex and any age over six, are all adept. Most day-time meals are cooked in this way, by individuals for themselves.

However, the women of a domestic group are responsible for cooking, not all meals, but certain kinds of meals, for the consumption of the entire group. These meals may be simple boiled foods, though men sometimes also boil food for themselves. But preferably women should cook for men the favourite staple meals of the Majangir, either a stiff grain porridge (*kyu*) or a sweet grain cake (*shoe*). These dishes require special sex-linked skills to prepare, including the hard labour of reducing the grain to flour or paste. Consequently, men depend entirely on women to provide them with these foods. Men also depend on females to prepare the most available kinds of relish, sesame paste and boiled greens.

These facts are summarized in Table 3.

The important considerations are these: (1) a good meal, to Majangir, should include a relish (*malan*) as well as a staple, and the best staples are grain cooked as porridge (*kyu*) or cake (*shoe*); (2) a good life, to Majangir, should include frequent good meals; (3) good meals can be prepared only by females.

TABLE 3. *Methods of preparing different foods, by sex*

		Cooked by women only	Cooked by men or women	
		Pounding, or grinding, plus boiling, or steaming (*keji*)	Boiling only (*keji*)	Roasting on spit (*medee*); baking in embers (*tuje*); or toasting on shard (*waye*), etc.
Starch staples	Dry maize, sorghum	× (*kyu*)	×	×
	Sweet maize, sorghum	× (*shoe*)	×	×
	Tubers and pumpkins		×	×
Relishes (*malan*)	Greens and mushrooms		× *	
	Sesame, pumpkin seeds	×		×
	Meat and fish		×	×

Women cook for entire domestic group

Individuals, men or women, cook for themselves

* Ideally done only by women.

These considerations explain the importance of the women's responsibility to prepare some meals for their domestic groups. The domestic partnership is often summarized by men: *Pura aguto jati, le ko keje kyu,* 'I make fields for a woman, so she will make porridge.' Ideally women should make for their group one meal a day, usually for the evening. In actual practice, a man is usually satisfied to receive a meal about every other night from the women of his group. For other meals, he depends on his own cooking.

Drink. Only males provide honeywine, for only they practise apiculture. Only females provide grain beer, for its preparation requires their sex-linked skills. Neither drink is brewed for consumption only within the domestic group; drink is made to be offered especially to persons outside the group. But often drink is brewed for working parties to help make fields, huts, etc., which will belong to the domestic group as a whole. In these cases, as I have said, any member of the domestic group may make the drink or provide its ingredients; the group as a whole benefits. When a working party is necessary, every member of the domestic group is obliged to contribute whatever he or she can at the time to make drink for the party. Failure to fulfil such obligations leads in course to sharp dissension and perhaps to dissolution of the group (see later chapters).

Trade goods. Men personally own the honey their hives produce. If a man's domestic group needs his honey for a drinking party then he should use it for this. But if it is not needed for this purpose, then according to Majangir a man is theoretically free to sell the honey and buy whatever he wants for his personal use or to give to whomever he wants. In practice, of course, such freedom is constricted by actual social relations. Also, men are expected to provide their domestic units with such items as machetes, axes, bullets, salt, and in times of famine purchased food: any item related to the unit's subsistence needs.

Home-made tools and utensils. Men should provide the females of their domestic group with any home-made items that are necessary to the subsistence of the group, but which women cannot make well for themselves. These include baskets, wooden mortar and pestle for pounding grain, handles for iron tools, etc. Women, however, are responsible for making their own pottery.

Shelter. Men construct all the huts for their domestic unit, except for occasional, very flimsy shelters put up by women or children, usually for field-watching.

Water. The females of a domestic group should provide for all its members' cooking and drinking needs. This task requires several trips a day to stream or spring.

Certain items such as tobacco, beads, cloth, cosmetics, pipes, leather, etc., are not produced or pooled or distributed on the basis of domestic group affiliations. Persons belonging to the same domestic group cannot borrow or take these items from each other without asking for them (as they can do food, tools, etc.). Rather, they must ask each other to lend or give them these things, just as they would ask members of other domestic groups. These items are noticeably further removed from subsistence in its narrower sense – the means for staying alive – than the items which are shared freely within the domestic group. The essential function of the domestic group among the Majangir is simply to provide a livelihood for its members by the means described.

The domestic group jointly owns and uses an 'estate': a collection of property including fields, huts, tools and stores of foods. The Majang domestic group may be called a 'corporate' group, but unlike groups normally called 'corporate', it does not have a continuous existence independent of that of its members. No doubt this fact is related to the nature of its property, its estate, which in the Majang economy has no permanent value. Its fields and food stores must be renewed every year, even every season, if a domestic group is to continue. Labour, not property, is the crucial factor. Some domestic groups have very short lives. If partners fail in their obligations to each other, or if for any other reason they should not want to continue in partnership, their domestic unit easily breaks up and the persons in it find others with whom to join (see chapter 5).

The domestic group which continues over a long period of time is usually based on nuclear family ties. But the developmental cycle of a family establishes its own limits to the lifetime of a domestic group composed of a nuclear family. As a corporate unit having no permanent estate, but depending on its members' labour, the domestic group must rely for its coherence over time on the constant inter-relationship of its members, organized to renew periodically the estate. But the existence of the domestic group is then subject to the breakdown of these working relationships, a breakdown which can be brought about not only by its members' diverse wills and at their convenience, but also by inevitable or accidental developments in its members' lives.

These factors will be explored in the next chapter. So far the Majang domestic group has been described mainly in terms of norms and abstractions. Subsequent chapters will explore how these norms work in practice, in actual cases.

5

THE DOMESTIC GROUP: COMPOSITION AND DEVELOPMENT

I THE MAJANG MODEL OF DOMESTIC ARRANGEMENTS (I)

Before entering in detail into the numerical composition of domestic groups and the factors which generate these numbers, we may consider briefly the ideal and abstract view the actors themselves hold of their domestic organization. Their 'home-made' model considerably simplifies reality, even to the point of distortion; but such simplification lends their model a forcefulness which makes it an appropriate introduction to the actual, observed complexities of domestic organization.

The Majangir have no word for the domestic group, just as they have no term for the nuclear family. But they do have a term, *wai*, which implies both these units, and may be used to indicate domestic affiliations.

The several uses of the word *wai* all involve a concept of domesticity. In its broadest sense, *wai* is used to refer to 'settlement' in general as opposed to *jang*, 'bush' or 'wilderness'. The *jang* is associated with the purely masculine activities of hunting and honey-gathering taking place there, in unsettled and uncultivated areas, outside the domain of 'domestic' activities involving women and taking place in settlement, near home, fields, human domiciles. These latter activities are associated with *wai*. *Wai* is appropriate for this use because its primary material referent is the closed hut where, ideally and usually in fact, a woman sleeps with her young children and sometimes her husband. *Wai* in this sense is opposed to *depo*, the open hut where only males eat and sleep (see chapter 6).

Wai thus implies the nuclear family, or at least the unit of mother and children, which sleeps in it. In my first months among the Majangir, I attempted to learn the Majang term for the nuclear family by describing its composition; I was told by an intelligent informant that I was thinking of '*wai*'. However, I never subsequently heard the term used by Majangir to refer to a group of persons we would call a 'family' – or to refer to any group of persons at all. The references of *wai* are only to places: settlement, married woman's hut, home.

Wai is often used to mean not only the one hut where a wife and children and sometimes the husband sleep, but by extension to mean an entire

The Domestic Group: Composition and Development

'homestead', which in Majang society is not a single edifice but a complex of fields and huts and the things they contain (see chapter 6). Here it is important to note that Majangir can use the word *wai* to indicate attachment to a particular set of fields and huts, and thus indirectly to the domestic group which owns and uses this homestead. The *wai* is the 'estate' of the corporate domestic unit.

Thus one cannot ask 'Who is your *wai*?' But if one asks a Majang 'Where is your *wai*?' (*Wai nok ar et?*), he or she may give three alternative kinds of answer, depending on the context in which the question was asked. The answer may be (1) the geographical location of the one *wai* hut within a homestead; (2) the geographical location of the entire homestead; or (3) 'so-and-so's homestead', e.g. '*wai Lempeshe*', 'the *wai* of Lempeshe'. Lempeshe would be a senior member of the domestic group owning the homestead. (Homesteads may be called after any member, but are usually called after the most prominent members.) The last answer would be a statement, in effect, of domestic group affiliation, by claiming affiliation to this group's estate.

If one asks Majangir to what *wai* they belong, one may thus discover how they group themselves by homesteads and by the domestic groups owning the homesteads. Almost invariably the Majangir assign themselves to the same units as the outside observer would assign them, using the economic criteria presented in the previous chapter to define 'the domestic group'.

Wai, while implying the domestic group, also implies the nuclear family. These implications coincide because ideally, in the Majang model of domestic relations, the domestic group is composed of a nuclear family. This model is clearly articulated by Majangir, not as a systematic whole but rather in responses to hypothetical questions regarding domestic relations, and in voluntary statements of what they consider to be a normal situation. If one arranges the remarks of informants to present a composite text, their 'home-made' model of the domestic group and its developmental cycle emerges. Condensed, but in their words, it translates as follows:

A young man marries a girl, and after he has paid the bridewealth she comes to live with him. He makes fields for her and she cooks him porridge (*kyu*). [This is the Majang way of summarizing the several domestic responsibilities of male towards female, and vice versa.] They have their own homestead (*wai*). They have children. The children grow up, the boys help their father make fields for their mother and sisters, and the girls help their mother cook for their father and brothers. A man and wife and their children live (*bede*) at one homestead (*wai omong*).

Eventually a man's children marry. His daughters leave to go live with their husbands, who must pay bridewealth to the girls' parents and brothers. But a man's sons marry wives who come to live with them. Each new wife must have her own homestead (*wai*) of huts and fields made for her by her husband, for whom she cooks meals. He and their children live at her homestead (*wai*). They live near his parents and brothers. They help his parents and give them things, but their things are separate (*aler gengk mo*).

The above sentences were repeated to me many times by many informants. I have only organized them into a composite whole and an economical sequence, for informants were not interested or able to do this. In any case, the sentences indicate what Majangir regard, in general terms, as the expected and desired state of domestic arrangements, at different stages of a family's development. The Majang 'model', as I have put it together, embodies their ideal norms. If Majangir always conformed to these norms, the norms would generate actual domestic arrangements always according to the model. In reality this is of course impossible, not only due to individual deviations by choice from ideal behaviour, but also due to certain intractable demographic factors. The two succeeding sections will attempt to account for these factors, and also to elaborate the ideal norms involved.

2   THE COMPOSITION OF THE DOMESTIC GROUP

Virtually every Majang who is able to work takes part in subsistence activities. Children begin early in life to help their parents, and their contribution becomes useful at about the age of eight when they can watch fields, fetch tools and food and water, etc. As they enter adolescence they begin to play a major role in subsistence activities, helping in all the hard work of their sex. At the other end of the life cycle, older men and women, as they become feebler, give less help in more demanding work, but continue to assist in minor ways.

For subsistence all persons work not independently for themselves, but as members of domestic groups on which they depend for sustenance. A domestic unit must contain at least one male and one female old enough to assume full responsibility for their sex-linked tasks. Minimally, therefore, two persons may form a domestic group. Maximally, the number of members appears to be limited mainly by the ambition of every married woman to have her own homestead and household economy, separate from those of other married women. I encountered no domestic group containing two able-bodied married couples.

Table 4 presents statistics on the numerical composition of a representative sample of sixty-four domestic groups in two communities (Til-Emyekai and Gilishi-Gabwi-Je-Geshoi-Lesheshi).

A Majang is free to partner in a domestic unit with any other persons. There are no restrictions, except the temporary one that a man should not partner with his prospective wife or affines until he has substantially satisfied the demands of the latter for bridewealth. Even this rule is occasionally broken, and in fact persons with a very wide variety of different relationships, kin and non-kin, are found belonging to the same domestic groups.

However, a numerical sampling of the composition of domestic groups or even casual observation soon shows that far from being randomly composed, these groups tend in the great majority of cases to contain persons related in only a comparatively few ways through kinship and marriage. This phenomenon is perhaps best explained by considering that, while a domestic group does not have to contain persons related in any particular way, persons who are related in certain ways should belong to the same domestic group.

Who then do Majangir partner with, domestically? This question has many possible answers, depending on the level of complexity or generality we wish to reach. The simplest view of the matter is that of the Majangir, which I have described. Ideally, the Majangir think of the domestic group as composed in effect of a nuclear family. And in fact it tends to be so composed, owing to Majang recognition of two important sets of obligations within the family.

The first set of obligations is that a husband and wife must cooperate in domestic activities. A husband must make fields, etc., for his wife, and she must cook, etc., for him. In our terms, they must form a domestic group. Unless they do so they will not long remain husband and wife, for a marriage, though involving also matters of bridewealth and sexual relations and children, is contingent on the mutual obligation of husband and wife to be partners in subsistence activities. If a man who is able does not make fields, etc., for his wife and does not in future intend to do so, they cease to be regarded as husband and wife, and the woman may marry another man. If a woman does not discharge her household responsibilities, her husband will no longer make fields, etc., for her, with the same consequences of *de facto* divorce. (There is no other, formal way to dissolve a marriage in Majang society.)

Another important rule of domestic organization is that a parent and child are mutually obliged to help each other subsist when either needs help. If the child is too young or the parent too old, he or she must be supported as a dependant by the other. Though stated as categorical imperatives by the Majangir, these obligations are not enforced by any sanctions except the moral ones arising from personal conscience and public criticism. But parents and children rarely refuse to accept their responsibilities towards each other.

To summarize these two sets of obligations which we shall see to be

TABLE 4. *Numerical composition of domestic groups*
(sample of 64 groups)

A. Total number of persons (members and their dependants) per domestic group

No. of persons	...2	3	4	5	6	7	8	9	10	11	12
Frequency (no. of groups)	...2	10	10	12	10	6	7	4	2	—	1

B. Breakdown of composition according to labour contribution

		No. of persons in each category, per group						Total persons	Average no. per group
		1	2	3	4	5	6		
Fully able	∫ Male*	39	13	8	2	2	—	107*	1·67
	∖ Female	31	20	9	2	1	1	117	1·83
Partially able, aged	∫ Male	10	—	—	—	—	—	10	0·16
or crippled	∖ Female	9	—	—	—	—	—	9	0·14
Partially able, under	∫ Male	19	1	—	—	—	—	21	0·33
12 years	∖ Female	18	4	1	—	—	—	29	0·45
Unable, dependent children under 7 (approx.)	∫ Both ∖ sexes	16	16	5	—	1	—	68	1·06
								361*	5·64

* These figures include ten males counted twice, as each belonged to two separate groups (one belonged also to a third group outside the sample); and one male counted three times, as belonging to three separate groups (he also belonged to three others outside the sample). The significance of plural membership will be explained later in this chapter.

important factors in the composition of domestic units: husband and wife are necessarily members of the same unit if they are fully husband and wife; while parent and child are members of the same unit if necessary.

What I have said of parents and children applies in a less categorical way to kin relations in general, including siblings. Kin of any kind should join in domestic group partnership when they find it necessary or convenient to do so. Any kinsman or kinswoman who needs to join with others should not be excluded. The same principle should apply, more vaguely, to any sort of friend or quasi-kinsman. However, the sorts of kin and friends whom Majangir actually prefer to join, emerge more clearly in statistics than in the statements of the Majangir. The only persons who are expected to belong to the same domestic group are husband and wife; and, at certain times in their life cycles, parents and children.

Indeed, if the Majang model of domestic organization were to work perfectly, a person need never combine in the same unit with any other person than his or her parents, children, spouse and unmarried siblings.

One would belong to only two or three domestic groups during one's lifetime. The first would be one's nuclear family of orientation: father, mother, siblings, with perhaps a grandparent or two added. The second would be one's family of procreation with one's spouse and children and perhaps a parent or two. And the third would be, in old age, with one's son and son's wife and children. This home-made model is of utmost simplicity because it is identified with the ideal developmental cycle of the family. But how accurately does the Majang model represent reality?

It is not surprising to find reality deviating from the ideal. Table 5A presents the numbers of males and females in the sample over eight years old, according to age group and according to whether they belong, as ideally should be the case, either to the domestic group of both their parents, if they have never married; or to a group containing a spouse, after their having been married. Marriage here is defined as being joined with one's spouse in a domestic partnership. Forty-seven per cent of the persons in the sample – those included in the totals marked by asterisks – belonged to neither: that is, they did not perfectly fit into the Majang model of the complete nuclear family as the domestic group.

Some of the reasons why these persons are not members of the same domestic group as either both parents or a spouse are indicated in Tables 5B and 5C. In the case of unmarried persons, they have in most instances lost one parent by death or by the separation of their parents. Nevertheless, they usually remain with one parent. As is evident in Table 5D, only twenty-six persons not yet married belong to a domestic group including neither parent. They constitute only 17 per cent of the total number of persons not yet married. Of the category of persons 'once married' but no longer, due to death or separation, all but six of the men and one of the women were members of the same domestic group as one or more of their children (Table 5E).

Therefore of the total of 278 persons over seven years old in the whole sample, only thirty-three or 12 per cent did not belong to a domestic unit including either a parent, a child or a spouse. Several of the thirty-three did belong to the same unit as a sibling. The others were members of units containing a variety of other kinds of relatives or simply friends.

These figures may be set against the 47 per cent of the whole sample who did not belong to the same group as either both parents or a spouse – that is, did not belong to a unit containing their complete nuclear family (perhaps minus siblings) either of orientation or of procreation. The total picture which emerges from these statistics is that although there is evidently a very strong bias towards partnering with primary kin – the kin

TABLE 5. *Persons belonging to same domestic group*
as parents or spouse

A. By age distribution and marital career. ('Married' here means joined with a spouse in a domestic unit.)

Males	8–17	18–27	28–37	38–47	48+	Totals	
Never married, group incl. both parents	16	7	1	—	—	24	—
Never married, group not incl. both parents	25	22	2	1	—	—	50*
Married, group incl. spouse	—	9	15	11	6	41	—
Once married, present group not incl. spouse	—	—	1	2	7	—	10*
						65	60*
						(52%)	(48%)

Females	8–17	18–27	28–37	38–47	48+		
Never married, group incl. both parents	27	6	—	—	—	33	—
Never married, group not incl. both parents	28	17	—	—	—	—	45*
Married, group incl. spouse	—	13	22	13	1	49	—
Once married, present group not incl. spouse	—	—	8	9	9	—	26*
						82	71*
						(54%)	(46%)

B. Causes for persons, not yet married, not belonging to same domestic group as both parents.

	Males	Females	Both sexes
Father dead	21 (42%)	17 (38%)	38 (40%)
Mother dead	9 (18%)	3 (7%)	12 (13%)
Both parents dead	7 (14%)	1 (2%)	8 (8%)
Parents separated	11 (22%)	18 (40%)	29 (31%)
Parted from parents (parents alive and unseparated)	2 (4%)	6 (13%)	8 (8%)
	50 (100%)	45 (100%)	95 (100%)

C. Causes for formerly married persons no longer belonging to group including spouse.

	Males	Females	Both sexes
Spouse dead	6 (60%)	16 (62%)	22 (61%)
Separated from spouse	4 (40%)	10 (38%)	14 (39%)
	10 (100%)	26 (100%)	36 (100%)

TABLE 5 (*cont.*)

D. Numbers of persons, not yet married, belonging to group including both, one, or no parent.

	Males	Females	Both sexes
Group including both parents	24 (32 %)	33 (42 %)	57 (38 %)
Group including only one parent	34 (46 %)	35 (45 %)	69 (45 %)
Group including neither parent	16 (22 %)	10 (13 %)	26 (17 %)
	74 (100 %)	78 (100 %)	152 (100 %)

E. Numbers of married or formerly married persons belonging to group of spouse or child.

	Males	Females	Both sexes
Group including spouse	41 (80 %)	49 (65 %)	90 (71 %)
Group including child but no spouse	4 (8 %)	25 (33 %)	29 (23 %)
Group including no child or spouse	6 (12 %)	1 (1 %)	7 (6 %)
	51 (100 %)	75 (99 %)	126 (100 %)

* Totals of persons not members of a domestic group ideally composed, i.e. not members of a group containing either both parents or spouse.

types we reckon as constituting the nuclear family – nevertheless the ideal Majang model of the complete nuclear family as the domestic group is very often not realized. In fact, the ideal is not realized by about half the population at any given time.

Another way of looking at the data is to take the domestic groups themselves, instead of the individuals composing them, as our units of analysis. The total sample contains sixty-four domestic groups. Every one of these groups (though I noted exceptions outside the sample) included at least two members related by a primary kin tie. Yet only about a third of the groups were composed simply of a nuclear family. The persons in the other groups were either fewer or more than a nuclear family.

These data may be inspected in Table 6, which catalogues the domestic groups found in this sample according to their composition by kinship. The presentation of the data is made difficult by the fact that there are no recognized 'heads' of domestic groups. No one person formally or invariably organizes the domestic activities of the others. Only children will be constantly subordinate to the wishes of their elders. But among adult members seniority, while acknowledged, is usually irrelevant to the

TABLE 6. *Catalogue of the composition of the sixty-four domestic groups included in the sample*

NOTE: genealogical notations indicate the relation of persons to the 'man' or 'woman' initially mentioned. 'Ch' means children of both or either sex, of any number. The plural ending '.s' means more than one person in any particular category.

23 units: man, W, Ch if any, WCh (if different) if any

1 unit: man, W, W

1 unit: man, W, S.s, D, SW, SCh

6 units: man, W, Ch plus attached primary kin (1. WZ, WZCh   2. WB   3. WB   4. Z   5. M   6. WM)

12 units: man, W, Ch plus attached persons not primary kin (1. 'SS'   2. WMBD, WZS.s   3. BS   4. MZ   5. 'FS', 'FB', WZD   6. friend, S's friend   7. W's friend and friend's D.s   8. friend   9. friend, WBD   10. BD   11. BW, BS, BD   12. BD, BDS, BDD)

4 units: woman, Ch

2 units: woman, Ch, HB

3 units: woman, Ch, plus attached persons (1. M   2. FBSD   3. HBS)

1 unit: woman, S, HW, HS (i.e. two former co-wives and sons)

2 units: woman, S.s, SW, SCh

1 unit: woman, D.s, DH, DCh

2 units: woman, D, HS.s

2 units: man, S, D

1 unit: man, S.s, D, SW, SWB, DCh

1 unit: man, B, Z, plus attached 'FS' (all never married)

2 units: man, Z (both formerly married), Ch, ZCh

responsibilities involved. Cooperation is achieved through agreement in informal conversations. Some members of a group may be more influential than others, but it is impossible to define influence in terms of any particular status found in all groups.

Another difficulty in presenting this material is the wide variety of ways in which these units are composed. Despite the lumping together of siblings of the junior generation of a group, the sets of relationships found in the different units are too many to arrange economically while specifying the structure of each. Among the sixty-four units, thirty-three different sets of relationships are found.

Table 6 does not attempt to eliminate this complexity. Rather it catalogues the data so as to leave the structure of each group retrievable for re-ordering, if anyone should wish to do so. Nevertheless, an attempt has been made to simplify the presentation by distinguishing between 'attached' and 'core' members of a group.

By 'core' members I mean those persons who have been members of the domestic unit since its formation, or who have been born into it, or who have joined subsequently but whose labour is now essential to the group's viability. 'Attached' members, on the other hand, are defined as those who have joined previously existing and viable units, and whose labour has not become necessary to the viability of their units. By a 'viable' unit I mean, as defined earlier, a unit containing at least one male and one female each able to assume the full agricultural duties of his or her sex. The core members of a group must, as I have defined them, be at least a potentially viable unit in themselves; attached members are superfluous to the group's continuance.

These definitions and criteria are somewhat arbitrary, as they are not recognized by the actors. Nevertheless, they are essential to describing the genesis and development of domestic groups over time. It is this sort of description to which I now turn, for it is only by looking at the rather cumbersome data of Table 6 in a developmental perspective, that any order emerges out of this apparent *mélange* of nuclear, extended, polygynous, matricentral, patricentral, etc., family types of domestic group composition.

3 THE DEVELOPMENTAL CYCLE OF THE DOMESTIC GROUP

Fortes, in his introductory essay to *The Developmental Cycle in Domestic Groups* (1958: 3), predicts that superficially different types of domestic groups encountered in a society may likely be only variations of a 'single general form' if domestic groups are seen in terms of their development and of their age-specific characters. I believe this statement can be shown to be valid in the case of the Majangir. Majang domestic groups, at least those in the sample, if looked at in the terms recommended by Fortes, all fall into place in the developmental cycle of a 'single general form'. This section will describe how this is so.

It is unnecessary to outline again the developmental cycle in a succinct and general way, because I did this earlier when I described the ideal views the Majangir have of their own domestic organization. It is unnecessary to improve on their 'homemade' model except to take account of the deviations from it. The 'single general form' of Majang domestic groups reduces essentially to the nuclear family over its developmental cycle. Groups which are not actually nuclear families can nevertheless be shown to be derivations from this form.

All of the cases in the sample can be subsumed under the general schema I propose if we take into account the circumstances which led to the formation of exceptionally composed units. For invariably these cases can be seen as attempts to reconstitute or repair units which were previously complete nuclear families but which had lost their economic viability due to the loss of either the father or mother of the family. Because they previously were nuclear families, these cases can be included in our model if we make allowance for such developments.

The Majang ideal scheme of the developmental cycle of the nuclear family as domestic group does not make allowance for 'accidental' as opposed to natural developments in the cycle. Majangir ignore, in general terms, the very frequent occurrences of death and divorce, which were shown in Table 5 to be the main reasons why the ideal pattern is often not fulfilled. In practice, however, when faced with such developments, Majangir find several solutions to them, involving either the replacement of the lost member by another person, so preserving the independence of the domestic unit, or by joining, often temporarily, another group, before eventually forming a new unit.

I want now to discuss, in terms of the cases found in my sample, some of the alternative solutions to the different situations which arise. For the sake of exposition, I have arranged my data schematically in Figure 3. Although I have simplified the material considerably, excluding 'attached' and superfluous members of groups, this presentation is still of a statistical nature, as I have tried to account for every case found in the sample, and only these. But the scheme by which they are presented would presumably fit, or could be adjusted to fit, any other case.

What I have tried to do is to take into account, in one dimension, the factors of death and separation as they affect the composition of domestic groups, while in another dimension to take into account the 'age-specific' characters of the groups found in the sample. I have used Fortes' paradigm of the three main phases in the developmental cycle of the domestic group (Fortes 1958: 4–5) but I have adapted the paradigm to fit certain crucial aspects of Majang subsistence economy.

The first phase of development corresponds not necessarily with the fertility of a marriage but rather with the ages of its children. In Phase I none of the children are yet old enough to bear the full share of subsistence labour required of their sex. That is, they are not yet old enough to support themselves in partnership with a person of the opposite sex. Therefore they are by Majang definition too young to marry, and must be dependent on their parents. The effective subsistence partnership is that of their parents, between husband and wife. Twenty-two units, or more than a third of the sample, fit this description. They consist of young married couples with or without young children, and perhaps with various attached persons detailed in Table 6.

But if the unit is dependent on the married couple, the children being too young to contribute much work, what happens in the event of the couple

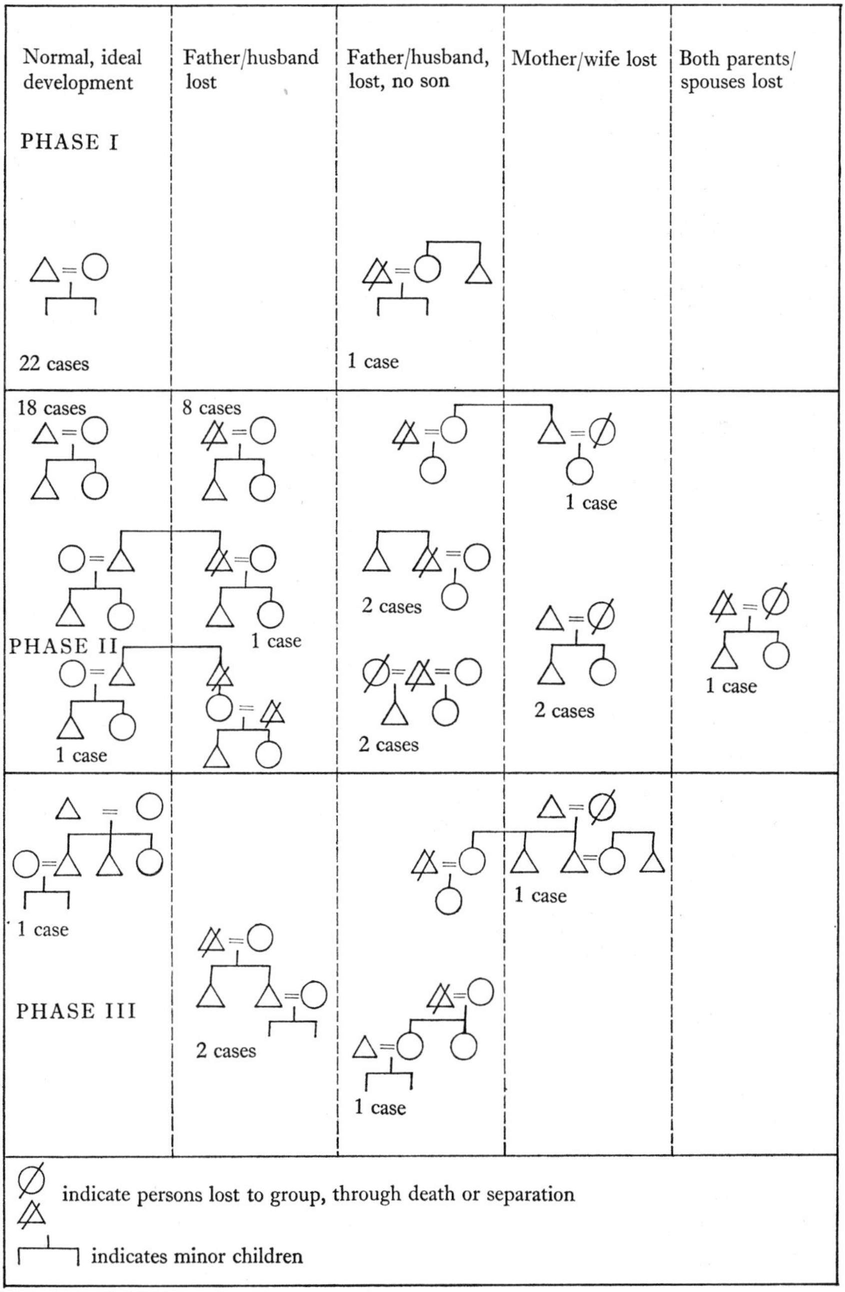

Normal, ideal development	Father/husband lost	Father/husband, lost, no son	Mother/wife lost	Both parents/spouses lost

Fig. 3. Developmental cycle of the domestic group.

separating, or one of them dying? A young woman who loses or leaves her husband will usually soon remarry, thus reconstituting a nuclear family unit. A young widow should preferably marry a classificatory 'brother' of her husband – in effect, any of his kin of his generation. If she has children this type of relative is obliged to care for her and them if she wants. Many widows do in fact marry a 'husband's brother' (*reg*). Even if she chooses not to, it is always easy for a young woman, whether widowed or separated from a previous husband, to find another spouse unrelated to her previous husband.

Almost all young women remarry, but for the short period between their marriages they may find it necessary to attach to another domestic group. In the sample there are three such cases of young women, divorced or widowed, with small children, and not yet remarried. One of them has joined her sister's and sister's husband's domestic group; another has joined a friend's and friend's husband's group; and the other who appears alone in Phase I of Figure 3 maintains her own domestic unit with the help of her brother, who took up the domestic responsibilities of her dead husband.

A young man who loses a wife also remarries soon, and indeed may already have taken a second wife. But again for some men there is a period between marriages when they must make some other sort of domestic arrangement. Two men in the sample are in this situation. One has formed a domestic unit with a 'brother's wife' – too old to marry – and her daughters. The other has attached to the household of his sister and her husband. (In passing it may be noted that in the sample there are three oldish bachelors, that is, over thirty. Two of them have joined their sisters and sisters' husbands, and one, a cripple, lives with a classificatory 'son' and 'son's wife'.)

These examples of widowed and separated young men and women ('young' here meaning without children at or past puberty), who were caught presumably between marriages at the time of the sample, are too few to indicate the wide variety of domestic arrangements possible for them in this situation. They may join any relative or friend with whom they are on good terms. As labour is the most important factor in the Majang subsistence economy, anyone who can contribute work to a household is not unwanted on economic grounds.

In the cases where one man works for two or more women each having her separate household, this does not mean he must necessarily expend twice as much, or more, labour in fufilling his responsibilities. Most of the heavy agricultural work is usually done by drinking work parties (see chapter 9). The man's duties in these are only to manage the work and the distribution of drink. Honey, meat, trade goods, and the products of his other subsistence activities he simply divides between the domestic groups of which he is a member. His benefits from plural membership are to enjoy beer and proper (boiled) meals more often.

Only eleven men (no women) in the sample belong to more than one domestic group. Four make fields, etc., each for the separate households of two wives; one for three wives (one wife outside the sample); one for six wives (three outside the sample); two for wife and sister; one for mother and sister; one for mother and wife; and one for wife and 'brother's wife'. These women have separate homesteads and independent household economies. Many other men, of course, belong to domestic groups containing two or more women who share one household and homestead.

To summarize, there is little economic restriction on the possible domestic arrangements individuals can make. Nevertheless, younger widowed and divorced persons with small or no children apparently prefer to remarry quickly rather than attach themselves for long to another domestic group. The reasons probably have less to do with domestic economy than with other reasons – such as the desire for legitimate sexual relations, and desire for children – which I cannot discuss here. However, Majangir also feel that each able adult should have, together with a partner of opposite sex, his or her own homestead independent of others. This feeling is especially strong in the case of women. Although joining another woman's domestic group is a suitable short-term solution to divorce or widowhood, an able woman will eventually try to make another arrangement giving her an independent homestead and household economy – independent, that is, of other adult women. Marriage is apparently the most satisfactory arrangement for achieving independence – at least, for younger women.

These tendencies may be illustrated by means of an example. In the dry season of 1965–6, we found living at the homestead of a man, Robn, and his wife, Kabul, a woman named Garati, who was Robn's sister. She had been married twice and had two small girls by these marriages. She had left her more recent husband because, Robn claimed, the husband had refused to clear fields for her. Garati herself would not acknowledge her former husband – a way of indicating one considers oneself unmarried, that is, 'divorced'. As is customary, the small children of the broken marriage had accompanied their mother.

The previous season Robn's brother's son Ngayak, who belonged to the domestic group of his parents and siblings near by, had undertaken to clear fields for Garati, and a small hut had been built for her. It was intended that she should have her independent homestead, with Ngayak as her partner. Before we arrived in the area this arrangement had collapsed for obscure reasons: she would not discuss them, but Ngayak and Robn held that she 'would not guard the fields' (*kwe ko tebit*) – probably a condensed way of saying she had not fulfilled her several obligations as a domestic partner.

In any case, her field had come to little, and she had moved from her own hut to live in the cooking hut at Robn's and Kabul's homestead, presumably so she could easily share their food. Robn accepted her joining their household – he justified it on grounds of her kin relation to him – but she contributed a large, even disproportionate, amount of the drudging labour of the household, cooking, getting wood and water, etc.

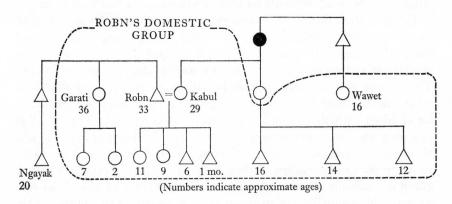

(Numbers indicate approximate ages)

Robn's wife Kabul possessed a strong personality, and to an unusual degree for a Majang woman she disciplined and directed the minors of her domestic group, and even Robn seemed generally intimidated by her. Nor was Garati an exception: Kabul treated her not as an equal but as an inferior, rather in the same way Kabul treated the children of the household, giving Garati orders and enforcing them by browbeating and heavy sarcasm. This sort of relationship was not normal or justifiable in terms of their relative ages, which were roughly the same; or in terms of the stereotypical relationship of mild respect, equality, and good will which should obtain between brother's wife and husband's sister. Nor was it justifiable in terms of the normal attitude of one woman towards another temporarily joining her domestic unit: an attitude of friendly acceptance and willingness to have someone to help in the work, rather as Majangir accept any visitors.

Apart from their personalities – Kabul fierce and dominating against Garati not too proud but good-natured – the source of their untypical relationship seemed to be Kabul's resentment of Garati because the latter apparently did not want to have her own separate homestead. When we asked their neighbours about Kabul's bad treatment of Garati, treatment the neighbours acknowledged was 'bad' (*ngyewen*), they stated that it was wrong for a woman to reside with (*bede agutumo*) her brother's wife. However, we had observed other cases of temporary arrangements of this kind, where brother's wife and husband's sister lived together quite amicably. The difference in Garati's case appears to have been that her joining Robn's domestic group did not seem to be temporary. In view of the failure of her separate domestic enterprise with Robn's brother's son, it appeared that she might not be willing or sufficiently responsible to establish her own separate domestic unit.

After Garati, to Kabul's delight, had left Robn's homestead, Kabul criticized her, saying that Robn had offered to make separate fields for Garati but she had not been interested. Garati's attitudes were at odds with the Majang expectation that an adult, able, once-married woman (*jati*) should at first opportunity establish her own household. From my discussion with the persons involved, who were not willing to be quite frank about the tensions between them, Garati's unconventional behaviour emerged as the most likely basic cause of the situation described.

Garati left Robn's abruptly in the rainy season of 1966 when her pregnancy by a secret lover was discovered. Kabul was consumed by an indignation about the discovered liaison which such an affair normally does not warrant or arouse among Majangir. She threatened Garati that Robn would beat her. Brothers are nominally responsible for preventing their sisters from economically or sexually serving other men until bridewealth is paid, though in the case of Garati, hardly any bridewealth could have been demanded. Whatever Robn felt, he was relieved she had left, and he took his wife's part against his sister. At last report Garati had joined her lover and was his 'wife', i.e. she had become his economic as well as sexual partner.

The second phase of development of a domestic group is reached when one of the children of a marriage becomes old enough – about fourteen or fifteen – to participate fully in subsistence activities and, if necessary, to take up all the sex-linked tasks of the male or female side of the domestic partnership. By Majang definition a child is then marriageable, and no longer intrinsically dependent on its parents or substitute parents. Neither is the child's family domestic group any longer dependent on both of the parents, the husband and wife.

In fact, after reaching the second phase, many groups survive the loss of one parent, relying on an elder child of the same sex to replace the parent.

5-2

The Domestic Group: Composition and Development

The domestic group, in its form of the nuclear family, is also a unit of reproduction, and after a lapse of years may have provided its own replacements for the necessary economic roles in it.

Thus we find numerous cases in the second phase of the developmental cycle, of units composed of only mother and children or father and children. In fact, separation of spouses at this stage of marriage is perhaps facilitated by the possibility of the separated person managing independently if he or she keeps a child of the opposite sex. Older women, whether separated or widowed, do not remarry as readily as younger women, perhaps partly because they often do not have to remarry to maintain an independent homestead. They can often rely on their adult or adolescent sons.

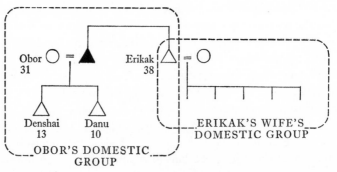

In one case, a widow Obor had, for several years prior to our coming, been dependent on her husband's brother Erikak as the male partner for her household, though apparently he had never slept with her or been given food by her regularly. He lived with his wife and now lent only token labour to Obor's domestic enterprise. She would brew beer from the grain of her last crop, to provide drink for a party to clear a field for the next crop.

Once a woman controls a certain amount of capital in grain stores she is in some ways able to support herself, barring a bad crop which would leave no surplus for beer. Only in the absence of capital surplus in grain does a woman have to rely entirely on the actual labour of her partner to clear her a field. But for some things Obor had needed Erikak even after she achieved a surplus: he had managed the work done by the drinking parties, and had provided her with some meat, honeywine, trade goods, etc. He also had helped her growing sons acquire the skills to provide these.

At the time of the census, however, Obor's domestic group was in transition with her son Denshai, then about thirteen years old, taking over most of the functions of his father's brother in the domestic group. Obor and her

68

children had become in effect domestically independent of Erikak, and constituted a viable unit without him.

To return to Figure 3, we see that of the thirty-six domestic groups of the sample in Phase II, only eighteen or fifty per cent have a nuclear family as core. Eight, or 22 per cent, have as cores a unit of mother and children, without a father/husband but with a son taking the father/husband's place in the domestic economy. In two other cases, woman and children have attached themselves to other units despite one of the children being a son over fifteen years old.

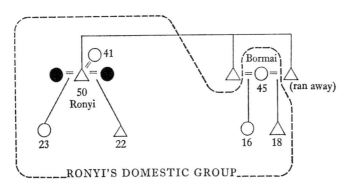

RONYI'S DOMESTIC GROUP

In one of these cases, a woman named Gorki and her children had left their husband/father and had joined Gorki's father's half-brother and his family. The two sets of persons were on still very friendly terms several seasons after the merger. Although no one could or would explain to me why Gorki and her children – a boy, sixteen, and a girl, fourteen – had not yet set up a separate homestead, everyone expected them to do so eventually. The persons involved were apparently living so harmoniously together that they had not yet felt the impulse to separate.

The other case is more explicable: a woman, Bormai, and her near-adult son and daughter had joined the group of Bormai's husband's brother Ronyi and his wife and children. Bormai herself was old, and nearly blind and somewhat addled; she could do little work. Her children had first left home after quarrelling with their father, and had gone to join Ronyi. Bormai had followed them. Though the son and daughter could have formed together an independent unit, they said they felt no need for it, they felt quite satisfied to be a part of Ronyi's group.

Typically, young unmarried persons show less inclination than older persons to form their own independent domestic units. As in this case, they prefer to attach to another, larger group. Although unmarried persons of this age group, called *atinye* – older adolescent to young adult – work very hard, they do not like responsibilities which tie them to a particular place. This is the age at which they like to travel and visit around, returning home to help when they are needed for heavy labour.

In the sample only two cases or 6 per cent of the units in Phase II have a core of father and children without a wife/mother. In one other case a man and daughters had combined in a unit with the man's sister and her daughters. Apart from the advantage of polygynous males who are able to lose one wife and yet remain married, there are other probable reasons for the existence of fewer units with father–children cores than of units with mother–children cores. In cases of separation children usually remain with their mothers. Also, the constant nature of a woman's duties in the house-hold – cooking, watching fields, getting water – makes unmarried girls during their teens and early twenties, when they want to court and visit about, generally unreliable for regularly carrying out the necessary domestic tasks.

The men of the two groups in the sample who depended only on teenage girls complained constantly of their unreliability. Indeed, these men's standard of living was low: they received few 'proper' meals, they often had to guard fields and draw water themselves, etc. The inconvenience and inappropriateness of such a situation may lead to dissolution of the unit, or to finding another woman to depend on. One of the father–children core units in the sample was in fact caught in the census at a time of transition from a recently ended partnership with a widow, the father's 'brother's wife', and her family, to a new partnership with the father's brother and brother's wife. The father and his sons realized after a season's trial that they could not really depend on their sixteen-year-old daughter/sister.

On the other hand, mothers can depend on their sons more easily, for a male's role in the domestic economy imposes tasks – hunting, honey-gathering, clearing forest, etc. – which may be done irregularly, and without interfering much with the boy's courting and visiting and other affairs. This is not true of a female's tasks.

However, not all mothers have sons, or fathers daughters. In the second phase of the developmental cycle, demographical inevitability impinges not only in the form of untimely death of spouses, but also in the birth and sex of children. Some women (or men) who lose or leave their husbands (wives) do not have sons (daughters) to replace them economically. In the sample, six women are in this situation, and have made various domestic arrange-ments to support themselves. (1) One woman and her daughters have temporarily attached themselves to the domestic unit of the woman's brother and brother's wife, but in the next season they expect to form a separate unit with another, unmarried, brother. (2) A woman and her daughters have combined as a unit with the woman's divorced brother and his daughters. (3) and (4) Two women have, with their daughters, continued their separate households with the help of 'husband's brothers' who for certain reasons have not cohabited with (married) the women. (5) and (6) Two women, with only daughters and no sons to depend on, have formed independent units in partnership with their dead husbands' sons by other wives.

Conversely, one man in the sample has lost his wife and is left with an adult unmarried son but no daughter. He and his son have split apart, the son attaching to a friend's domestic group and the father joining the domestic unit of his sister and sister's husband.

Again, the examples in the sample do not convey the wide variety of relatives whom a man or woman, lacking a spouse or older child of opposite sex, may join. Many combinations of kin types are possible. What is necessary is of course that the persons forming a domestic unit are personally friendly and able to cooperate. Kin relationship may dispose persons to friendship, but does not guarantee it.

Again, women in the second phase of the developmental cycle do not like to partner more than temporarily, and only while necessary, with a kinsman who supports another woman. For a woman without a husband or an older son, the alternative ideal solution, outside of remarriage, is to find a male partner similarly unmarried and uncommitted to another domestic unit.

Such *ad hoc* partnerships between unmarried men and women, not united by children or sexual relationship, are always likely to be short-lived, though they need not be. But Majangir are not concerned about the long-term durability or 'security' of particular domestic arrangements. Their view is that other equally satisfactory arrangements can be made whenever necessary.

The second phase of the developmental cycle ends with the marriage of the children of a family, and their forming with their spouses domestic units of their own. This is the phase of 'dispersion' and 'replacement', in Fortes' terminology. The composition of domestic groups at this stage of the developmental cycle is influenced by another demographical factor, old age. As children grow towards physical adulthood they are able gradually to take on a larger share of the work, and eventually the responsibilities, of their domestic group's subsistence activities. Correspondingly, the parents of the group grow older and less able to do hard labour. The problem at this point of the developmental cycle is that just at the time when the labour of the younger children of the group is becoming essential to the group's support, the children as young adults have become ready and able to marry.

The Domestic Group: Composition and Development

At this stage there are broadly two courses of development open to a domestic group. If the parents' group is able to continue as a viable unit despite the loss of a particular son, that son on marriage will set up with his wife as a separate unit independent of the parents' group. Subsequently if the parents' group breaks down, particularly at the death of one parent, the surviving parent may attach to the son's group. By right parents too old to work can become dependent on their children. When a daughter marries she must be allowed to join her husband. A parent may subsequently attach to her unit also.

Cases of parents attached to their children's domestic groups are not shown separately in Figure 3. In the sample, there are three aged parents attached in this way, two women to their daughter's group and one woman to her son's. Old persons do not necessarily attach to a child's group: three old men preferred to join friends, and a woman without children has become dependent on her sister's son's group.

The alternative course of development for a domestic group, including old parents, is for it to extend itself by incorporating a child's spouse and children. On marriage, if necessary, a son will remain a member of his parents' group, he and his wife working the same fields as his parents. There are four cases of this type of group in the sample; in two cases one parent has died. The parents in these extended units are all unable to contribute much labour, and so are more or less dependent on their son and son's wife. The extended family group allows the son to marry, yet his parents to keep his support. In fact, the resulting arrangement is not much different, except in a developmental perspective, from an old parent attaching to a child's initially separate group.

While for a daughter-in-law to join her husband's parents' group is an acceptable arrangement, it is unthinkable in usual circumstances for a son-in-law to join his wife's parents' group. Exceptionally it does happen, and one example appears in the sample. I cannot here go into all the reasons for the rule or this exception. But notable about this case is that the mother of the group had recently lost her husband yet she had no son. It was a logical solution to find a partner in the daughter's husband, who until then had not been permitted to make fields for his wife because of bridewealth difficulties. With the departure of his father-in-law, however, he joined his mother-in-law's group, in violation of ideal norms, but in satisfaction of their subsistence needs.

Extensions of the domestic unit into a three-generational family group are the most frequent cause of 'divided ownership' within the domestic group. 'Divided ownership' occurs when a domestic group functions as one unit in most activities, and cultivates the same fields, yet formally divides

72

1 (a)　Young man with beer on his lips

1 (b)　*Shonggwidike*: young people making music following a beer party

2 (*a*)   Two women drinking together from a pot during a ritual drink for a *waldi* spirit

2 (*b*)   Young girl digging holes to plant taro in a recently cut and burned *gedi* field

3 (a)   Man dancing in the clearing around a *wai* and a *pan* hut

3 (b)   Man smoking 'Galla' tobacco from a waterpipe

4 (*a*)   *Tapat* (on right, with bracelets) and others holding the spear in sacrificing a goat

4 (*b*)   Girls and children grouped around a hut during a ritual beer drink

the crop into two parts. Some members of the group will then own one part, and some members own the other: 'owning' meaning the right to use freely without asking or receiving permission. Some members of the group will have ownership rights in both parts. Normally, a domestic unit owns its entire crop jointly and stores it all together. But eight, or 12·5 per cent of the domestic groups in the sample, were internally divided into two crop-owning units each.

Crop division is necessary when a domestic group contains two married or formerly married women who are related to each other as affines. Dividing the crop in these cases is explained by Majangir as a measure to prevent disputes between women who are not kin nor necessarily friends, and thus are potentially hostile to or jealous of one another.

Usually co-wives are well separated, each having her own homestead and independent domestic economy, the husband contributing separately to each. But in the sample there is one instance of a young man and his two wives, as yet childless, who share one homestead: one set of fields, one cooking hut and one set of household items. The only separation is that each wife has her own closed *wai* hut four yards from the other's (most co-wives' huts are fifty or so yards distant). Each wife sleeps in her own hut, and the husband alternates his sleeping between them. When the joint fields of the group are harvested, the husband divides the crop into two equal portions, each wife to store hers in her own hut. The two women are on very close terms, and cook together and share food as if it comes from one stock. But nominally each wife 'owns' her separate store, and the husband 'owns' both.

The histories of other domestic groups indicate that such groups, containing two young co-wives, are not rare, but that the arrangement is temporary. The women will separate their domestic economies and homesteads later in the marriage, especially after the birth of children.

Another example appears in the sample of two co-wives whose husband left them. They have one son each. These boys, near-adults, clear a single set of fields for the group, and one of the co-wives does most of the female tasks, as the other woman is decrepit and nearly blind. Although they form a single domestic unit for all practical purposes, and share one homestead, the two women nominally each own a separate half of the crops, and cannot take from each other's half without the courtesy of asking or at least informing the other. These requests would be almost impossible to refuse, as one woman has to depend on the other, and the two sons can use food from either store.

The other six cases of divided crops concern affines other than co-wives. In three of these cases, an old woman belongs to the domestic group of her son and son's wife; in one case, to the group of her sister's son and his wife. In these four cases the older women are physically incapable of managing their own separate domestic units. Although nominally they are given their own separate stores of grain, they are not able to care for a separate set of fields and they are not able to do much of the heavy work of making flour for beer and porridge, carrying water from the river, etc. The older women in fact depend on their daughters-in-law to do most of the female work in the household. But the rule is that female affines who have reached the status of *jati* (wife or once wived) should have physically separate stores of food, even if the two stores come from the same fields, are used in the same way, are prepared at the same place by the same cooks for distribution to the same persons.

In one case an old couple are sharing a homestead with their daughter and two sons and one son's wife. Unlike the units described above, it would be possible for this group to split into two viable units, the old couple to depend on their unmarried children and to be independent of the married son and his wife and children. However, the single son had been absent much of the time and had left his married elder brother most of the work of supporting their parents. Instead of maintaining two homesteads the elder son, with a little help from the old father, cleared only one set of fields. The produce from these will be divided between the mother-in-law and daughter-in-law. The former is not dependent on the latter because she can depend on the labour of her own daughter, who prepares meals separately from her brother's wife. This domestic group could split into two, and perhaps will later do so, but I have counted it as one because at the time of the census it had a single set of fields farmed collectively by all the members of the group.

The final case was mentioned previously: the man who has joined his wife's mother's unit. He clears fields for her and her daughters, but he also clears a separate set of fields for himself which his wife cares for. The produce of these fields will be kept separate, he explained, so he will be able to cook meals for himself without having to ask for food from his wife's mother. By custom a man should never ask things of this relative. However, food from both stores can be removed by his wife, and she and her mother and sisters will prepare food, as they were doing at the time of the study, for the consumption of the entire group, including the son-in-law.

This domestic group therefore functions as one unit, and indeed cannot become two viable units until the man pays the bridewealth to persuade his wife's family to allow her to set up with him an independent household – whether or not he continues to make fields also for his wife's mother and sisters. But it is necessary that the crops be divided between the son-in-law and mother-in-law, just as between mother-in-law and daughter-in-law, or co-wife and co-wife, in accordance with the formal requirements of their affinal relationship, and despite their domestic relation of cooperation and effective pooling and sharing.

All the above arrangements may be fitted into the developmental cycle of the Majang domestic group. One case of crop division, of the young co-wives, belongs at the very beginning of the cycle, before the young wives have set up their separate household economies as they will eventually do. The other cases are those at the very end of the cycle, when older women must depend for sustenance on an affine, generally a spouse of their child. Thereby they form domestic groups which are extended, not nuclear, families. But such extension is accompanied by crop division between women within the domestic group. This division is a concession to the ideal that the women should maintain separate household economies though in reality they cannot or do not.

Here I want to close my analysis of the developmental cycle of the Majang domestic group. The point I have tried to make is that the domestic group and the nuclear family, while not identical statistically, would be almost so if it were not for the intervention of such intractable demographical and social factors as old age, failure to bear male or female children, and frequent, untimely death and divorce. Such factors inevitably leave some Majangir unable to fulfil their abstract ideal of domestic partnership with their complete nuclear family. Either individuals must attach themselves elsewhere, or their units must be rearranged or amended in composition so as to remain economically self-sufficient. I have tried to describe and order these rearrangements and amendments within a developmental framework relating the deviant cases to the ideal and statistically modal form of the domestic group as a nuclear family.

6

THE DOMESTIC GROUP: EATING AND SLEEPING

I THE MAJANG MODEL OF DOMESTIC ARRANGEMENTS (II)

The two previous chapters have described and analysed the 'domestic group', the corporate economic unit engaged in the production and pooling of subsistence goods and the distribution of rights in them. Other, related 'domestic' activities remain to be considered: sleeping, cooking, eating. Before entering into a description of how these matters are actually arranged, I would like to sketch how these are ideally and abstractly viewed by the actors themselves – in other words, to extend my earlier account of the Majang 'homemade' model of domestic arrangements.

In the earlier description I noted that the Majang word *wai* could refer either to the sleeping-hut of a wife/mother or to the residence of members of a single domestic group, their 'homestead' consisting of all their corporate property in huts and fields and tools and stores. This identification by one word, *wai*, of both the entire homestead and one particular type of hut, is a case of the part (*wai* hut) representing the whole (*wai* homestead).

In the previous chapter I discussed how a Majang woman, married or once married, normally desires her own homestead and domestic unit in which she is the senior active female partner. She also will want her own sleeping hut, called her *wai*. Because two married or once married women ideally should not belong to the same domestic unit sharing one homestead, there ideally should be only one *wai* hut to one *wai* homestead. Exceptions occur, with two *wai* huts, or none, in a homestead. These occurrences will be examined in the next section; but here the examination is confined to the ideal norm.

Just as a homestead should contain one *wai*, or married woman's hut, it should also contain one *depo*, or men's hut. These two huts should be well apart from each other, in different parts of the homestead. The *wai* should be on the downhill (female) side of the homestead, among the fields. The *depo* should be on the uphill (male) side of the homestead, on the edge of the forest, and in the direction the homestead is agriculturally shifting, away from the river. The *depo* should be fairly hidden and off the main paths – against enemy attack but also against the intrusion of women on

76

men sleeping and eating. The *depo* should be open: that is, with no walls except the few posts necessary to support the roof. Thus men, say the Majangir, may watch for game in the forest behind them, and for people arriving at their homestead before them.

The *wai*, however, should be closed (*rikatan*) with a closely spaced paled wall, because, say Majangir, women are afraid of leopards. Some also add, so that men may have sexual relations with their wives in privacy. The *wai* should have its entrance (*tuga*) on its west or downhill side. The entrance should be closed at night with a wicker door. The *wai* should also have a small escape door (*bur*, from *bureng*, 'to fear') at its back in case of attack by enemies. Finally it should have a drying platform (*pali*) under the roof, to store the homestead's produce.

Near the *wai* hut, but apart from it, should be the *pan* or wooden mortar, buried to its top in hard-packed earth, which women use to pound grain. The *pan* may have an open hut built over it or near it and called by its name. A woman should have a *pan* and an open hut in which to prepare food and to sit during the day, as it would be antisocial to stay by day in a closed hut. The *wai* and *pan* may be situated along the path to other homesteads, for a woman likes to gossip with persons passing.

A homestead should also include, when necessary, a sleeping hut for older girls (*gode petakung*, 'girls' hut'), a hut or huts to guard fields (*tebungk*, from *tebike*, 'guarding, watching out'), and any other sort of hut necessary for storing food, cooking, sleeping children, etc. But the *wai*, *depo* and *pan* are the necessary set of huts without one of which a homestead is not ideally complete. The Majang model of domestic relations presumes each domestic group in its homestead to have all three.

The Majangir describe their relations in the following terms (as in chapter 5, this is a composite text I have arranged from informants' actual sentences):

A man sleeps at his *depo* and his wife sleeps at her *wai*. He visits her at night and they lie together (*dunger agutumo*, have sexual intercourse). A woman's small children sleep with her in the *wai*, but they do not see what their father and mother do because they are asleep and stupid. Older boys go to sleep with their father at the *depo*. Older girls sleep in another hut with their friends. Male visitors sleep at the *depo*, female visitors in the *wai*. Because of embarrassment (*king*) men do not sleep in the same huts with women. Only husbands sometimes sleep with their wives.

Men eat at their *depo*. Women cook food and bring it to them. Or a man can send his sons to ask food from their mother. She sends food back with them to the man. Boys eat with their father at the *depo*, and their male friends share with them. Women and their daughters and small children eat at the *pan*. Brothers and sisters may eat together but younger men avoid (*kireng*) eating with their wives, because this would cause them embarrassment (*king*). Only when they are old, with several children, will a man and wife stop avoiding eating together. But men should eat together at the *depo*, away from women.

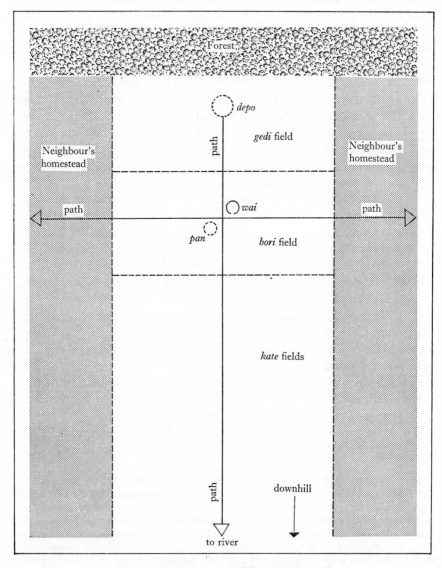

Fig. 4. Ideal plan of a Majang homestead.
(Huts as represented are over-sized.)

The Domestic Group: Eating and Sleeping

This simple picture, while essentially as true as the Majang view of the obligations which unite a nuclear family into a domestic group, is a picture similarly complicated in actuality, which I will describe in the following section.

2 HUTS

Members of a Majang domestic group inhabit together no single structure or house. Therefore, to call this group a 'household' has misleading connotations. The domestic group is a 'household', however, in the economic sense, as employed for instance in Fortes' study of the Tallensi (1949) or, loosely, in our own society: to mean a unit with a pooled income, providing sustenance and shelter for its members. The difference is only that members of a Majang domestic group will usually sleep and eat apart from each other, in different huts. They tend, however, all to sleep and eat in huts within the homestead boundaries of their domestic group. The domicile of a domestic group is thus not a single 'house' but a set of huts within the fields of a homestead.

Even if, as happens, some persons over a period of time eat and sleep outside the boundaries of their own homestead, their affiliation to it is not obscured. When they are asked where they live (*bede*, 'reside', 'stay', 'remain') they will reply '*wai* X', X being a senior person of the domestic group to which they belong. '*Wai* X' is the homestead of this group. Persons regard their 'residence' to be their homestead, and not the particular hut which they might presently, temporarily, be using for sleeping and eating. Nor can the groupings of persons using a single hut at any time for eating or sleeping together be considered, on that basis alone, to form a very significant social unit. The reasons for this will become apparent in this chapter.

Majang huts are relatively small and simply and crudely constructed. The materials consist of wood from the forest, vines for tying poles, and grass or bark for thatching. The favourite shape is a round hut (*lotan*), but rectangular huts (*shakari*) with or without rounded ends are also made. Huts used for sleeping are usually from ten to fifteen feet in diameter, or an equivalent size if rectangular; very few huts are larger, and some are smaller. Roofs, with the platforms (*pali*) to store grain, are invariably too low to permit standing upright in a hut except where the grain platform does not extend. Floors are always earth and ashes except in a *pan* where special mud is spread around the mortar to dry into a hard smooth surface for sweeping up flour.

The fire's place in a sleeping hut is in the centre, a spot marked by an accumulated heap of ashes and smouldering large logs. Often the fire is surrounded by several rack-like 'beds' made of bound sticks and raised somewhat off the ground by supports. There is not much space for movement, especially in closed huts, and indeed Majang huts are not used for any activities except those involving only sitting or lying. Even then, few persons can comfortably remain inside a hut. Rarely is a hut internally partitioned: huts are normally too small to permit this, even if there were a reason for it, which there normally is not.

The size, shape and amenities of a hut are insignificant in terms of social differentiation. The huts of a homestead are generally similar to those of every other homestead. Within a homestead, the *wai*, *depo* and *pan* are normally larger and more solidly constructed than auxiliary huts, but except for the *pan* which is distinguished by its equipment for food preparation, the functions of huts are not distinguishable by their form. Despite the ideal that a *depo* should be an open hut and a *wai* a closed hut, this is not always so in practice. Huts are instead defined by their functions. A *wai* is where the adult woman, or women, of the domestic group sleep, and a *depo* is where only men sleep. If their functions change, huts change names. In the course of their short lives, some *depo* become *wai*, and vice-versa. Other types of huts also change function when necessary.

Huts are easily constructed. Although men do not like to undertake the work alone, preferring to rely on the help of a work party or a few visitors or relatives to put up a large hut, one man with his own labour can construct a medium-sized closed hut by working several hours a day over a week's time. Usually even less labour than this is necessary, for when possible Majangir will take the roof of an abandoned hut and, with the help of neighbours, transport it whole a hundred yards or so to place on a new hut. This stratagem eliminates the need to make a roof frame and thatch it, a more laborious job than building the walls and supports of a hut.

The rather mean and rude nature of Majang housing fits the exigencies of their system of shifting field cultivation. Every year the locus of a homestead's agricultural activity partially shifts. As I explained in chapter 3, fields do not rotate around a fixed point, and in any case it is necessary that Majangir live in the midst or on the border of their major fields in order to guard them properly from animal and human theft. Possibly Majangir could relate their residence to their cultivations in a different way than they do, similar to one of the many other ways devised by swidden cultivators in other parts of the world. The custom Majangir do practise, however, is to live in the midst of their cultivations, and this requires that they shift their huts to follow their fields.

Therefore, although a Majang hut might presumably be kept up indefinitely by the replacement of its parts when necessary, in fact its life is limited by its position, not its physical condition. Most hut sites are occupied for not more than four or five years, many for only two or three years, after which they are useless: the homestead has advanced to leave them behind. New huts must constantly be made at new sites to keep up

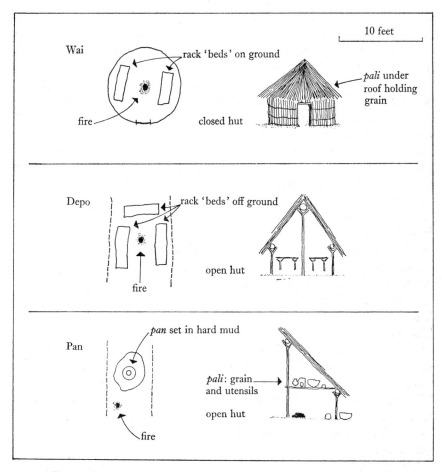

Fig. 5. Common hut types. (Examples taken from one homestead.)

with the new fields of a homestead. A whole new set of huts is not usually necessary within one year, unless a group moves to an entirely new location discontinuous with the old. But a homestead will need at least one or two new *tebungk* huts yearly from which to guard its new fields. In succeeding seasons these huts often become *wai, depo* or *pan*.

Other factors contributing to the transience of particular huts and hut-sites are (1) the ease and frequency with which domestic groups move, discontinuously, from settlement to settlement (see chapter 10); and (2) the custom of abandoning huts, if not the entire homestead, on the death of someone there, or after persistent sickness or bad luck.

The temporary and primitive nature of Majang housing is presumably responsible for the absence of strong personal and social attachments to particular huts. Persons and groups do not identify themselves by the particular shelters they use, but rather by the whole homestead which is the corporate property of their domestic group.

A homestead ideally consists of a set of different kinds of fields together with a set of different kinds of huts. These have been described in chapter 3 and in the previous section. The ideal arrangement of these fields and huts can be indicated by Majangir (see Figure 4, p. 78). The actual layout of a homestead is however determined by a complex of factors, ecological and social, which need not be elaborated here. Plans of actual homesteads are given later in this chapter. Despite aberrations in the actual layouts of homesteads in relation to the ideal pattern, most homesteads bear enough similarity to each other and to the ideal layout to show that Majangir do indeed tend to re-create on the ground a single pattern (that of Figure 4) modified to fit particular local and social circumstances.

But where the huts of a homestead are located is less important than whether a homestead includes a full complement, or set, of huts. Ideally a homestead should contain a *wai*, a *depo*, and a *pan*. Figures are presented in Table 7 of numbers of homesteads having or lacking these types of hut. The sample of thirty-nine homesteads (i.e. domestic groups) is a reduction of the size of sample used in the previous chapter, because here I will be concerned with activities such as eating and sleeping which had to be directly and regularly observed at night to determine groupings accurately. Therefore the range of information I could obtain was more limited than that about domestic group composition, which was ascertainable by daytime activity, was formally recognized by informants, and was more stable over time.

Table 7 indicates that only half of the homesteads in the sample contained the ideal complement of huts. More than a fourth included both *wai* and *pan* but no *depo*. Two out of every five homesteads had no *depo*. This phenomenon is explainable. While an adult male Majang wants, or should want, his own *depo*, he does not want to sleep and eat in it alone – no Majang likes to do these things alone. Ideally a man should always have male children and visitors to keep him company in his *depo*. In actuality, however, many men do not have male children old enough (from about eight years old) to stay with them in a *depo*, and visitors are not always about. In

TABLE 7. *Numbers of homesteads having or lacking* wai, depo *and/or* pan* *huts. Sample of thirty-nine homesteads*

A.	Homesteads having full set of huts	20	(51 %)
	Homesteads lacking *depo* only	11	(28 %)
	Homesteads lacking *wai* only	1	
	Homesteads lacking *pan* only	1	
	Homesteads lacking *wai* and *depo* only	2	(21 %)
	Homesteads lacking *pan* and *depo* only	2	
	Homesteads lacking *wai* and *pan* only	1	
	Homesteads lacking *wai*, *depo* and *pan*	1	
		39	(100 %)
B.	Homesteads lacking *depo*	16 (41 %)	
	Homesteads lacking *wai*	5 (13 %)	
	Homesteads lacking *pan*	5 (13 %)	
C.	Homesteads having two *wai*	4	
	Homesteads having two *depo*	1	

* '*pan* hut' includes cooking huts with mortar (*pan*) outside as well as inside the hut.
NOTE: Where a hut was both a *wai* and a *pan* because it served both functions – sleeping and cooking – it was counted as both. Seven (17 %) of homesteads had *pan* and *wai* combined in one hut.

fact, men who foresee a shortage of food in their domestic group often avoid maintaining a *depo* so they will not have to host guests. This is not ideal behaviour, of course, and is felt to lower one's social standing.

Therefore married men without their own *depo* are usually younger men who care less for the prestige of being a host, and who have no adolescent sons. Instead of sleeping and eating in their own *depo* men may sleep and eat regularly at a neighbour's *depo*. Or they may sleep and in cases eat with their wives. Or they may do both, use neighbour's *depo* and wife's *wai* as they wish. These arrangements will be analysed below.

One of every five homesteads in the sample had either no *pan* or no *wai*. These homesteads were all those of domestic groups which had only recently been formed, or had recently moved to the area, and the women were temporarily using the mortars and sleeping huts of neighbours until their male partners eventually would make them their own. Significantly, none of the women without a *wai* were married: they did not need a private *wai* hut for sexual purposes.

The significance of a homestead's huts, however, becomes clear only if we consider the domestic activities for which huts are necessary: sleeping, cooking, eating.

The Domestic Group: Eating and Sleeping

Owing to the long and heavy rains, Majangir must sleep under shelter for most of the year, and they prefer to do so even in the dry season. While most huts are used, even if occasionally, for sleeping, the *wai* and the *depo* and sometimes a hut called the *gode petakung*, 'girls' hut', are specifically meant to be used for sleeping.

These types of huts usually contain racks (*ye* or *jolakan*, 'rack bed') raised by supports from a few inches to a few feet off the ground to keep persons 'out of the ashes', as Majangir say. Neither the supports nor the sleeping racks themselves are very substantial; they are easily made and easily broken. They are used for sitting, resting and sleeping through the day and night. Often the racks are detachable from their supports and can be put away to clear the cramped interior of the hut; or they can be moved to a *pan* or other place when they are needed to sleep or rest on.

Girls and small children are often content to sleep on a barkcloth on the ground without a rack. Majangir think it very distasteful to sleep with nothing between them and the ground. The reason is not that they like soft surfaces – the racks are very hard – but they do not like to get dirt or ashes on their bodies.

Sleeping racks and the persons who sleep on them are never randomly distributed but are always gathered around the fire. Nights are chilly, especially after a rain, and Majang housing does little if anything to keep out the cold. Nor do Majangir have much clothing. Blankets are rare and barkcloth, while more common, is not sufficient protection against rain and cold. All Majangir rely on fires to keep them warm throughout the night. Large slow-burning logs (*gegie*) are best for this purpose, and several of them are kept burning throughout the night in the centre of the hut. The sleepers on their racks cluster around the fire. Few huts are so large as to accommodate two fires, and one fire can only warm three or four persons lying alongside it. These factors set the effective limit to the number of persons who sleep in one hut.

I mentioned previously that Majangir do not like to sleep alone. Partly this preference stems from the value they place on human company in most situations. But also a practical reason exists for sleeping in groups. A sleeping fire requires several heavy logs to burn through the night. Several persons can share one fire, each person on his own side of it, without interfering with the warmth each derives. Therefore if they cooperate in bringing logs for the fire the work of each is reduced without reducing the warmth of each.

The rule therefore that binds together a sleeping group is that every able member contribute one log to the fire each night. Persons who regularly fail to do this, I was told, will not be wanted in the hut by the others. In fact, almost everyone will contribute, not necessarily every night but frequently enough to be accepted by the others as welcome to sleep with them. Women get their own wood, just as men do. Only very old persons and children, and occasionally respected older guests, escape the necessity.

Every evening Majangir with their axes go into the nearby fields and forests to find their night logs (*gegie*). No one lays up logs for the future, and no one can claim to own a log before he cuts it and takes it home; it does not matter who owns the field a log is in, as all firewood is public property to belong to the taker. There is rarely a shortage of wood, as the Majang system of shifting agriculture provides each year new fields of half-burned logs and stumps. Indeed, as I mentioned in chapter 3, the reliance of Majangir on fire logs instead of on housing or clothing to keep them warm at night may be seen as a reason for, as well as a result of, their particular form of agriculture.

Other than the egalitarian requirement that all its members contribute fuel, there are no other obligations binding together a sleeping group. They usually, but not necessarily, share their evening meal (see below). Generally they should be friendly towards each other, and if not members of the same domestic group they will be neighbours. Irregularly the group will include visitors from outside the neighbourhood. Each regular sleeper will own or be the recognized user of a particular sleeping-rack and place by the fire.

When, as often happens, visitors or neighbours come to sleep in a hut where they have no sleeping rack or barkcloth, then the possession of these is altered for the night on the principle of seniority: older persons claim the better beds and cloths for themselves and younger persons must make do with the worse places and sleeping-things, or go to find somewhere else to sleep temporarily. This is mainly a matter of courtesy. Ownership of the hut itself means little. Several times I have seen an owner give up his hut and bed to a senior visitor and go to find another place to sleep.

The important point, perhaps, is that Majangir are quite willing to re-arrange their sleeping groups, because such groupings are formed out of convenience. Unlike the 'domestic group', whose interest is focused in an exclusively and corporately owned estate lasting at least a season, the sleeping group – which is technically also a kind of 'domestic' grouping – is based as a group on no shared interest except a fire which lasts one night only.

Huts are easy enough to build and freely enough available – in a neigh-bourhood there are usually several *tebungk* and *pan* huts vacant for sleeping – that the ownership of huts is not a critical factor. No important 'rights' are involved, no long-term relationships are set up merely by sleeping in the same hut together. Sleeping groups can, and often do, change composition frequently, overnight. Nevertheless, who sleeps with whom is an interesting index of certain factors which do impose some regularity on sleeping arrangements. These factors arise from relations within the domestic group and family.

Most men sleep away from women. Unmarried males and females sleep apart, in different huts, after about the age of eight. For them to sleep together in normal circumstances would imply the probability of sexual relations between them, raising, in the case of unrelated persons, not only the question of the nominal impropriety of such liaisons; but also, more deterring to lovers, the question of marriage and bridewealth, leading to interference by the girl's relatives. A married woman would not of course sleep in the same hut with a man not her husband, for this would imply adultery and would also lead to troublesome repercussions. And for a male to sleep in a hut with a female relative would imply something akin to our notion of incest. In short, male and female would not sleep in the same hut unless they were (1) husband and wife; (2) small children; (3) parents and small children; (4) lovers or friends, outside of situations where the female's relatives could intervene.

Questions of sexual intercourse are not the only ones involved. Men and women are anxiously shy of the other sex seeing them in an immodest position, i.e. with their private parts uncovered. This is a more serious danger for men, whose loincloths are much scantier than women's skirts and more likely to be deranged while they sleep. This fact is often adduced by men to explain why they want to keep their *depo* hidden and off the public path.

This modesty is not necessary with members of one's own sex or with anyone sexually familiar, that is, one's spouse. Men may sleep with their wives, and, because small children are thought 'stupid' and unobservant, both parents may sleep with them in the *wai* (females never sleep in the *depo*). Men will state abstractly, ideally, that males belong in the *depo*, but except when a man has visitors to keep company at the *depo*, it is a quite respectable alternative to sleep instead with one's wife at the *wai*. Many men prefer to do this.

In the survey, twelve men at the time were sleeping in the *wai* with their wives while eleven men with wives were sleeping at their *depo*. Men without *depo*, as I have noted, may sleep either at a neighbour's *depo* or at their own *wai*; often they seem to do both alternatively. But some men whose homestead includes a *depo* do not use it regularly, leaving it to their sons or other males while they sleep usually with their wives. The ages of the couples seems an irrelevant factor, except in the case of fairly old and presumably sexually inactive couples who usually sleep apart. But some young and some middle-aged couples slept together more regularly than they slept apart, and some of each category slept more regularly apart.

In some cases informants admitted that post-partum sexual avoidance – ideally until weaning but in practice considered breakable a year or two after birth – is a factor in determining whether men sleep or not in the *wai* with their wives. Men would sleep with their wives when the women did not have babies at breast, but would sleep in the *depo* when the women did. However, some couples with recently born babies slept in the same hut but on opposite sides of the fire.

Sleeping in the same hut is not necessary for sexual relations, for men may have such relations with their wives by visiting the *wai* for a short time at night, and then returning to the *depo* to sleep.

Older boy children find a *depo* in which to sleep. Girls may continue to sleep with their mother if she has no husband sleeping with her. But where a couple is sexually active, the older girl children must also sleep outside the *wai*. They may either sleep at a neighbour's *wai* where no man sleeps; or, more often, at their homestead's *pan* or even in a special hut with other unmarried females. The same is true of any unmarried women attached to a household. Female visitors sometimes will sleep in the *wai* with a wife while the husband temporarily moves to a *depo*.

There is a significant statistical difference between older, married persons, and younger, unmarried persons, as to how likely they are to sleep in a hut that belongs to their homestead and not to a neighbour's (see Table 8A). Only seven married or formerly married persons in the sample did not sleep at their own homesteads, and these seven all belonged to domestic groups which had recently been formed or had moved, and had not yet built the ideally requisite huts for their homesteads. But young persons as yet unmarried often slept outside their own homestead in a neighbour's hut. One-third of them were doing so regularly at the time of the survey. Boys, especially, tended to sleep away from home: four out of every ten were doing so in the sample.

Another way of looking at this phenomenon is to count the numbers of huts sleeping only members of one (the owning) domestic group, and huts sleeping members of two or more groups (see Table 8B). Four out of five *wai* huts in the sample slept only members of the owning domestic group. Partly this is due to the desire of older women to have their own *wai* hut, to sleep in their own homestead. This is virtually a condition of marriage. Also, when a married couple is sexually active, they cannot permit persons of another domestic group to share their *wai*. Three out of five *depo*, on

TABLE 8. *Sleeping arrangements (counting the statistically most regular arrangements within thirty-nine homesteads)*

A. Married* and unmarried persons sleeping at own or other homestead (includes only children over 8 years old, i.e. too old to sleep with both parents).

	unmarried	married*
Males sleeping at own homestead	26 (59 %)	29 (91 %)
Males sleeping at other homestead	18 (41 %)	3 (9 %)
	44 (100 %)	32 (100 %)
Females sleeping at own homestead	37 (70 %)	40 (91 %)
Females sleeping at other homestead	16 (30 %)	4 (9 %)
	53 (100 %)	44 (100 %)
Both sexes sleeping at own homestead	63 (65 %)	69 (91 %)
Both sexes sleeping at other homestead	34 (35 %)	7 (9 %)
	97 (100 %)	76 (100 %)

* 'Married' here includes single persons once married but now widowed or separated.

B. Huts sleeping members of one or more than one domestic group.

	wai	*depo*	Other huts
Sleeping members of owning domestic group only	31 (82 %)	8 (38 %)	4
Sleeping members of two or more domestic groups	7 (18 %)	13 (62 %)	3
	38 (100 %)	21 (100 %)	7

C. *Wai* huts sleeping nuclear family unit or matricentral unit of women and children (most regular arrangement):

	wai
Sleeping husband, wife and children, if any	14 (37 %)*
Sleeping only women and children	24 (63 %)
	38 (100 %)

* Includes two polygynous situations where one man was sleeping at two *wai* alternately.

the other hand, were sleeping a mixed group from different homesteads. This statistic is related to the shortage of *depo* and to the absence of any reasons to restrict male additions to the group.

The picture which emerges from the statistics is that while older and married Majangir normally sleep at their own homesteads, a good proportion of younger and unmarried persons at any one time are sleeping elsewhere. The sleeping arrangements of young persons are usually quite temporary, changing not only with the availability of places to sleep but also with the availability in their neighbourhood of friends of the same age and sex. After they reach adolescence, and until marriage, young persons often prefer to sleep with their age-mates rather than with older or younger members of their own families. Boys try to find a *depo*, and girls some other hut, in their neighbourhood where no older person is sleeping, a place they may use as a centre for the courting and music-making activities attractive to adolescents and young adults.

Another factor which influences the composition of sleeping groups is food: persons who sleep together usually also, by virtue of being together at night, share the same evening meal. A person's sleeping place is therefore often determined or limited by where he may expect a meal. To explain this factor it is necessary to describe cooking and eating among the Majangir.

4 COOKING AND EATING

In chapter 4 I described the obligation of females to cook certain foods for all members of their domestic group, and the ability of persons of either sex to cook for themselves some other kinds of foods. Thus there are in effect two different types of meals.

The kind of meal which one cooks for oneself requires little labour and may be prepared anywhere there is a fire, with little or no cooking equipment. I call this a 'simple' meal. The other kind of meal, which I will call a 'main' meal, is prepared only by females because of convention and, in the case of porridge and corn cake, because only females are adept at the techniques of preparation. To cook a 'main' meal requires more equipment than to cook a 'simple' meal, and this equipment is kept usually at one spot in a homestead. Most homesteads, as I have shown, possess the wooden mortar (*pan*) and pestle (*ude*) needed to make flour of grain. The *pan* is buried level with the earth, and normally is under or at least near a hut (called, by extension, the *pan*) where other cooking utensils and a cooking hearth are kept.

Females of the few homesteads at any one time without a *pan* will use their neighbours' equipment. Sometimes out of desire for company, a female, who has her own *pan* and other equipment at home, will visit a friendly neighbouring homestead to cook there. Such an arrangement is always irregular and temporary. The constant tendency is for all the females of one domestic group to share the same equipment to cook 'main' meals together, at their own homestead. If a group contains several females, each does not prepare a separate 'main' meal, but cooperating as a small team they prepare a single main meal. Cooperation is useful especially in preparing foods such as porridge which require much labour.

The women of a group individually prepare 'simple' meals for themselves just as men do. 'Simple' meals may be thought of as similar to 'snacks'. When a man or a woman is hungry he or she takes some food and cooks it quickly to eat. 'Simple' meals are thus prepared irregularly, at any time of day or night and anywhere there is a fire. It is impossible during the day to predict where and when one will find Majangir eating.

A 'main' meal, however, is normally prepared once a day, though some days twice and some days not at all. If it is porridge its preparation requires a number of hours' work. Partly for this reason, and partly because it should be shared by everyone in the domestic group, the main meal has normally finished cooking and is served towards evening when members of the group have returned home for the night. Thus there is some regularity about the time and place Majangir eat their 'main' meal.

I call this meal 'main' not because Majangir necessarily eat more food at it than at 'simple' meals – often the reverse is true – but because this meal cooked by women for the whole group is regarded by Majangir as the most important meal of the day. It is more important to them, first, because it will include foods cooked in the way Majangir prefer them (see chapter 4); and second, because of the importance of the social obligations involved. Men complain bitterly when they fail to receive 'main' meals from women, but the complaints are not basically about plain hunger, for men can cook 'simple' meals for themselves as they wish.

I have mentioned before that Majangir do not like to eat alone, but prefer company – at least when food is not scarce. Whether they are eating 'simple' or 'main' meals the same general rules define the persons who should and should not eat together:

(1) Males should not eat in the presence of females, and vice versa, unless they are 'familiar';

(2) Persons, male or female, who have at hand cooked food should offer a portion to anyone else present and eat together with them, unless this would conflict with rule (1) above.

To understand rule (1) one must understand what categories of males and females are 'familiar' with each other. (This word translates a distinction made by the Majangir, who, however, do not use a single term for it.) To Majangir the matter is fairly simple: generally, 'familiar' persons of the opposite sex with whom one may eat are those with whom one should not marry; but those one may marry are those with whom one should not eat. The significance of this principle will be developed in the next chapter. Here we need note that 'familiarity' is recognized only between males and females (1) who have grown up in the same domestic group or as near neighbours; or (2) who are close kin; or (3) who have been married for ten or so years. These males and females are not embarrassed to eat in the presence of each other if it is convenient to do so, though generally they will prefer to eat apart.

The Domestic Group: Eating and Sleeping

Males and females not 'familiar', however, would be very embarrassed to be seen eating by each other, so they must of course eat apart. Therefore males normally eat at the *depo*: for even if they might not have to avoid the females of their own domestic group, it is quite possible a non-'familiar' woman will be visiting at the *wai* or *pan* or will come passing through. Partly for this reason, a *depo* is preferably located off the main path. Women, on the other hand, may retire to the closed *wai*, or simply put away food when they see men approaching.

Similarly, older men put aside their food without hiding it when non-'familiar' women approach. But younger men, especially those unmarried or of marriageable age, carry the avoidance further, trying to hide all traces of their eating from girls and young women, putting their food out of sight when girls approach or yelling at them not to approach, and wiping out afterwards all signs of food having been eaten. Girls, on the other hand, follow more the behaviour of older women than of boys, and merely stop eating when males come near.

Small children, as in all things, are exempt from the rules until they can understand and practise them. Males gradually begin avoiding eating with females when they begin sleeping at the *depo*, but the avoidance becomes stringent only when they enter adolescence.

The practice of eating avoidance tends usually to divide a domestic group for most meals into two or more eating groups. The females and small children of a domestic unit usually eat apart from their male partners. However, eating arrangements are complicated by a number of other factors, including the second general rule stated above.

Women who have cooked a 'main' meal distribute it in portions taking or sending them to other huts and eating groups. But they keep a portion for their own consumption. When a woman individually cooks a 'simple' meal she does not distribute any of it away from the place she has made it. In both situations, however, the cook normally offers to share her food with other women or children who may be present, whether or not they are members of her domestic group, or whether they are neighbours or other visitors. Such offering to share is a matter of courtesy, and if one does not want to share – in times of shortage, for instance, or when scarce foods like meat are involved – one does not cook the food except at night or in a place out of the public way. Such secrecy is used to exclude members of other domestic groups, and never the members of one's own group. There is no secrecy within the domestic group, only between different groups.

Although persons should normally never ask to share food they do not 'own', in that they do not belong to the domestic group which produced it, they expect to be invited to share cooked food if they see it. Not to offer food in such circumstances, and to eat in front of another not invited to join, would be considered a very unfriendly act towards the excluded person and would offend not only the person but public opinion as well, as being very anti-social behaviour.

An eating group of women and children at the *wai* or *pan* is therefore likely to have an unpredictable composition, including frequently persons who happen to be visiting or passing through. Women of the same domestic group will tend to eat most meals together, as they spend much of their time together at their homestead. But at other times one or more may be absent during the day when 'simple' meals are taken. At night the females of the group will usually be at home, and neighbours and visitors are more likely to be absent. For the same reason the males of the group may feel freer at night to join the females and take meals with them. This is true especially of older men who sleep with their wives, and of women's sons who hope their mothers have saved out a portion of the main meal especially for them. But as I have said, most males prefer usually to receive and eat their food in their *depo*.

As well as avoiding eating in sight of non-'familiar' males, a woman should avoid seeing eating – or being seen eating by – her mother-in-law or daughter-in-law, real or classificatory. She may turn her back or go inside a hut to avoid this. Such avoidance does not prevent mother-in-law and daughter-in-law, when they are members of the same domestic group, from regularly cooking together and sharing meals, though not face to face. Father-in-law and daughter-in-law, and son-in-law and mother-in-law avoid each other eating also, but father-in-law and son-in-law do not have to avoid each other in this way.

Otherwise, when men eat, the rules that govern the sharing of meals, 'simple' or 'main', are similar to those described above, of females sharing. Men must offer to share with any other men present. Therefore the composition of daytime eating groups is likely to vary irregularly, including whoever is about at the time. It is in the evening when males return to their *depo* to sleep that the eating group is most predictable; and it is probably partly for this reason, as I mentioned, that the 'main' meal is usually then distributed to the *depo*. The evening eating groups tend to be the sleeping groups. But this is not always so: for there may be visits of near neighbours to each other's *depo*, to eat but not to sleep, or vice versa; and men who sleep at the *wai* may go to the *depo* to eat, or vice versa.

When women have finished cooking the main meal, they keep a portion for themselves and send a portion to the men who make them fields, the men of their domestic group. This is an obligation, as I have described. The women themselves may take the food to the *depo*, but they are more likely to send a child, male or female, with it. It would be embarrassing for a mature male to fetch it himself.

Where some or all the males of a group are sleeping outside the homestead, they will either return home to their group's *depo* or *wai* to eat their portions of the main meal laid aside for them; or their portions will be sent to them where they are sleeping. The first alternative is preferred in circumstances where the male(s) involved is a child or adolescent, or when a group is conservative due to shortage of food. But in many cases, food is sent to men at a *depo* where they share it with others not belonging to their domestic group. The others in turn will receive food from the women of their own domestic group and will share it also.

Thus a certain reciprocity is involved where these arrangements are regular. It is a less generalized reciprocity than that of sharing food simply with visitors happening to be about, in the knowledge that if the situation were reversed the visitors would share their food in a similar fashion. Men from different domestic groups who regularly sleep in the same *depo*, and are fed from different sources, pool their meals sent to them from these sources. If one man failed consistently to receive food from his women, he could still reciprocate by bringing raw food from his group's stores to cook and share 'simple' meals with the others. Even though reciprocity in these matters is not measured or accountable, Majangir are well aware of the obligation of each man to contribute some food to the common meals – not necessarily every day, but often enough so a man is not thought to be living continually off others. Lack of any reciprocation over time would lead to resentment and the breaking up of the sleeping–eating group.

A word should be said about the etiquette of meals. When tubers, cracked corn, etc., are eaten, each person helps himself as he eats to tubers or handfuls of corn, etc., until satisfied or no more is left. When porridge, corn-cake, relish, etc., is involved, it is brought in one lump (*gopak*) and if the eating group is small, the lump is left for each person to pull off mouthfuls to eat. Individual portions are not assigned except to certain categories of respected persons. Eating is rapid. The eaters of course must adjust their intake to that of others, no competition must be evident, and no one must be thought greedy. These factors are regulated according to conscience. Also, it may be thought somewhat bad and anti-social for a person to eat too little or to refuse to partake. Such behaviour is conventionally assumed to reflect either grievance or unfriendliness.

Between domestic groups there are other forms of sharing food than that of a mixed sleeping group. Men and also women who are neighbours and on friendly terms visit each others' homes frequently during the day and evening, and so share meals together often, though perhaps not regularly.

Sometimes the groups are friendly enough so that the women of one who have cooked a large 'main' meal will send a portion to the women of the neighbouring group. This gesture will eventually be reciprocated, but again there is no strict accounting of the flow of food between homesteads. The exchange is sporadic and irregular except in the cases of some co-wives, who ideally should send each other food more or less regularly; if they do not like each other, however, they will not do so. Also a woman should send food often to her husband's parents if they live nearby, even if they belong to a different domestic group; but the parents need not often reciprocate.

Another form of sharing food may occur in situations when a woman is sick, or absent on an extended visit. Her domestic group may then go to share 'main' meals with a sympathetic neighbouring group. Also when a domestic group exhausts its supply of food it may temporarily subsist off another group. And whenever one group needs girl-labour to make beer, the girls of another group may join it to help in the work and meanwhile to live off the household.

Therefore, although domestic groups are corporate units quite un-equivocally defined by certain bundles of rights and obligations, their separateness is in practice somewhat blurred by various activities including sleeping arrangements, the sharing of food, and the sharing of labour. This chapter has been more concerned with the internal nature of domestic groups than with their external relations. A fuller description of the inter-relations of domestic groups belongs properly to subsequent chapters on neighbourhood, settlement and community. It has been necessary here to describe the overlapping of eating and sleeping arrangements between households in order to complete the description of the domestic group.

5   CASE HISTORIES OF DOMESTIC GROUPS

The following case histories have been selected to illustrate the organiza-tion and functioning of domestic groups. The cases are untypical only in that for interest they have been drawn from complicated rather than straightforward domestic situations.

Wai Dilakan. In the dry season of 1965–6 Yigirkanti was living in Je (Gilishi) at the homestead of her mother's half-sister Ibalti. Yigirkanti's brother Dirgipin slept nearby at another homestead, but he made a field for his sister every season, and she and Ibalti cooked for him. The father of Yigirkanti and Dirgipin had long been dead, and their mother had re-married. Her children preferred to stay near their other relatives rather than go with their mother to her new husband's.

Yigirkanti had been betrothed for several years to Dilakan, and had borne one child. But they did not yet co-habit because, they said, Yigirkanti's mother was not satisfied with the bridewealth payments so far offered. So while Yigirkanti lived with a domestic group of her con-

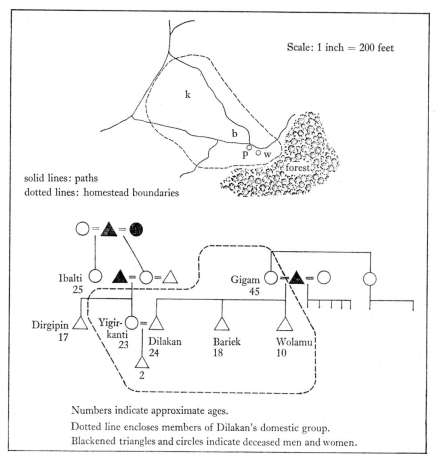

Plan 1. *Wai Dilakan*, August 1966.

w = *wai*   p = *pan*
b = *bori*   k = *kate*

sanguines, Dilakan lived about a mile away at the homestead of a ritual expert (*tapat*).

Dilakan's father died in January 1966, leaving Dilakan's mother dependent on her children. She moved with her two sons Bariek and Wolamu from their old homestead to their new *gedi*, cleared in 1965. There, with the help of a small beer party, they built a closed hut by an open *pan* hut left from the previous year, when Dilakan's mother had used it to watch the *gedi* (see plan). Bariek provided a little honey for an *ogol* party which cleared a small *bori* field. (A rainy 'dry' season prevented them clearing a new *gedi*.)

Off to a new start, the domestic group failed to prosper. The mother was old and becoming incompetent. She could not do hard work. The *bori* field was left to weeds which reduced its yield to almost nothing. The mother did not like to weed, neither did she make many meals. She depended mainly for food on her sister who lived nearby, and she even slept there, not using the new hut made for her. Her oldest son Dilakan, living with the *tapat*, had not helped the group, and her younger sons had not worked hard on their fields. They slept and ate at various other households, those of their friends and of their mother's co-wife, and also at their mother's sister's home.

At the same time Yigirkanti was having troubles. Her fields and those of Ibalti's had also partly failed, and they faced a shortage of food. Dirgipin had eloped with a girl related to a neighbouring family and even though the girl had returned home, Dirgipin could not return to Ibalti's for fear of the girl's relatives nearby. Yigirkanti could no longer depend on him to make her fields, and Ibalti's group was not that year otherwise well served by its other male partner, Ibalti's half-brother.

Neighbours in their gossip were of the opinion that now Dilakan should make fields for his wife, despite her 'bad' mother; and that he and his brothers should also make more fields for their mother. These developments they anticipated for the coming *tota* season, the making of *kate* fields. Some persons thought Dilakan would not be given permission by the *tapat* to leave him. Others said the *tapat* could not refuse if Dilakan told him he had to make fields to feed his and Yigirkanti's little son.

In fact, things came to pass as the neighbours had said they should. Dilakan and Bariek provided honey for two small parties to clear *kate* at their mother's homestead, and they added to the field with their own labour. The *tapat* gave Dilakan corn to plant. Dilakan's mother said happily that the field was for her son's wife and child. She was not only fond of her grandchild but welcomed her daughter-in-law coming to her household, probably partly because Yigirkanti could relieve her of much of the work.

Yigirkanti one day simply put her *ye* (sleeping rack) on her shoulder and went to live at her husband's mother's homestead. The two women began to sleep together in the *wai* there, and to cook food together though they had to eat out of sight of each other. Dilakan remained sleeping at the *tapat*'s and his brothers at their neighbouring mother's sister's son's *depo*.

They said they would eventually construct their own *depo*. Meanwhile, they came to the *wai* to receive what little food, at that time of shortage, was laid by for them.

Dilakan and Bariek had told me that they would clear two sets of fields, one for their mother and one for Yigirkanti; and that they would build them each a separate *wai*. This season, however, they did not, and the two women shared one *wai* and one set of fields. Bariek said that the produce would be divided after harvest and that while it would all be stored in the one *wai* hut, a partition could be made between the two stores.

Although ideally they had expected the two women's households to be separate, in practice this was impossible as Dilakan's mother was becoming unable to manage independently her own household. Nor did she want to do this. She was quite happy living with her daughter-in-law and depending on her. When Dilakan would move home to sleep with his wife (probably the next year) the two women would need two *wai* to sleep separately, but otherwise the new domestic arrangements were quite satisfactory to everyone involved.

Wai Maungkek. Since his other wife had left him, Maungkek lived with his remaining wife and small children in a simple domestic arrangement, he doing all the male tasks and she the female tasks of their domestic group.

In the rainy season of 1966, however, they were joined by Maungkek's sister, Ngingin, and her children. Ngingin's husband had become involved in a blood vendetta and had fled his former home with another wife. Ngingin and her sons also left home, but decided not to follow their husband/father but rather to settle with Maungkek.

Temporarily Ngingin's family simply lived off Maungkek's group, eating its food and using its huts and tools. Maungkek, who had previously slept always with his wife in the *wai*, built with his nephews' help a *depo* where they slept while Ngingin and Melengkai slept in the *wai* with the small children (see Plan 2).

The two families did not intend to remain one domestic group. Using some of Maungkek's *bori* land, Ngingin's sons cleared *kate* fields for her. Maungkek did not help them nor did they help him clear *kate* for his wife. The sons said they intended to build a *wai* and *pan* for their mother as soon as their crop was ready. When they attained their own food stores they would be independent of Maungkek's group. They had needed to join and depend on his domestic unit for only a season.

Wai Lapita, Wai Koinapi. In the dry season of 1964–5, Lapita was living in the settlement of Emyekai (Shiri) in a domestic unit containing his wife

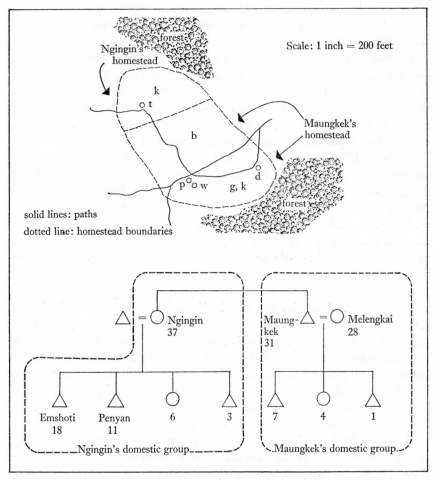

Plan 2. *Wai Maungkek*, August 1966.

p = *pan*	w = *wai*
d = *depo*	g = *gedi*
b = *bori*	k = *kate*
t = *tebungk*	

Ibalti and son Yanggan. At the edge of their homestead was a *wai* hut, the home of a woman Kwedejop and her four children. The two groups frequently exchanged food, shared meals, and cooperated closely. They justified their relationship by saying Kwedejop was Lapita's *reg*, 'brother's wife'. The 'brother' – actually only a close friend and not traceable kin to Lapita – was a man named Koinapi who was living about a mile away at the homestead of a second wife. He slept there and took most of his meals there.

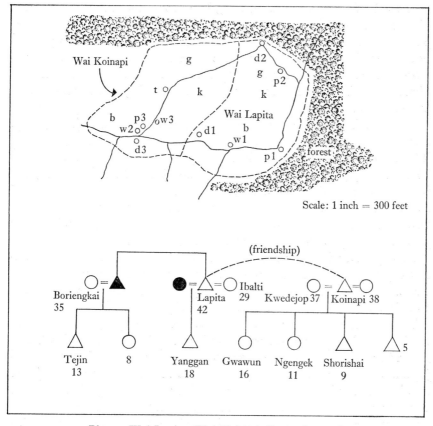

Plan 3. *Wai Lapita, Wai Koinapi*, September 1965.

g = *gedi*   b = *bori*
k = *kate*   t = *tebungk*
w1 = Ibalti's *wai*
w2 = Kwedejop's *wai*
w3 = Boriengkai's *wai*
d1 = *depo* abandoned April 1965
d2 = *depo* abandoned August 1965
d3 = *depo* September 1965
p1 = Ibalti's *pan*, abandoned April 1965, roof taken to p2
p2 = Gwawun's *pan*, abandoned August 1965
p3 = Kwedejop's *pan*

Kwedejop had until recently lived in that neighbourhood but, hating her co-wife, she was made a new home by Koinapi to separate her from her co-wife. In the dry season he began clearing a *gedi* for her, and she made beer for a working party to help him. Her *gedi* was adjacent to Lapita's, which was being cleared mainly by the efforts of Yanggan and a few honeywine parties.

The Domestic Group: Eating and Sleeping

At the beginning of the rains, 1965, Lapita's brother was murdered in a distant settlement. In the aftermath of the murder came troubles and disputes between Lapita and various relatives, neighbours, and other persons of his area. Full of grief and grievances, he was persuaded by a sister to move to her settlement, three days' walk away. His wife Ibalti went with him. His son Yanggan remained and continued caring for their homestead and the growing crops.

Yanggan, however, had to depend domestically on Kwedejop's group. Her oldest daughter Gwawun became partner in Yanggan's *gedi*, guarding it from monkeys as she worked in Ibalti's *pan* moved to a new location (see Plan 3). Yanggan received meals from Kwedejop and her daughters, and in return he gave them food. When Yanggan killed a wild boar, Koinapi acting as Yanggan's classificatory father took most of the meat for Koinapi's wives and children. Yanggan had moved to a new *depo* on the far side of his *gedi* and Koinapi's son Shorishai went there to sleep.

Koinapi had with the rains moved from his other wife's homestead to Kwedejop's, as part of the yearly alternation he said he practised between wives. He slept with Kwedejop and his youngest son in the *wai*, and the two girls began sleeping elsewhere in the neighbourhood.

Towards the middle of the rainy season Boriengkai, the widow of Lapita's dead brother, and her two children arrived at Kwedejop's. Her mourning over, she was seeking a new home. She began living at Kwedejop's but soon her son and Yanggan had built her a *wai* near Kwedejop's. She began sleeping there with her daughter and Kwedejop's daughters. Yanggan's harvest was stored here, and while Boriengkai kept cooking at Kwedejop's *pan* and sharing food with Koinapi's family, the persons involved were separating into two domestic units: Koinapi and his family in one and Yanggan and Boriengkai and her children in the other.

The only anomaly in the situation as I last saw it at the end of the rainy season, 1965, was that Boriengkai's *wai* was located outside of Yanggan's fields, within Koinapi's; and Yanggan and Tejin and Shorishai had moved back from the other side of the fields to occupy another *depo* near to Koinapi's *wai*. Boriengkai's group, however, would presumably have to move quarters in the next season to disperse itself around its new fields in order to guard them; then the two homesteads would have sorted themselves out from their temporary merger.

In 1966 I heard that Lapita had returned to his old homestead. Boriengkai, I was told, would continue to have her own fields apart from those of Lapita's wife. In fact, though I could not confirm it, it is possible that Boriengkai also became 'wife' to Lapita. But in any case she had a growing son to help her.

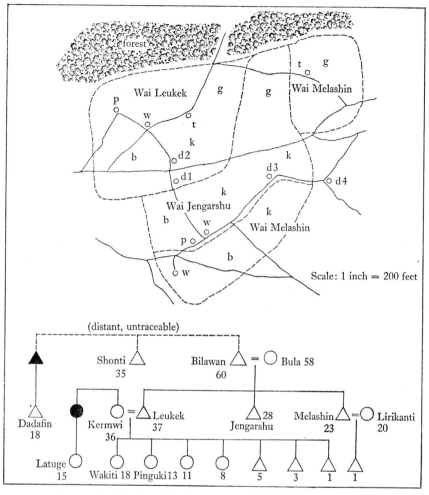

Plan 4. *Wai Leukek, Wai Jengarshu, Wai Melashin*, August 1966.

g = *gedi*   b = *bori*
k = *kate*   w = *wai*
p = *pan*   t = *tebungk*
d1 = Shonti's *depo*, abandoned January 1966
d2 = Shonti's *depo*, August 1966
d3 = Jengarshu's *depo*, abandoned May 1966
d4 = Jengarshu's *depo*, August 1966, built in May outside the home-
        stead to avoid danger of falling trees in the wind at d3.

The Domestic Group: Eating and Sleeping

Wai Leukek, Wai Jengarshu, Wai Melashin. In 1965–6, three adjacent homesteads in Gabwi (Gilishi) contained members of an extended family, the children of an old man, Bilawan, and his wife Bula. Bilawan was too old to work but his wife was still able. They formed a domestic unit with their son Jengarshu, who was engaged to marry, but had not yet given enough bridewealth to bring his wife home.

Jengarshu's younger brother Melashin was married and had, with his wife and baby, his own fields, food stores, and *wai* hut, though these were close to his parents' and brother's (see Plan 4).

Bilawan's oldest son Leukek lived also nearby at his own homestead with his wife and seven children, one foster-child and two distant male relatives, Dadafin and Shonti. Dadafin was an orphan, unmarried, and so had attached himself to the home of his classificatory 'half-brother' (*panya*) Leukek. Shonti was also a bachelor, without parents. He had been crippled since birth, though he could do token field labour. He was classificatory 'father' (*epen* or *washil*) to Leukek though they were about the same age.

The domestic economies of the three groups were essentially independent of each other, yet some of their domestic activities overlapped. For a period Jengarshu and Melashin used Shonti's and Dadafin's *depo* to sleep and eat, receiving food there from all three households. Leukek and Bilawan slept and ate with their wives. Later this *depo* was abandoned. Dadafin built a smaller one for himself and Shonti, and Melashin and Jengarshu built one for themselves and their father. The reason for this split was not conflict among the men but rather clashes of Jengarshu and Melashin with Leukek's wife. As Dadafin and Shonti's *depo* was at the edge of her homestead and received food from her group, Jengarshu and Melashin stopped living at it.

In the new arrangement Leukek and his wife and children continued eating together and, with their smaller three children, sleeping together. Dadafin and Shonti, who made fields and worked for Leukek's wife, continued to receive food from her family at their *depo*. Their affiliation with Leukek and not the other two brothers was logical because Leukek's group had an abundance, even surplus, of female labour available to provide better meals, to watch fields, etc. – in general, to match the labour of attached males.

The only regular sharing between Leukek's and the other groups was that Leukek's girl children slept and sometimes ate at their grandmother Bula's. Bula was indulgent to her own grandchildren, who would help her occasionally as well as eat with her. The four girls slept in the *pan* not far from Bula's *wai* where the latter slept.

Bilawan had moved to sleep in the new *depo* with Jengarshu. Melashin sometimes slept there, but he also had begun sleeping with his wife – on the opposite side of the fire, he told me, for their baby had only recently been born. Melashin continued to take his meals at the *depo* for he could not eat with his wife. His wife ate alone in her *wai* because she also had to avoid her mother-in-law Bula eating.

Melashin's wife did not have her own *pan*, however, though Melashin intended eventually to make her one. She did not need one because she worked happily with her mother-in-law Bula at the latter's *pan*. The two women often helped each other prepare the same meals, to which they might each contribute food from their separate stores. At night each would take a portion of the meal and together deliver it to the *depo* where Bilawan, Jengarshu and Melashin ate.

I asked Melashin why, since they shared the same meals, they bothered to cultivate different sets of fields. He replied that in this way they produced more. While possibly true, this answer evades what I believe to be a more important reason: that women, especially mother-in-law and daughter-in-law, want their own separate homesteads and domestic economies if they can so manage. As long as Bula was able to prepare food and her son Jengarshu provided her with a crop, she and her daughter-in-law could maintain their own domestic units independent of each other. Their cooperation was out of convenience and friendliness, not necessity or duty.

While the two sons and their parents shared food, they did not share with Leukek and his wife. I asked why, and Melashin said that Leukek had his children to provide for. He would give fresh corn to them, as a priority, and would not offer any to his brothers. But he would not refuse his father if Bilawan should ask. In fact, Jengarshu and Melashin had grievances towards Leukek, and vice versa, over some matters of honey and money. And their mother and father for obscure reasons were on bad terms with Leukek's wife. These tensions resulted in less cooperation and sharing between Leukek's homestead and those of his brothers and parents than by Majang standards would have been ideal between brothers, and fathers and sons.

Wai Ibalti, Wai Lempeshe, Wai Nyedekak. In the dry season of 1965–6 Lempeshe was an old man, the oldest in the area in which he lived. He had for many years been a widower, and although he had occasionally hoped to find a 'brother's wife' (*reg*) to replace his deceased wife in the household, he had never been successful. For a number of years while his children were young he had combined his group with that of Pilpil, a widow and distant 'sister' of his wife, and Pilpil's daughter Ibalti. Lempeshe could not marry or treat as freely a 'wife's sister' (*or*) as he could have done a

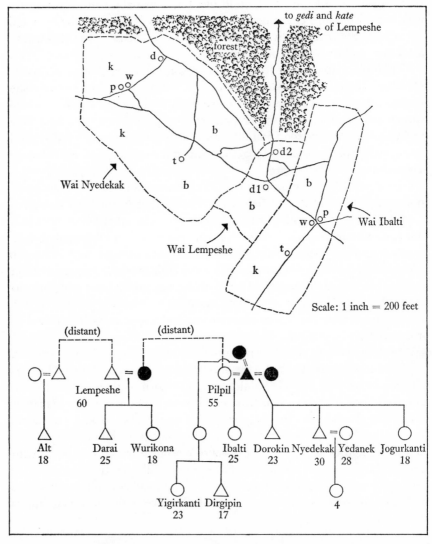

Plan 5. *Wai Ibalti, Wai Lempeshe, Wai Nyedekak*, August 1966.

    g = *gedi* (Nyedekak and Ibalti cleared no *gedi* in 1966 because of prolonged rains)

k = *kate*	b = *bori*
w = *wai*	p = *pan*
d = *depo*	t = *tebungk*
d1 = Lempeshe's *depo*	
d2 = Darai's *depo*	

'brother's wife' (*reg*). But the arrangement between Lempeshe and Pilpil and their children was satisfactory in terms of providing subsistence and raising the children. Lempeshe's daughter grew up working with Pilpil and Ibalti, and they sent cooked food to Lempeshe nearby in return for his and his son's contribution of raw food to their kitchen.

Ibalti and Pilpil had not depended only on Lempeshe, but had also been made fields by Ibalti's half-brothers Dorokin and Nyedekak. By 1965–6 Nyedekak was married and he and his wife Yedanek had their own separate household. Dorokin, unmarried, was left responsible for making fields for Ibalti and Pilpil. Lempeshe's daughter Wurikona had matured enough to assume most of the female responsibilities of her father's and brother's domestic unit, although Lempeshe often complained that she neglected them.

Lempeshe's group included a boy, Alt, who had been brought up by Lempeshe after he had refused, as an adolescent, to remain with his parents whom he disliked. Alt and Darai made fields together; Lempeshe gave them token help despite his age, and Wurikona cared for the fields and cooked a little for them. Alt and Darai, probably to escape Lempeshe's often tiresome old man's behaviour, built their own *depo* a couple of dozen yards from Lempeshe's. The two *depo* provided a haven for young male visitors and neighbours, including Ibalti's half-brother Dorokin and various classificatory nephews of Lempeshe and of Ibalti as well as friends of all the males involved.

Through 1966 there was a rapid turnover of persons who used these *depo* to sleep and eat, sometimes not contributing food themselves. Lempeshe was helpless against them but his son Darai and Alt finally abandoned their own *depo* and went to sleep at neighbours' *depo*. They would return home to eat by day when other boys were not around to share. During this time Alt became attached to another domestic group, helping them make fields and ceasing helping Darai and Lempeshe. Wurikona was now able however to make beer for working-parties, and so Lempeshe's group continued.

Ibalti and Pilpil had two large huts, *wai* and *pan*, and their home also became a haven, for female visitors and neighbours. Living with them for periods during 1966 were various women and girls, some who had crops made for them in the area by male partners and some who had none. Ibalti's half-sister's daughter Yigirkanti (see earlier, first case) had stayed at Ibalti's, and her brother Dirgipin had made fields for her. Dirgipin slept and ate usually at Lempeshe's *depo*. This arrangement collapsed in the middle of 1966, as I described earlier. But when I left, Wurikona still slept and cooked and ate at Ibalti's, as did Jogurkanti, a sister of Nyedekak and Dorokin.

Jogurkanti did most of her work for Nyedekak's group, however, and Nyedekak made her fields. Dorokin, though he ate sometimes at Nyedekak's and slept and ate around at various *depo*, worked for Ibalti and Pilpil and took nominal charge of their beer drinking parties which cleared most of their fields.

The domestic activities of Lempeshe's, Ibalti's and Nyedekak's domestic groups were very much interwoven:

Domestic groups (produce, own, draw from pooled income)	Commensal groups	Sleeping groups
1. Lempeshe, Darai, Wurikona, formerly Alt	1. Lempeshe, sometimes Darai, Alt, Dorokin and others (Darai, Alt, Dorokin often eat elsewhere)	1. Lempeshe and various others including sometimes Dorokin
2. Ibalti, Pilpil, Dorokin, formerly Yigirkanti and others	2. Ibalti, Pilpil, Wurikona, Jogurkanti, formerly Yigirkanti and others	2. Darai and others including sometimes Dorokin, Alt (Darai, Dorokin and Alt also often sleep around at others')
3. Nyedekak, Yedanek and Jogurkanti	3. Nyedekak, Yedanek, their child, sometimes Jogurkanti and Dorokin	3. Ibalti, Pilpil, Wurikona, Jogurkanti, formerly Yigirkanti and others
		4. Nyedekak, Yedanek and child

Nevertheless, these were three separate units in 1966, and not one, by the criteria discussed in chapter 4.

Dorokin explained the situation thus: though he could sleep at Lempeshe's and Nyedekak's and share food with them, he did not have the right to go to Lempeshe's *depo* or Nyedekak's *wai* or to their fields in order to help himself to their food. He had the right to take (*bonge*) food without asking (*kwe kalidi*), by himself (*duma*), only from Pilpil's and Ibalti's store, the store to which he was responsible for contributing. It is this economic relation which demarcates the domestic group, not kinship – Dorokin was more closely related to Nyedekak than Ibalti – and not arrangements for sleeping and taking meals – Dorokin did not sleep at Ibalti's and rarely took meals there. Instead, he removed raw food himself from Ibalti's or else was sent cooked food from there; for this food was the pooled income of his and their pooled labour.

7

THE NEIGHBOURHOOD
('THE SAME COFFEE')

The overlapping of domestic activities of different domestic groups leads us to a consideration of neighbourhood and, more generally, 'local organization'. Although all Majangir are united by a distinct common culture, they are not organized in any way as a tribal entity. They are organized, in the loosest sense, only at a local level. By virtue of residence, each Majang belongs to several recognized types of demographical aggregates and territorial units. We have looked at the domestic group and its homestead. Succeeding chapters will describe successively wider kinds of local groupings: the neighbourhood, the settlement, the community, and the territory. In this chapter I turn to the smallest of these groupings, the 'neighbourhood'.

It is apparent from earlier chapters that Majangir do not live in villages or nucleated settlements. Each domestic group maintains its residence, its huts, in the midst of the fields it is cultivating. Two groups cultivating adjacent homesteads will live in dwelling huts separated by at least twenty-five yards or so, but normally by a greater distance. Most of the time this distance will be grown up with crops or weeds keeping neighbouring households from sight.

Dispersal of living quarters gives Majangir the privacy they desire for two reasons: (1) to avoid embarrassment, as described in chapter 6, in their eating and sleeping and sexual relations; and (2) to maintain some secrecy, when necessary, in the preparation of food and drink. The insubstantial, open character of Majang housing would not suffice for these purposes, but dispersal of housing does. Dispersal of huts is primarily necessary, however, to protect fields from pests. Hut sites are chosen with an eye to this necessity. So huts are dispersed within the homestead as well as between homesteads.

Majangir realize that other tribes, such as the Anuak and Galla, guard their fields by other methods which allow them to maintain nucleated (and relatively permanent) settlements. Majangir regard this as a difference of custom, but see no advantages in other systems over their own, which indeed gives maximum protection to their fields with minimum bother. Nor do Majangir see an advantage in nucleated settlement as a possible means of defence against enemies. Given their lack of substantial property to defend, the dispersed settlement pattern of the Majangir in fact facilitates their traditional defence against attack by a superior force: to hide by fleeing into the covering forests (see chapter 1).

Although Majang huts are dispersed, the huts of each domestic group within its own fields, these fields may be adjacent to the fields of another homestead. The great majority of Majang homesteads at any given time will be contiguous with at least one other homestead: their fields will border. Single homesteads which are totally isolated – that is, surrounded only by forest or other uncultivated land – are occasionally found, but they are not common, and their occupants usually expect their isolation to be temporary. The norm, ideally and statistically, is for homesteads to be aggregated in clusters. Such aggregation creates 'settlements' which will be described in the next chapter; and it also creates neighbourhoods.

'Neighbourhood', as an ideal, is in fact the motive of Majangir in aggregating their homesteads. The question of whether to live isolated or aggregated appears as a real choice to Majangir, and their reasons for usually choosing to live together in adjacent homesteads are social reasons, not ecological ones. There are no important advantages to be gained in their particular system of agriculture by settling in clusters. But there are important social advantages to living in 'neighbourhood', very near to others.

These advantages centre largely on sharing. This includes the occasional lending of such things as labour, tools, utensils, etc. But a much more important aspect of neighbourly relations is the sharing of immediately consumable items such as porridge, relish, salt, fish, game, grain beer, honeywine and coffee – any consumable item, in fact, which is desirable yet is available only intermittently to a single household. By living in neighbourhood, the chances of Majangir consuming these things more regularly are greatly improved. Of course each household must then be prepared to share its consumables with others. But Majangir typically prefer to look at the positive side of sharing rather than the negative. 'Sharing' (*yoge*) as an ideal is the justification Majangir give for living in neighbourhood, and their deeds appear to uphold their words.

'Sharing', however, in its many forms, extends beyond the neighbourhood and into all sorts of relationships among the Majangir. What delimits the sphere of sharing that characterizes the neighbourhood? The Majangir recognize this sphere terminologically when they speak of persons living close enough to share '*kari omong*', 'the same coffee'. *Kari* is the infusion made from the leaves of wild coffee, with liberal addition of red peppers and occasionally various herbs, garlic, ginger, onions or salt if available.

The Neighbourhood ('The Same Coffee')

Coffee bushes, though scarce in a few areas, are plentiful in others, and as they are a forest product free to all for the taking and easily collected, *kari* is not as scarce and valued a drink as grain beer or honeywine. Neither is it seen as having the desirable effects wine and beer have, in intoxicating and satisfying hunger. Majangir say they like *kari* because it cleans the mouth of bad tastes. Probably they are also mildly physiologically and psychologically attached to it in the same way as many persons in our own society are attached to drinking coffee or tea regularly.

However this may be, most Majangir are fond of *kari*, and though less passionate towards it than towards beer or wine, they rarely pass up a chance to drink *kari*. Occasionally they will go out of their way to find some to drink. *Kari* is liked especially in the early morning, but also at other times in the day. Even in the areas where *kari* grows nearby, one household will not have *kari* at hand at all times, nor will it always have the requisite peppers, which take time to pick. In any case, a woman does not attempt to make all the *kari* the members of her household want. Persons desiring it go visiting looking for it, and undoubtedly this visiting accounts for much of the significance of *kari* to Majangir.

Since *kari* ready to drink is not usually difficult to find nearby, and since on the other hand it is not usually felt to be worth a long walk, the phrase '*kari omong*' indicates a narrow range of residential nearness. Members of a domestic group would share 'the same coffee' frequently with persons of adjacent homesteads, and the next homesteads adjacent to these. The sharing of *kari* would taper off in frequency with more distant households, rather than break off sharply at any one point, unless settlement ended there.

Thus *kari omong* suitably carries the notion of neighbourhood: it is not delimited definitely as anything resembling a unit, but rather is a vague sphere of settlement within which certain patterns of behaviour operate, more strongly the nearer persons live to each other and more weakly the further apart they live. Each domestic group has its own sphere of neighbourhood which may not be exactly the same as the sphere of neighbourhood of any other domestic group. But even the neighbourhood of one domestic group is not exactly defined.

Informants I asked to tell with whom they shared '*kari omong*' would name a number of other homesteads, the nearest half-dozen or so to their own. But the number could be expanded arbitrarily on different occasions to include other homesteads, especially if an informant wished to say something positive about his relationship with the members of these homesteads.

The same use is made of another word heard only in northern Majangirland: *olakak* (sing. *ola*), translatable as 'neighbours'. *Olakak* (perhaps related to the Majang terms *olakanak* meaning 'twins', or to *olanak* meaning 'sweethearts' in the north and 'spouses' in the south) expresses nearness of residence just as does *kari omong*. Informants who were asked to name their *olakak* would name the same persons with whom they claimed to share *kari omong*. Still another way of putting it is simply to say that two persons live in *nyon omong*, 'the same place', meaning not at the same homestead but in the same neighbourhood.

In southern Majangirland *olakak* is not heard, but informants told me that its equivalent, the term for persons sharing 'the same coffee', was *shakom*. *Shakom* may also be translated as 'friend' or 'age-equal'. Majangir explain that a *shakom* shares food freely with one. The term is thus useful for expressing neighbourliness, for every neighbour of roughly the same generation should be a *shakom* even if every *shakom* need not be a neighbour.

In explaining to me the terms *shakom*, *olakak*, and *kari omong*, and in discussing the implications of living in *nyon omong*, 'one place', with others, the Majangir showed that they are very well aware of the phenomenon I call 'neighbourhood'. This phenomenon is simply that certain kinds of behaviour usually obtain between persons living near to each other, irrespective of how or whether or not they may be related in other ways, such as by kinship or marriage. Furthermore, these kinds of behaviour tend to be more definitely manifested the nearer the residential propinquity, whereas they tend not to obtain at all when persons live further than fifteen or twenty minutes' walk from each other.

I have indicated that these kinds of behaviour have to do with 'sharing', in the widest sense. It remains to describe more specifically the content of neighbourly behaviour, and to show how residential propinquity encourages it.

In the previous chapter I described how the domestic arrangements of neighbouring households may overlap. Persons are often found regularly sharing meals or exchanging food or sleeping or cooking, etc., with members of different but nearby homesteads. The reasons behind such arrangements may be for convenience or from necessity or simply to avoid isolation, to do things in the company of others. Such arrangements may extend over long periods.

Only domestic groups which are spatially close will be able to share food, accommodation or labour regularly. Males, for instance, may share the same sleeping hut (*depo*) and the same meals on a regular basis only if the *depo* is near enough to the cooking sites of both their female partners for these to send the men food at night. This range is restricted to within about ten minutes' walk, because women will not bother to take food further to men, and because a long walk would alert too many possible unwelcome mouths to the food, along the route. Thus men who share a common *depo* and meals over a long period of time, regularly or even frequently, must be neighbours in order to remain near both of their sources of cooked food. For the same reasons females, to exchange food regularly or to use each other's cooking equipment, also must be neighbours.

Non-neighbours may come to visit a homestead and receive food and shelter, and they may stay for even a month or two, but unless they join that household as new members they eventually must leave it and return home to care for and draw on their own sources of livelihood. Neighbours, on the other hand, may continue to be involved with each other in domestic activities while continuing to maintain and be maintained by their own domestic economies.

Most non-neighbour visitors will visit one's home only occasionally, and stay for only a short time. Neighbours, however, can and often do 'visit' (*jodeng*) each other continually, and share each other's food and drink frequently. (Thus the concept of *kari omong* is appropriate, as coffee is the most commonly shared item and pretext for visiting.) This sort of sharing, which is outside of the set arrangement of domestic activity, but rather 'happens' in favourable circumstances – when both neighbours and food or drink appear at the same time – is the basic constituent of neighbourly relations.

A domestic group which comes into possession of any valuable consumable item such as beer or wine, or meat or fish, is practically obliged to share some of the item with its nearest neighbours, those of adjacent homesteads. If the quantity of the item is small, non-neighbours may and will be excluded from sharing, simply by secrecy. If these non-neighbours discover later that something was consumed without them sharing, they will normally accept the fact without perturbation. It does not matter how closely non-neighbours may be related to members of a domestic group by kinship, friendship, etc. But a group's neighbours, even if they are unrelated to it except by spatial nearness, feel that they should share their neighbours' good fortune. If they should discover their neighbours have been consuming good things in secrecy from them, the discovery leads to antipathy and strained relations between the groups, and possibly to reciprocal exclusion eventuating in a rupture of relations.

Of course, it is just within this range of nearest neighbourhood (adjacent homesteads) with its frequent visiting, especially of children, between households, that secrets can hardly be kept. Majangir therefore come to expect, almost as a right, to share in their nearest neighbours' good things; whereas those at a distance might hope, by love or luck, to be invited to share, but cannot expect to be. In every case I witnessed of a man killing a game animal, he distributed portions to his nearest neighbours. At the same time, men would not normally give any meat to a non-neighbour kinsman if the latter were not present.

The sharing of neighbours thus has a character compounded both of inevitability and obligation. I mentioned in the previous chapter that Majangir feel obliged to share food or drink with any others who may be present at the time of consumption. It is one's neighbours who naturally are always most likely to be present. Not only are they most likely to be aware of a neighbour's affairs, but they are in the easiest position to visit when they think something is available to share. A domestic group with a small amount of meat or fish will save it to eat at night to avoid too many visitors; for the same reason, small amounts of honeywine will be drunk at dawn. But neighbours may visit each other at night, when no one likes to travel further; and neighbours can easily attend each other's small drinks at dawn, when paths are wet with dew and no one likes to travel further.

In short, patterns of sharing immediately consumable items are more developed among neighbours than among any class of non-neighbours. And in this, the ties of neighbourhood appear to operate independently of the existence of any other kinds of ties, such as kinship.

The same tendencies are evident, though less pronounced, in the lending and giving of some other goods such as clothing, tools, use of land, etc. Neighbours, rather than kinsmen or other non-neighbours, usually form the small groups which a domestic group sometimes raises to help it *kanshe*, 'for free' (without drink), in some task such as moving a roof, building a bridge, or clearing a field. (This latter type of drink-less work party, called a *dadu*, is often held with the implicit understanding that the host will, when able in the future, provide drink to compensate the men who helped.)

When someone dies, that person's neighbours will usually do most of the work of preparing the grave. In the subsequent mourning neighbours of the deceased often evince as great a grief as the deceased's kinsmen. For a number of months afterwards no music should be made in the neighbourhood of the death. (There is no restriction on individuals or particular relatives of the deceased making music if it is made outside the neighbourhood.)

In several significant ways, Majangir tend to assimilate neighbourly relations into their model of kin relations. Sometimes Majangir make this explicit. I asked an informant named Kukash whether his neighbour Wolangat – they lived about seven minutes' walk apart – was his *tekan*, 'kinsman'. Kukash replied: 'Not kin. But we live in the same place (*nyon omong*) together, and when we live together we share food together and we act like kin (*tekanikin*).'

To Majangir, generosity in sharing things and helping each other is the ideal pattern of behaviour between kinsmen (*tekanir*) – those related by traceable genealogical ties or assumed common descent. The same ideal behaviour, as I have shown, obtains among neighbours; and in practice some forms of sharing are more developed among neighbours than among non-neighbouring kin. Majangir, however, do not conceive of the similarity between behaviour towards kin and behaviour towards neighbours in terms of kinsmen behaving like neighbours – there is no expression of this – but rather they conceive it as neighbours 'behaving like kin', *tekanikin*.

In fact, a substantial minority of a person's neighbours are likely to be actual kin, as I will later discuss. But here I am interested in the majority of one's neighbours, who are not genealogically related and do not belong to the same descent group. Many of these are able to assume quasi-kinship links by virtue of some remembered but untraceable relationship between two parents or grandparents. Even without such a precedent, persons can assume kin terms on the basis of friendship or long association. Being neighbours, or even having once been neighbours, is sufficient in itself to use kin terms.

For instance, a visitor named Amshelakin from another part of Majangirland was once passing through the settlement in which I was living, and I asked him if he had any kin in the settlement. Among others he named a woman who he said was his 'sibling' (*manya*) because they had lived in the same neighbourhood when they were children and had shared maize together. I asked her later, separately, whether Amshelakin was related to her and she said he was a 'kinsman' (*tekan*). Both of them admitted that the basis to this claim of kinship was not any presumed biological connection, but rather a previous relationship of neighbourhood and the common experience this entailed.

The Majang conception of 'kinship' and its extensions cannot be fully discussed here. But it is sufficient here to note that it merges at points with their conception of neighbourhood. That is, the Majangir tend to look on neighbours as 'kin', as similar in some ways to persons who are related genealogically or by descent.

This attitude takes many forms in their behaviour. I have described it in their sharing of goods. It also extends to matters of marriage and bridewealth. When a man wants to raise wealth to give to his prospective wife's relatives, he will ask for contributions not only from his kinsmen but also from his neighbours and even former neighbours. The contribution he may expect from neighbours (Eth. $1, or its equivalent) is the same amount he expects from most of his kinsmen. On the other hand, neighbours are not equated with kin in the distribution of received bridewealth, of which neighbours receive none. Nor does a marriage involve the neighbours of the persons married in new affinal relationships, as it does the persons' close kin.

Clearly neighbours are treated as kin only in certain respects, but not in others. Another example is eating and marriage prohibitions. Majangir state as a maxim that males and females should avoid (*kireng*) eating in the presence of each other (see chapter 6) unless they are kin, in which case it does not matter. They also state that one may marry non-kin, those one avoids in eating, but that one should not marry kin, those one eats with. So stated, the rule is quite clear.

In practice, however, and by admission of the Majangir, the rule is skewed by neighbourhood. Preadolescent children may all eat together, and if a male and female grow into adolescence together in the same neighbourhood they do not begin avoiding eating together, even if they are not related by kinship. As I pointed out earlier, however, because they grew up in the same neighbourhood they like to look on each other as kin, and their non-avoidance of eating together as well as their use of kin terms, claims for hospitality, etc., are all manifestations of this attitude. Because they look on each other as kin, it also follows from Majang rules that they should not marry. And indeed, Majangir also state as a maxim that one should not marry from nearby but should marry from afar. One should not marry neighbours or kin. The two are similar.

In fact persons do sometimes marry from within the neighbourhood. Such marriages are certainly more frequent and less resisted than marriage between close kin such as first cousins or members of the same descent group (*komwoi*). But the exigencies of affinal behaviour – a mixture of hostility and avoidance – are such that it becomes difficult if not impossible for an affianced pair and their domestic groups to remain neighbours. They will almost inevitably move apart to become non-neighbours. Only after bridewealth has been paid and a marriage has been in existence for a number of years, are affines able to live in neighbourhood with each other.

A change from neighbourly to affinal relations axiomatically entails the dropping of claims of kinship and the adopting of eating avoidance. While marriage within the neighbourhood is thus awkward because of the changes in relationships it causes, the fact that the parties were not actually kin – i.e. had no remembered genealogical links – makes it easier for them to assert non-kinship (*gatiat*), the ideal pre-requisite for marriage.

However, despite resistance, marriage also occasionally takes place between actual kin, persons related by known genealogical ties or presumed common descent. Difficult as it is for Majangir to rationalize these marriages, they admit that, depending on certain circumstances, it is possible for kin as close even as first cousins to marry. An important determining circumstance they cite (though I do not have enough data to confirm this) is that it is easier for kin to marry if they live at a distance, but especially difficult if they live near to each other. In a sense, then, neighbourhood appears to be a factor determining the strength of kinship – how easily a kin relationship can be supplanted by the opposing relationship, to Majangir, of affinity/non-kinship.

In keeping with the Majang conception of marriage being more possible with non-neighbouring kin than with neighbouring kin, it is interesting to note that males and females who are kin, but who did not grow up in the same neighbourhood and thus did not eat together when young, will often avoid eating with each other later in life when the possibility arises. 'Familiarity' in eating apparently stems more from ties of neighbourhood than from ties of kinship, though Majangir tend to express it in terms of the latter.

The tendency of Majangir to treat neighbours in ways as kin, and to regard the practices of neighbourhood as within the ambit of kinship, is a tendency perhaps encouraged by an ideal assumption of theirs. Of course in actual situations Majangir can, and in some circumstances must, distinguish between kinship and neighbourhood; they recognize the difference between persons related by genealogy or descent, and persons related merely by residential propinquity. Ideally, however, according to their own model of neighbourhood, the distinction between kinsmen and neighbours should be irrelevant. One's neighbours should be kin.

Majangir think this for a number of reasons. For defence in war and especially in feuds or vendettas, Majangir ideally prefer to reside in the midst of close relatives. Kinsmen, and particularly those of the same patrilineal descent group, are regarded as one's best source of support in times of troubles. Therefore it is thought best that such kinsmen live near each other.

Non-kin neighbours may also help each other in times of fighting, but such help is not dependable, for it is not morally obligatory. Only kinsmen are morally bound to fight for each other, and only kinsmen share collective responsibility for each other's actions. In practice this ideal is skewed somewhat by neighbourhood. Kinsmen not closely related genealogically, yet living near together, tend to group themselves, and to be grouped by their enemies, as collectively responsible; while often kinsmen more closely related, but living far apart, may dissociate themselves from each other's affairs, and such dissociation will be accepted by others. In this way neighbourhood plays a part in feuds and vendettas. But even the closest neighbours, who are not kin, are not held by others as collectively responsible in fights and disputes.

Another factor contributes to the assumption that one's neighbours should be kin. This is the ideal of patrilocality described in chapter 5. When a man marries, ideally he leaves the domestic group of his parents to establish his own homestead, with his wife and children, adjacent to his parents' homestead. Parents and married sons, and also brothers, would then theoretically live together in the same neighbourhood. If this settlement pattern were maintained and extended over several generations, one would expect to find neighbourhood clusters of patrilineally related kin and their wives and mothers. Allowing for some cases of men moving to live with their wives' or mothers' people (*tukudike*, v.), this pattern is indeed the one conceived by Majangir as the ideal norm.

In fact, they realize that most settlements and neighbourhoods do not conform to this ideal, and some hardly approach it. The reason is not that most newly married couples do not establish their homes near the husband's parents and brothers – most do, though some do not. Rather, the reason is found in the residential mobility of Majangir: the ease and frequency with which domestic groups move their homesteads, not only in the yearly shifts required agriculturally, but further distances to discontinuous sites and different settlements. In this moving, the large patrilineal kin clusters, which might form if settlement were relatively permanent or stable, tend to break up or not to emerge.

The forces behind residential mobility will be examined in chapter 10. To appreciate the results of such mobility, as well as the nature of the neighbourhood itself, we may look at the composition of neighbourhoods in the two settlements of which I have the most complete census information.

As 'neighbourhood' has no exact definition in practice, it is necessary for our purposes to define a sphere within which strong neighbourly relations would invariably be expected. By this criterion, the sphere of a domestic group's 'neighbours' should include all the groups living in adjacent homesteads, and in the next homesteads adjacent to these. All of one's 'neighbours' should live at most within ten minutes' walk from one's home.

Using these more or less arbitrary criteria, the census provides complete information about the 'neighbourhoods' of forty-five domestic groups. The 'neighbourhoods' of different groups include a range of from three to fifteen other domestic groups. The number of dyadic ties between 'neighbouring' groups is 230. To assess the coincidence of neighbourhood and kinship ties between these groups, we can look at the relationships between the senior male core members of 'neighbouring' homesteads. The results are tabulated in Table 9.

TABLE 9. *Neighbourhood composition by kin*

NOTE: 'Men' and 'neighbours' of this sample are the senior male members of adjacent or adjacent-but-one homesteads. The relationship between each pair of neighbours is a 'neighbourhood tie'. Some of the ties counted are to men not themselves included in the sample, as living on the edge of the neighbourhoods censused.

Category of relationship	Neighbourhood ties (230 total) of this category	Number of men (total 45) having one or more neighbours in this category
1. Patrilineal kinship, traceable	31 (13%)	23 (51%)
2. Patrilineal kinship, un- traceable: same descent group only	12 (5%)	10 (22%)
3. Patrilineal kinship (1 & 2)	43 (19%)	29 (64%)
4. Non-patrilineal cognatic kinship, traceable	11 (5%)	16 (35%)
5. Affinal relationship, traceable	27 (12%)	20 (44%)
6. Any traceable kinship or affinity (1, 4, 5)	69 (30%)	32 (71%)
7. No traceable kinship or affinity	161 (70%)	45 (100%)
8. Any traceable kinship or affinity, or common descent group membership (3, 4, 5)	81 (35%)	36 (80%)
9. No traceable kinship or affinity, or common descent group membership	149 (65%)	45 (100%)

The two communities sampled showed similar figures and thus are lumped together. In these communities, only about one-third of neighbouring domestic groups were related by traceable ties of kinship or affinity or by common descent group membership. Of the related groups, the senior male members of about half were related patrilineally; of the other half, the males were related by affinity or non-patrilineal kinship.

Between two-thirds of the neighbouring domestic groups in the sample there were no ties of traceable kinship, affinity or common descent group membership. However, two-thirds of the domestic groups were related to at least one neighbouring group by ties of patrilineal descent between their senior male members; four-fifths were related to at least one neighbouring group by some sort of tie of traceable kinship or affinity or of descent group membership. On the other hand, all groups had one or more neighbouring groups which were not related to them in any way.

The Neighbourhood ('The Same Coffee')

One figure does not appear in the table: forty-one (91 per cent) of the forty-five domestic groups in the sample were unrelated to half or more of their neighbouring domestic groups.

The figures indicate that while the neighbourhoods sampled certainly deviate greatly in composition from the ideal pattern described earlier, the pull of this pattern is not entirely absent. The bias towards patrilocality – or, more exactly, towards patrilineally related males settling together – is quite evident, though in a small and incomplete way. Furthermore, given the fact that kin ties are usually untraceable and forgotten beyond two or three generations, Majangir here would appear to live in neighbourhood with kinsmen to a much greater degree than would be expected if they settled randomly, without regard to kin ties.

Thus the figures indicate a tendency towards the ideal of men living in the neighbourhood of their kinsmen, especially patrilineal ones. From my impressions of other settlements, I believe the neighbourhoods sampled here are probably representative of the majority of Majang settlements, although perhaps there is a substantial minority in which the composition of neighbourhoods approaches much nearer the ideal. Settlements do exist in which nearly all the males are related, most of them patrilineally. I visited several such settlements in my travels, and my informants described others. In the absence of checked and complete census information on such settlements, I cannot analyse them numerically. The figures I have presented should therefore not be taken as typical of Majang neighbourhood composition everywhere, but rather as representative of what I believe to be the prevalent situation: in the majority of settlements, most neighbours are *not* kin.

Certainly the figures indicate the operation of factors other than the ideal of settling with one's brothers and other kin. The analysis of these other factors belongs to chapter 10. The morphology of neighbourhoods, as well as their shifts and developments over time, can be fully discussed only in the wider context of the 'settlement', to which I now turn.

8

THE SETTLEMENT
('THE SAME FIELDS')

In discussing neighbourhoods it was mentioned that most Majang homesteads border others. It is rare to find single homesteads which are totally isolated: surrounded only by forest or fallow, and not bordering at least approximately the fields of another homestead. Much more commonly found are clusters of two or three or four homesteads isolated from others. Clusters of five to ten and more homesteads are common also. But certain conditions work against clusterings of many homesteads, and aggregates of more than twenty or so homesteads are not often found. I will come eventually to describe the conditions which discourage large aggregations of homesteads; but first it is necessary to explore the nature of the aggregates we find.

I have spoken of 'aggregates' and 'clusters' of homesteads: these aggregates or clusters exist whenever a number of homesteads' fields are adjacent one to another, thus forming a continuous area of cultivated land. A settlement cluster exists also by virtue of its isolation: it is surrounded at the outer borders of its homesteads by uncultivated forest or abandoned fallow lands which separate it, more or less distantly, from other settled areas. Such a separate cluster of contiguous homesteads I call a 'settlement'.

If seen on large-scale maps or in aerial photographs, settlements would appear quite plainly to an outside observer as discrete demographic and ecological units. This is *prima facie* evidence for regarding the settlement as an entity for ethnographical attention. But how are these entities regarded by the Majangir themselves, and what social importance is attached to them?

The Majangir recognize that they usually live in clusters of adjacent homesteads, and they occasionally express this recognition when they say of persons living in the same settlement, that they live in '*bori omong*', 'the same fields'. As described in chapter 3, a *bori* is a previously cropped field still in use for cultivation. Therefore the phrase, 'the same *bori*', expresses quite exactly the ecological unity and distinctness of a settlement, the occupants of which inhabit a single unbroken extent of cultivated fields.

But although by this use of the term *bori* – which normally means the fields of one domestic group or the one *bori* field of this group – the

The Settlement ('The Same Fields')

Majangir recognize the concept of a 'settlement', they do not appear to treat the concept as particularly useful or important. *Bori* in its extended meaning of 'settlement' is used by Majangir only infrequently and in limited contexts, usually to express the nearness of residence of persons living in *bori omong*, the same settlement. But the word *bori* cannot be used to express such notions as, for instance, 'my settlement', 'the settlement he comes from', 'two different settlements', 'a number of settlements', and so on, because in these as in most contexts *bori* retains its other meanings as 'the fields of a household' or 'a previously cropped field', and does not mean a 'settlement', in the sense I am using the word.

The term *bori*, therefore, is not a very useful term for discussing localities and local affiliations: at least I did not find it so, and the Majangir themselves rarely make use of it for these purposes. Yet there is no other term in Majang to express the notion of a discrete unit of contiguous homesteads – what I am calling the settlement.

Verbal difficulties exist also at the level of identifying particular settlements by proper names. No Majang settlement has a verbal identity independent of its locale. A settlement is invariably referred to by the name of a particular geographical feature: a stream, mountain, gully, pond, type of vegetation, etc., which characterizes the particular locale that the settlement is exploiting. But the Majangir are shifting cultivators of the sort that all their settlements are continually, gradually shifting location; and almost always as the settlements shift they adopt new names from the geographical features of their new localities, and abandon their previous names together with the localities which furnish them. Any names by which a settlement is known are thus as temporary as the settlement's locale; and a settlement as an aggregate of shifting homesteads carries no verbal identity over time.

But even at any given point in time, many settlements are known by no single, exclusive name. A single settlement, especially if it is extensive, may be treated terminologically as two or more places, one end of the settlement being designated by one proper name, the other end by another. Or two quite separate but nearby settlements may be known by one name from a common geographical referent. Or settlements which are separate and distant, but border an extensive geographical feature so that they are at different points on the same river or on opposite sides of the same mountain, may share the same proper name derived from this feature. In such cases confusion is avoided by general qualifications such as 'upriver', 'downhill', etc.; or more specifically, by simply referring to settlements as the homes of well-known persons living there.

This kind of linguistic behaviour might seem to indicate that Majangir do not unambiguously recognize settlements as significant units, or 'the settlement' as a significant concept. But to understand this matter let us pass from linguistic to other kinds of social behaviour.

The behaviour described in the previous chapter as characterizing the 'neighbourhood' is also the behaviour which obtains to some extent within the settlement, for of course a settlement is composed of one or more neighbourhoods. But it is obvious also that what I have described as the neighbourhood, and what I have defined as the settlement, are not the same thing. The reasons for this are twofold. First, except in the case of smaller settlements, the range of neighbourhood is too limited to be co-extensive with the whole settlement. Second, while settlements are discrete units isolated ecologically without overlap, neighbourhoods are usually not this. Different spheres of neighbourhood in a larger settlement will overlap. Each household has its own sphere of neighbourhood which may be different from the spheres of neighbourhood of all other households.

Therefore neighbourhood and settlement cannot be regarded as the same thing, except in the case of the smaller 'neighbourhood settlement', which is compact enough for all its households to include each other in neighbourly patterns of behaviour. Such a settlement will contain only about a half-dozen or fewer homesteads. A larger settlement will be too extensive for all its residents to belong to one neighbourhood; it is composed instead of a number of overlapping spheres of neighbourhood.

If a larger settlement is not a neighbourhood, the question arises of whether it has any basis for existence except as an accidental accretion of domestic groups seeking to associate in neighbourhood. Is a settlement, as a settlement, apart from the neighbourhood ties I have described, a significant social unit in its own right?

It is possible to evaluate what the settlement is and is not. It does not form a distinct unit for participation in drinking parties for work and ritual: these activities will usually draw participants from a much wider area than one settlement (see next chapter). The inhabitants of a settlement never, in my experience, form a group for cooperative effort of any kind on the basis of settlement membership. The inhabitants of a settlement own no property in common, not even a land or territory. Each domestic group owns the land it has cultivated, and each has rights to new forest land adjacent to its cultivations; but rights to other land about a settlement may be claimed or obtained by outsiders without reference to the settlement's members (see chapter 11). Except for the area its homesteads occupy, a settlement is in fact never associated with any delimited territory, pertaining to it as opposed to other settlements.

Just as a settlement is not a corporate group for economic purposes, neither is it one for political purposes. Social control among the Majangir operates without reference to settlement affiliation. Settlement membership also does not serve as a basis for collective defence against enemy raids. Nor do settlements act collectively to face present-day incursions of government tax-collecting expeditions. All of these actions, in cases where collective action is taken at all, are based on other organization than the settlement.

Corresponding to its lack of economic or political purpose, the settlement is not regarded sentimentally or ideologically. I pointed out earlier that the Majang concept of settlement is undeveloped, and that often a settlement will have no single unambiguous name. It is not surprising then to find that the settlement is not recognized as a unit for any ritual purpose; or that inhabitants of one settlement manifest no in-group feelings in regard to inhabitants of other settlements. Majangir simply do not use settlement membership to define themselves as social groups in opposition to other settlements.

The members of a settlement may be related to each other in any number of ways: there is no predictable pattern. Most of them will usually be connected either directly or through others to many of the other settlement members either by kin ties, affinal ties, clanship or assumed kinship. (For examples, see Figure 6 below, with Map 2.) But settlements are not kin communities in the sense that composition and recruitment would tend to follow any single principle of kinship which would organize or give a predictable structure to such communities.

Theoretically, a domestic group is free to add itself to any settlement it would like, whether there exists any relationship or not between members of that domestic group and anyone in the settlement. Actually, a domestic group will not move to make a new homestead at a different settlement or neighbourhood except on the basis of understandings reached with at least one resident of the neighbourhood being moved to. And such understandings presume pre-existing relations of some kind. The point is that almost any kind of real or assumed relationship, of kinship, clanship, affinity, or simply friendship, can be used to justify the entry of new domestic groups into existing neighbourhoods. What matters is not the formal aspect of the relationship, but simply whether the parties are friendly at the time. Therefore the compositions of different settlements are likely to be quite varied, as can be seen in the mixed compositions of neighbourhoods shown in Table 9 of the previous chapter. Moreover, settlement and neighbourhood composition is subject to rapid change, owing to the mobility of Majang domestic groups (see chapter 10).

An assessment of the settlement leads to the conclusion that as a unit it has no particular social significance for Majangir. The small neighbourhood settlement shares only the ties of neighbourhood I described, while the larger settlement does not emerge as a social unit of any kind: its unity is merely spatial and ecological, while socially it is best viewed as a cluster or series of overlapping neighbourhoods.

To understand why such a definite spatial unit acquires no particular social significance for Majangir, Majang settlement must be considered in its temporal dimension. Individual settlements, seen at any one point of time, appear quite definitely to be units. But such unity dissolves when settlement is seen over a number of years' time. Historically, individual settlements are seen to be transient, *ad hoc* accretions of homesteads or neighbourhoods. Settlements, large and small, are constantly springing up, merging, shifting, dividing and disintegrating in ways which leave a single settlement no continuity. Settlements certainly do not live longer than their members. Most settlements which exist today could probably not be identified as ones which had existed ten years previously, or as ones that will exist ten years in the future.

Behind such impermanence is an admixture of social and ecological factors which militate against the stability and continuity of settlement. Essentially, perhaps all these factors stem from the nature of the Majang system of shifting field cultivation. This system was described in chapter 3. As the fields of a domestic group gradually shift, the huts of the homestead shift with them, for they must be located in the currently planted fields in order to guard them properly and conveniently. The main huts of a homestead are then moved every few years. Each year a large portion, often more than half, of the domestic groups of any given settlement will shift their residences. It is apparent that in the course of several years a settlement may lose its form: that is, the spatial relations between its constituent households may be altered. In several more years a settlement may simply break apart, if its homesteads are moving away from each other in different directions.

Under the constant necessity for all homesteads to be continually shifting their locations, an aggregate of domestic groups, a settlement, would probably remain together as one unit only if there were some advantage or compulsion or desire to remain so. But we have seen that there are no particular common interests or social activities involved in settlement membership – indeed, strictly speaking, there is nothing about a settlement involving 'membership' for those living there. The settlement, as a settlement, provides no inducement to its constituent units to shift together and not gradually apart.

Ties of neighbourhood, on the other hand, do have social meaning for the Majangir, and Majangir in many cases explicitly try to preserve neighbour relations when shifting residence. Neighbours who want to remain such try to do so by making fields in the same direction, advancing along a common front, so to speak. I have said how a large settlement can be regarded as a cluster or chain of interlocking spheres of neighbourhood. This cluster or chain of neighbour relations might then theoretically also advance along a common front on the basis of a general desire to preserve the existing spatial relations on which neighbour relations depend.

Although such linkages might and occasionally do occur over a few years, the chain, as it is, will only be as strong as its weakest links. But neighbour relations are not so strong or permanent as to keep many neighbourhoods intact for many years, and certainly not to keep settlements intact for more than a few years. Neighbour relations are based initially on the close, friendly personal relations which induce domestic groups to immigrate into particular neighbourhoods. It is through such recruitment by personal ties that small settlements expand into large ones if ecological conditions permit.

Neighbour relations are maintained by intense sharing and social interaction based on the initial friendly relations. But it is perhaps because ties of neighbourhood depend simply on the strength of personal relations – rather than on more durable ties of a formal, jural or economic nature – that neighbour relations are ultimately fragile. They are easily disturbed by any petty conflict or dissatisfaction between neighbours, and the high ideals Majangir hold of neighbourly behaviour may easily lead to dissatisfaction or conflict. When neighbours fall out, or simply become cool towards each other, there remains no reason for them to keep living in neighbourhood, and personal disaffection will sooner or later be translated into spatial separation.

Disaffected neighbours either shift gradually away from each other, or leave altogether to migrate to another settlement. I mentioned before that it is easy for Majangir to find alternative locales in which to settle, owing essentially to the surplus of cultivable land in Majangirland. Thus the mobility of the Majangir, and their freedom to break out of one set of residential affiliations and to establish others, depend essentially on their ecology which permits this. Therefore ties of neighbourhood are usually not durable enough to keep a settlement together, either to keep domestic groups from leaving, or, more important, to persuade domestic groups to move together, year after year, as a unit. In fact, the falling apart of neighbourhoods causes the falling apart of settlements.

If there is no social compulsion to maintain settlements as units, neither are there ecological reasons to do so. In fact, the Majang ecology not only permits the breaking up and rearranging of settlement patterns through the general availability of land; but it also encourages these developments by limitations it places on the specific availability of land: that is, limits to available land in particular places.

For instance, we have seen that Majangir must be continually clearing the forest and moving their homesteads because their system of agriculture cannot cope with the declining fertility of old fields, and especially with their invasion by grass. Normally, when land has been cleared in the midst of forest, the intrusion of grass does not become a problem for at least four or five years, during which the old fields, the *bori*, may be cultivated every year until they lose fertility. But inevitably grass invades them, and often the invasion begins to spread rapidly even into fields which have been cultivated only one or two years. A domestic group must then expend much more labour to clear a larger *gedi* field every year, and depend mainly on new fields because old ones must be quickly abandoned. Finally, however, Majangir will avoid the problem by moving altogether to another location where grass has not set in.

This development encourages the total break-up of settlements: instead of moving together on a common front, clearing a continuous wide swath of land with old fields at their backs, and forest and new fields at their front, the settlers fleeing from the grass must break away from their old fields altogether. Since they must move anyway, and since nothing constrains them to move at the same time to the same place, settlers will usually move, in individual households or neighbourhood blocs, at different times to different places. They will use the need to move as an excuse to join or begin other neighbourhoods and settlements, rather than re-form their old settlement in a new place. Settlements which cannot continue geographically will normally not continue in any form, their settlers dispersing rather than transplanting the old settlement.

Another ecological factor restricting the permanence of settlements is the Majang insistence on having their households located near water. This is simply because women dislike the work and inconvenience of carrying water long distances; and men dislike the inconvenience of doing without water for drinking or brewing honeywine, simply because their wives and daughters have shirked going to get it. Normally, a walk of more than ten or fifteen minutes to water is considered intolerable, although the range can vary widely, depending on the number of females in a domestic group and their willingness to work. The Majangir could presumably, if necessary, live much further from water than they do, but there is enough available land and water in Majangirland to make the extra work seem unnecessary. So at a certain point, and perhaps often in conjunction with other reasons, a domestic group will decide it is no longer worthwhile to live so far from water, and will choose to move to a new location nearer it.

The Settlement ('The Same Fields')

It is also thought advantageous, if living near a permanently flowing river, to have one's fields right on its banks if the land is suitable: for on such land a household can manage to grow a dry season crop in addition to the usual two rainy season crops (see chapter 3).

The result of the Majang desire to live as close as possible to water is reflected in the shapes of their settlements: elongated when on streams or rivers, clustered when around springs or waterholes. Settlements on rivers will shift up or down the rivers, their households keeping near the water. If at both ends of a river settlement there happens to be cultivable forest, it is very likely that a large settlement will simply break into two parts, and each end go in a different direction. If, however, both ends of a river settlement are uncultivable – for instance, if a settlement arrives at an area which has too recently been abandoned by other homesteads – then the settlement will break up, as it cannot continue spatially. Few settlements in fact can travel for many years along a river in Majangirland without encountering another settlement. If two meet each other moving in opposite directions, they will temporarily unite, then break up, as no more land is available in either direction.

The permanence of larger settlements on rivers is also discouraged by another set of ecological factors. A large settlement cannot often continue as a unit because it is too awkward for it to shift as a unit. The space at the advancing end of the settlement, the end where there is cultivable land, will be too narrow to permit all the households to be near water yet to move on a single front, the only way they could preserve their patterns of neighbourhood relations.

The alternative way for all homesteads to continue as one large river settlement would entail the continual leapfrogging of all the homesteads: the ones in back of the settlement jumping over the ones in front to get to suitable forest land near water. But such overjumping would derange existing neighbourhood ties and require the forging of other ties where perhaps this was impossible, and would be continually depriving persons of the use of their *shompai* lands, since they would have to leave them too far behind in order to jump an extensive settlement. None of these obstacles arise in the case of small neighbourhood settlements, but they do arise for larger settlements, and serve to encourage their fragmentation.

In the case of a settlement depending on a spring for its water, it must be impermanent; and the larger it is, the fewer years it can exist, for it will use up all the sooner available land within a tolerable walking distance from the water. When homesteads of a settlement around a spring must abandon the site, again they will do so at different times and will move to different places, dispersing rather than reconstituting the old settlement.

The Settlement ('The Same Fields')

I have discussed some of the ecological and social factors which contribute to render Majang settlements unstable and transient. These factors emerge more clearly in actual cases than in generalizations, so I wish to describe one such case in detail.

The five maps (2-1, 2-2, 2-3, 2-4, 2-5) show settlement at five different points of time, along one small section of the Shiri River. This river is small, from twenty to forty feet across, but it is swift in this area, and may be forded without difficulty only at certain places at certain seasons if bridges are not made by felling trees across it.

Homesteads are indicated on the maps by capital letters, which also serve to identify the senior male members of these homesteads on the genealogical chart (Figure 6) showing the kin connections between them. Where on the maps the same letter is raised by different numbers, these indicate separate homesteads belonging to different wives of one man, who belongs to both homesteads. Land recently abandoned to fallow is indicated on the maps by shaded areas. The areas being cultivated at the time represented by the map are shown occupied by homesteads and are in outline: these outlined blocs are what I speak of as 'settlement'. Forested, uncultivated areas are left blank.

Map 2-1 shows the neighbourhood settlement of Koya in the upper left-hand corner, as it was around 1950 according to informants. It took its name from a whirlpool (koya) in the river at that location.

Map 2-2 shows the large settlement of Til as it was in 1959. 'Koya' has disappeared, although its inhabitants have not. Between 1950 and 1959 the homesteads of Koya gradually shifted south-eastward, keeping near the river for the sake of easy access to water. Settlement was forced to abandon one bank of the river, however, because of outcroppings of rock there at the base of the hill. Between 1950 and 1959 the settlement lost domestic groups D and E due to the death of their father/husbands; but the other members were absorbed by B and A. C's group broke up on the death of his wife, but his son H has established a new homestead. The settlers from Koya have been joined by a number of immigrant groups, as is evident on the map.

By approaching a new source of water, a wet-season spring called a *til*, the settlement has not only taken this as its name, but one end of the settlement is partly freed of its dependence on the river for water. Thus eleven domestic groups are able to make fields for a time along a common front, none of them being far from water, at least during the rainy season lasting eight or nine months of the year.

Map 2-3 shows the settlement three years later, in 1962. More immigrants have come, and settlement has pushed again across the river. The

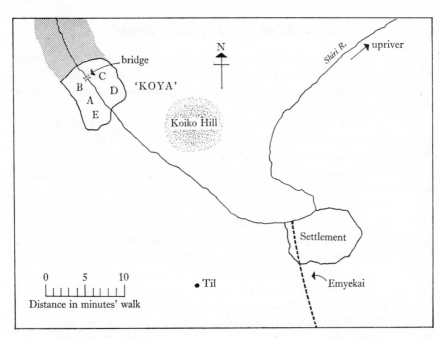

Map 2-1. Til-Emyekai 1950. Enclosed areas = settlements; shading = abandoned fallow; capital letters = homesteads; blank areas = forest (see text for full explanation).

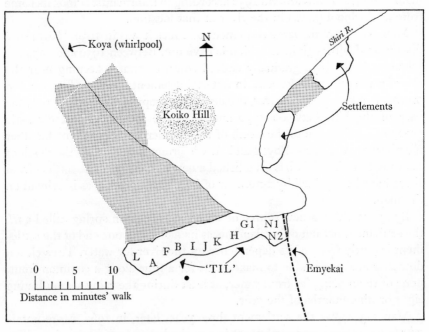

Map 2-2. Til-Emyekai 1959 (for key see Map 2-1).

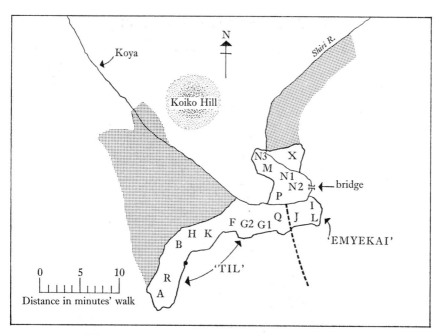

Map 2-3. Til-Emyekai 1962 (for key see Map 2-1).

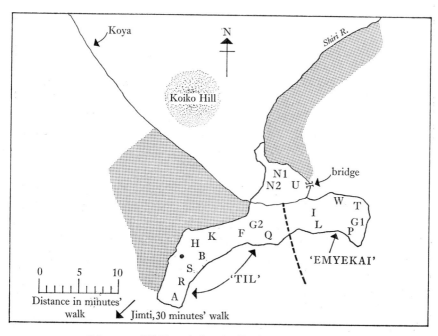

Map 2-4. Til-Emyekai 1964 (for key see Map 2-1).

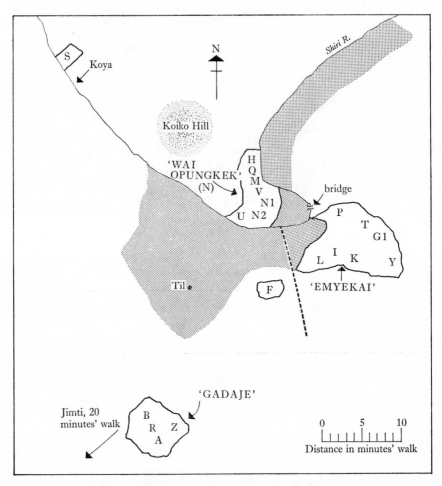

Map 2-5. Til-Emyekai 1966 (for key see Map 2-1).

settlement has become so extended that it takes as much time to walk from homestead M to homestead A, forty minutes, as it takes to walk from A to another settlement directly south. Notice also that there has been a re-alignment of some homesteads within the settlement. J, L and I, for instance, have broken from the Til area to cross the dry gully called Emyekai. This end of the settlement is now called Emyekai as opposed to the other end, Til. The settlement has now become terminologically two, while still geographically one unit of contiguous homesteads.

The men of J, L and I claimed that they had moved from their previous neighbourhoods because they had been too far from water, Til waterhole

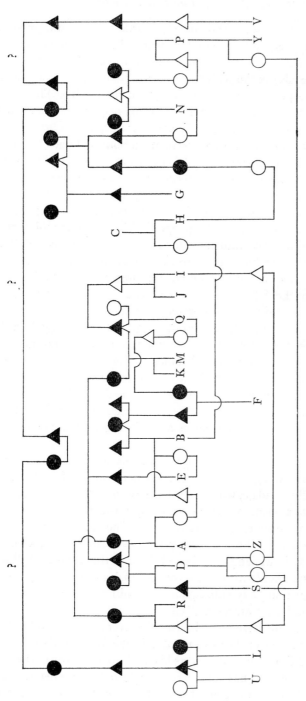

Fig. 6. Genealogy of Tïl-Emyekai: kin connections of senior male members of domestic groups of Koya, Tïl, Emyekai, Gadaje and 'Wai Opungkek' settlements, 1950–66.

Note: capital letters indicate the senior male owners of homesteads denoted by the same letters in Map 2. T, W and X on Map 2 are not connected by kinship to the others. ? question mark indicates a claimed but dubious connection. ⊔ indicates marriage. Purely clan connections (without known genealogical links) are excluded.

being dry in the dry season. And more important, they said, grass was beginning to invade fields too soon in the Til area. Personal factors may also have played a part in the break, though my informants would not admit this. Homestead F also broke with the Til area, its members complaining of grass and of the poor quality of Til water for honeywine. The man of homestead H, however, married a relative of his neighbour G and found himself subsequently beaten and tied up by G for purposes of bridewealth; so H moved away from his brother-in-law neighbour and back to Til.

Map 2-4 shows the settlement of Til-Emyekai as I knew it in 1964. It is still held together as one settlement, but certain strains are developing in the Til area. Some of the residents are complaining about their distance from water, and are hesitating to move their huts further away to keep up with their new clearings. More seriously, people in Til are complaining about the rapid invasion of grass into their fields. Settlement about the Til is doomed, but people are reluctant to leave. The Til homesteads theoretically could all move further upriver beyond N, thus preserving the settlement as one. But several of the Til men for personal reasons would not like to live near N, and the other side of the upriver is unsuitable recent fallow. But also simply no necessity is felt to keep the large settlement together. The senior male member of A feels it is more important, in terms of his social activities, to be living within easy distance of Jimti, another settlement directly to the south. H and K are thinking of moving downriver to reopen the old Koya lands. A remonstrates against this: he thinks this place would be too far from the drinking activities of Emyekai and Jimti. A in fact regards the place he lives at present as a good geographical position, for social purposes.

In Map 2-5, only two years later, 1966, the one settlement has become five. Til is no more. A, together with B, R and Z, has moved far out into the forest to a spot called Gadaje, where they have escaped the grass completely and have moved to a position, as they see it, equidistant from the drinking parties of Jimti to the south and Emyekai to the north. The price of this move is that these households are further than ever from water, an extraordinarily long way in Majang eyes, half an hour in the dry season. But A, B and R are all households with many young females who can be got to do the work. They plan anyway subsequently to shift their homesteads in a northerly direction back towards the Til.

Other Til homesteads have moved across the river and to Emyekai. Two domestic groups have elected to live isolated in the forest. F also wants to live near Jimti and Emyekai, and expects his fields to join those of the latter settlement in a few years. S has gone to resettle the old Koya area, where he hopes eventually to persuade some friends to settle with him. S did not move to Gadaje with his classificatory father A and brother Z, because he had fought with them.

The part of the settlement across the river, which has always been known by the name '*wai Opungkek*', i.e. the home of N, has technically become a separate settlement from Emyekai, owing to the abandoning of the fields between them. The two are still very close (1966), though they are moving in different directions which will separate them further in the future. Emyekai itself will probably divide in another few years, as P, T, G and Y are making fields in one direction and L, I, K in another.

This example, which we have followed cursorily through these five maps and sixteen years, is not untypical. It shows why it is difficult to see a Majang 'settlement' as anything more than a temporary, *ad hoc* aggregation of homesteads. At any particular point in time, as in these maps, Majangir demographically may be seen grouped into discrete settlements; but over time, as the maps show, Majangir ungroup and regroup in ways which deny continuity of form or unity to any particular settlement grouping.

By looking at settlement over time it is understandable why 'the settlement' does not emerge in Majang life as a significant social unit. In explaining this negative aspect, the insignificance of 'the settlement', I have attempted to explain some of the positive factors which determine settlement patterns among the Majangir.

The significance of ecological factors is obvious. In chapters 9, 10 and 11 some of the social factors involved in settlement patterns, touched on in this chapter, will be described further.

9

THE COMMUNITY ('THE SAME BEER')

I have mentioned the absence of any sort of in-group solidarity among members of the same settlement. Thus in their intercourse with members of other settlements Majangir are not divided by local allegiances based on settlement membership. Put in another way, there are no 'inter-settlement relations' *per se*. The relationship is one only of distance. Owing to this factor, of course, persons will generally be more familiar with members of their own settlement than with those of other settlements, but the difference is one of degree, not of kind.

Because of their mobility and the shifting transience of their settlements, Majangir are likely in the past to have resided in the same settlement if not the same neighbourhood with many persons who subsequently have come to reside in other neighbourhoods and settlements. Thus Majangir are usually closely acquainted with many persons outside their current settlements. But also, the important collective activities which gather Majangir together frequently for work, ritual and fun are not restricted to the members of one settlement: they typically engage the members of a larger area encompassing a number of settlements.

This area is recognized by the Majangir, who call it '*tajan omong*', 'the same beer'. The reason for this name is that it is grain-beer (*tajan*) which normally serves as the indispensable focus for these large gatherings. Alcoholic drink is highly valued and desired by Majangir for a complex of reasons which I cannot discuss here. Of the two kinds of intoxicants Majangir know, they generally prefer honeywine (*ogol*) for its taste. But in grain-beer Majangir recognize two advantages: (1) unlike honeywine, it is filling enough to be a sustaining substitute for food; (2) unlike honeywine, it can be provided in great enough quantities to host many people.

Ogol drinks, while held often for the same purposes as *tajan* drinks, are almost invariably small, attended primarily by neighbours and persons arriving by chance. They are kept relatively secret until they happen. Beer drinks are usually a more public occasion. The preparation of beer, unlike that of honeywine, requires many stages lasting over many days, and persons from a wide area hear of the imminence of the beer drink, and come to attend it. Once at the drink, they may remain all day and often longer because the beer by its quantity and substance can satisfy the hunger of a crowd.

The Community ('The Same Beer')

The overt purpose of a beer drink may be one of several. Small drinks called *shuki* are sometimes held for no purpose except simply to drink. But the larger drinks, with which we are here concerned, always are planned for a purpose either ritual or economic.

Most Majang ritual does not absolutely require drink, which is not always available. But when possible Majangir make drink to accompany rites. Drink contributes to the efficacy of ritual in two ways. It is regarded as one of the best means, sometimes the only means, of propitiating the various dangerous spirits on which Majang ritual focuses. The spirits value drink, not so much because they themselves like to drink the libations offered them – though they do like this – but because they appreciate the dedication of the whole drinking party to them. And they simply favour the act of drinking. So Majangir explain it. Secondly, drink is required to attract the large congregation of persons whose presence is desirable at most rituals, and necessary at some, in order to muster an impressive demonstration of human solidarity to persuade the spirits to relent in their evil-doing.

The other purpose of a large drink is to host a working party (*gamat*). Practically all subsistence tasks can be done by the members of a single domestic group, one or two persons. It is not from practical necessity but from social preference that much of the heavy work of agriculture, as well as of hut-building and occasionally hive-making, is done by means of large working parties.

A number of times each year, a domestic group will provide beer to attract and host other persons to help them finish in a day some piece of work, such as clearing a field, which would have taken many days for the members of the domestic group working alone to finish. Those who are freed in this way from having to work for themselves can devote their time instead to attending the drinking parties of other domestic groups and working for them. The basic economics of the situation are obvious. What the average household loses in grain when it makes beer to host others, it gains in the meals it saves when its members drink the beer of others.

In practice, of course, this system does not even out perfectly. Some persons undoubtedly drink more beer in a season than they provide; and vice versa. Some persons give more labour than others. These things are not accounted by Majangir. Also, for lack of resources a domestic group will occasionally not be able to provide drink during a season and must do its own work. Labour cannot be exchanged for money or goods or food or, except in a very limited way, for labour in return; nor can labour normally be commanded from outside the domestic group through kin or other types of obligation.

On the whole, however, the drinking party, and especially the beer drink, serve to organize the bulk of the heavier agricultural work done by the Majangir. Each domestic group, as the sponsor of the party and provider of the drink which is shared by the drinking group, retains sole ownership and control of the product of the drinking group's labour. The domestic group remains autonomous. But instead of each domestic group tediously labouring in isolation, Majang agricultural activity is characterized by the festive gatherings and communal efforts of drinking groups.

The importance of the drinking party is not confined to its overt purposes of work and ritual. Drinking parties are occasions of other important activities of Majang social life. Music, dancing, fighting, courting, gossiping and disputing all find their main opportunities at these gatherings. Without drink, more than a dozen Majangir will rarely congregate; only under the pressure of an outside threat, such as an enemy raid or a visit of government tax-collectors, is it sometimes possible to muster a large group for collective action. Yet with drink hundreds of persons from wide areas are easily and frequently gathered. The community life of the Majangir is based on the drinking party.

When it is said by Majangir of persons or settlements that they share '*tajan omong*', 'the same beer', it means that they live near enough to hear about and regularly attend each other's large drinking parties. A publicized drink will normally attract the people living within a radius of five to ten miles. Who comes to a drink, and from where, depends of course on many factors, such as the density of population in an area, the availability elsewhere of competing drinks on the same day, various kinds of social ties, etc. Generally, however, the nearer persons live to each other the more frequently they will attend the same drinking parties.

The sphere of beer-sharing, however, is limited at the outside by the distance a man can easily travel, have time to share the drink, and return home by nightfall. This maximum distance seems to be between five and ten miles (two or three hours' walk). Majangir do occasionally go further to visit and drink, but it is only within the sphere described, *tajan omong*, that persons attend each other's drink fairly regularly. Within this sphere a person can maintain close acquaintance with most other adults, because he works, sings, drinks, joins in ritual and talks with them frequently. For each Majang, therefore, this sphere of 'the same beer' constitutes what we may call his 'community'.

The 'community' is similar to the Majang 'neighbourhood' in that it is not a discrete unit: just as every homestead has its own neighbourhood, every neighbourhood has its own community. The effective communities of different settlements overlap. The community, like the neighbourhood and the settlement, has no nucleus and does not constitute an on-going exclusive group. But – unlike the settlement – neighbourhood and community do emerge at gatherings: the community at the large drinking party and the neighbourhood at small drinks, including *kari* drinks, and in a few other activities. But, depending on the site and host of the drink, different 'neighbourhood' and 'community' groups gather on different occasions.

Ambiguous as these concepts of 'neighbourhood' and 'community' appear, they are recognized by the Majangir themselves and they appropriately convey what are two socially very important spheres of action. The inner sphere, the neighbourhood, has been described as entailing the sharing of many items including, in a sense, the sharing of kinship and kinship values. The outer sphere, the community, entails sharing of a different sort: not of many material items, but only of alcoholic drink; and not of kinship, but rather of acquaintance, and the modes of social intercourse this allows.

The 'settlement', on the other hand, while an ecologically distinct unit, entails no forms of behaviour particular to it. The more amorphous phenomena of neighbourhood and community are the socially significant ones.

10

MOBILITY

Depending for their livelihood on fields which must be watched closely, the Majangir cannot move at random. Their residences must be fixed during the growing seasons of their crops. Their homesteads also contain an amount of immovable property in huts and cleared fields (*shompai* land), as well as property difficult to transport by back, such as stored crops and cooking utensils. This property encourages a certain stability in their residence.

Nevertheless, within these limitations Majangir may be said to be very mobile. They change residence frequently. I do not mean here the annual slight shifting of homesteads as required by their system of agriculture, and described in chapters 3 and 8. By 'moving' and 'mobility' here I mean persons abandoning their former homestead and leaving to make or join another homestead at a discontinuous location – at a new neighbourhood if not a new settlement. Instead of its normal shift, a domestic group which moves, breaks away to settle in an altogether different spot.

Individuals may 'move' separately just as domestic groups may 'move' as units. In this chapter I am interested primarily in the mobility of domestic groups, although much of what I will say applies equally well to individuals.

The frequency of moving is difficult to quantify. Informants tend not to recall or recount their less important moves – that is, those within the same settlement or community – especially if those moves occurred at a distant time or place. But it seems safe to say, from the information I have, that the great majority of Majangir aged over thirty have moved residence at least a half dozen times in their lives, and many of them a dozen times or more – the number of moves being generally proportionate, of course, to persons' ages. Most of their moves were of only short distances, less than ten miles or so. But more distant moves were not infrequent.

Some ideas of the range of Majang mobility can be obtained from comparing where persons of different ages are living at any given time, with where they were born. This information is tabulated in Table 10. The figures seem to indicate that the older a person is, the further that person's residence is likely to be from his or her birthplace. Also, relatively few persons over thirty are living within five hours' walk (about fifteen miles) of their birthplaces.

TABLE 10. *Relation of birthplace to present residence: distances in walking time between them. (One hour equals approximately three miles; one day, thirty miles.)*

	Age-groups					
	10–19	20–9	30–9	40–9	50+	Total
A. Gilishi males						
Less than 1 hour	18	10	—	—	1	29
1 to 5 hours	3	3	2	1	—	9
5 hours to 1 day	2	5	3	1	—	11
More than 1 day	3	7	5	7	3	25
B. Gilishi females						
Less than 1 hour	8	7	2	—	—	17
1 to 5 hours	5	4	1	2	1	13
5 hours to 1 day	—	2	2	3	—	7
More than 1 day	9	4	7	9	4	33
C. Shiri males						
Less than 1 hour	1	—	1	3	—	5
1 to 5 hours	1	3	—	1	2	7
5 hours to 1 day	2	1	—	—	1	4
More than 1 day	4	3	4	1	3	15
D. Shiri females						
Less than 1 hour	4	2	—	1	—	7
1 to 5 hours	1	1	—	—	—	2
5 hours to 1 day	4	—	2	—	—	6
More than 1 day	10	3	7	3	1	24

These figures cannot be guaranteed as typical of Majangir in general, because mobility in any one area has been affected by the peculiar conditions and history of that area. For instance, both communities censused, Gilishi and Shiri, were subjected in the past to the raids of foreign tribes which drove out most Majangir from these areas for long periods of time. In Gilishi this fact explains why few persons were born there from between thirty and fifty years previously; in Shiri, from between twenty and forty years previously. However, such raiding in the past affected most areas of Majangirland. The Majangir who eventually resettled the raided areas were partly different settlers from those who had fled, but partly the same people with their children born in the interim elsewhere. Raiding and warfare, as we shall see, were once an important factor in Majang mobility.

The birthplaces of persons under twenty, most of them living with parents, indicate the distances from which their parents have moved, if at all, in the last twenty years, to their present communities. Of Gilishi youths between ten and nineteen, 58 per cent were born within one hour (three miles) of their present residence; of Shiri youths, only 22 per cent. But in Gilishi special and temporary circumstances (to be described below) have been operating for a number of years to discourage emigration from the area.

Therefore the figures of Table 10 should not be taken as a necessarily accurate general picture of the Majang range of mobility. This picture will emerge more clearly after a discussion of the factors which impel persons to move, and to where; and from figures presented later in this chapter describing the dispersal of family members (Table 11). These figures will confirm the impression given by Table 10, that most Majangir do not remain in the same area for a lifetime.

Although as a general principle Majangir say they favour stable residence, they recognize and accept the fact that in practice they tend to be mobile. They say simply that they like to 'travel' (*enyeke*). And, as one man told me, 'If we did not leave our kin and go live apart, then we could not say "*teleme!*" ("hello!") when we met.'

Despite their acceptance of mobility and the transience of residential alignments, Majangir do not move about simply from restlessness. In most cases they are more or less compelled to move by circumstances. The reasons behind particular moves are sometimes clear, and other times obscure. For their past moves, Majangir will often present motives which conflict with more plausible reasons given by others who know them. Or Majangir will often refuse to discuss their motives seriously, saying, for instance, 'I wanted new forest fields (*gedi*)' when in fact there was *gedi* available in the neighbourhood they left. Sometimes Majangir will disclaim any motives for moving other than *kobako ngodo*, 'I felt like it' (literally, 'my throat thought'); or *ke karn, beda dakeda*, 'nothing the matter, simply to live here'. But in the cases I was able to probe, substantial reasons for moving always emerged. Often, of course, a complex of factors appeared likely to have been involved in the decision to move. But the major factors behind Majang mobility can be sorted out and described separately, as I propose to do.

One of the most important factors is Majang ecology. As described in chapter 8, Majangir are often forced to move when it becomes difficult for them to extend their cultivations, either because of encroaching grass, or increasing distance from water, or meeting obstacles to further expansion, such as rocky ground, another settlement, absence of forest vegetation, etc. If Majangir cannot shift their fields as required by their agricultural system, then they must move to a new location.

But if suitable land often becomes scarce in certain restricted locales, there is a general abundance of land available elsewhere in all parts of

Majangirland. This abundance is the permissive condition for Majang mobility: it is never difficult to find an alternative site for one's homestead. The population is simply not large enough to be using at any one time more than a fraction of the land suitable for agriculture, despite the extravagant way in which Majangir use land (see chapter 3); and the slight social restrictions on the use of land (see next chapter) never prevent anyone from finding a place to move to.

Ecological conditions often make it necessary for Majangir to move, and at the same time always make it possible for them to do so. Ecological reasons also play a part in where Majangir decide to move. If asked why they have moved from their former settlement to their new one, Majangir often say because they found in the new place good forest for *gedi*, water close at hand, no grass, no monkeys, a place where tobacco can be grown well, etc. But while such considerations are no doubt taken into account, on further investigation they seem usually to be secondary to other, social reasons more troublesome for Majangir to explain. Certainly many locations can be found which have equally good forest for *gedi*, water close at hand, etc.

Apicultural considerations are often more important than agricultural ones, simply because while land is free and tools and labour are easily transportable, bee-hives are valuable but virtually fixed property. A man must make new fields each year, whether he moves or not. This is not true of hives. It takes much labour and a number of years to make and bring to production the many hives Majangir want (see chapter 2), and if a man moves a great distance – more than one or two days' walk – he will not be able to keep up and use the hives he owns near his former home.

As explained in chapter 2 Majangir place hives not only in spots they select in the bush (*jang*) but also near their homesteads. As they shift and move their homes, men leave behind them what is in effect a trail of hives marking the history of their residence. It is advantageous to maintain hives in different locations, as long as these locations are within a day or so walking distance of one's current home. Therefore, while apiculture does not discourage mobility, it encourages men to move about only within a limited area, the area within which they have lived and have hives.

Men in fact often like to move back to a place where they previously farmed, after the place has regenerated to suitable forest land. The reason they give is so they may live near their hives left there, to watch after them and to be able to brew and drink honeywine as soon as possible whenever they crave it.

The area within which a man might move about, yet keep up all his accumulated hives, could be a fairly large area, a sphere about twenty-five miles or so in diameter. Nevertheless, not infrequently men do sacrifice their hives by moving far away. Their possible reasons for doing so, or having to do so, will be made clear below.

Of ecological factors, hunting is a minor consideration. Sometimes men say they have moved from a more populated to a less populated area to be nearer game. But this usually appears to be only a secondary reason for their move.

Of other factors behind Majang mobility, an important and inevitable one is misfortune, particularly death (*rir*). Majang custom, always followed, is to abandon a homestead where a death has occurred. The abandonment need not cause a group to 'move'; they may only shift residence to an adjacent spot, building a new set of huts. But the survivors in the deceased's domestic group always contemplate moving to a completely separate location; their decision usually depends on other factors such as their relations with their neighbours, or whether friends or kinsmen try to persuade them to come to another settlement. Often the survivors take the occasion to move: they say they want to erase the associations that link them with the recently dead, and so to avoid continuous grief – which in itself is thought dangerous. In cases where the dead person was necessary to the viability of a domestic group, the other persons in it may be forced to move elsewhere to join or form a new unit, as described in chapter 5.

Sometimes when several deaths have occurred within a short time (a number of months or a year), and within the same neighbourhood, everyone living there will want to move away. They say *bade dok*, 'the land is lost (broken, spoiled, dead)'. They feel it is dangerous to remain. The people of the area may all move together to a new place, but more likely different domestic groups will disperse to different places. Other misfortunes which bode death, such as lingering illnesses or epidemics or certain kinds of curses, may also cause individuals, families, or whole neighbourhoods to move, in hope of evading the misfortune.

Misfortune and death, as factors impelling Majangir to move, do not determine where they move to, or whether the move is to a near or distant location. Only rarely will a person claim to feel so grieved that he must leave his previous life, his 'community', altogether.

But given the high rate of mortality among Majangir, especially among children, it is obvious that the Majang reaction to death, moving to escape it, must be a very important factor contributing to instability of settlement and high mobility among the Majangir.

The Majangir also move to escape their human enemies. In the past (see chapter 1) Majangir were often raided for slaves by parties from neighbouring tribes, most prominently the Anuak, Shakko and Galla; and also by Ethiopian government forces. The last of these raids ended in the late 1940s when the Ethiopian government established a sort of peace over the area. But many Majangir are alive now who once fled foreign attack.

These raids greatly scrambled settlement. In the hunt for slaves, the raiders not only killed and kidnapped many Majangir, but drove many more into hiding to escape them. The areas bordering the raiding tribes Majangir did not dare to re-occupy, so they fled to settle elsewhere. But even in more interior areas Majang settlement was disrupted by raids. The raiders usually destroyed their huts and food stores. For lack of food, seed and perhaps tools, Majang refugees often could not simply reconstitute their settlements in the same place or elsewhere. They were forced to apply for succour to their friends and relatives in other settlements, and as Majang households do not have much surplus it was necessary for refugees to scatter to different places, to spread the burden. After a number of years, some refugees would return to the area of their former settlements. But others remained in the areas to which they had fled.

If nowadays intertribal warfare and raiding has been largely suppressed, foreign pressures continue to affect Majang settlement in more subtle ways. The Ethiopian government, in the form of its police and tax-gatherers, is accepted now by most Majangir, but in the past and less frequently today some Majangir have reacted to the tax-gathering expeditions by moving to the recesses of Majangirland where these expeditions still do not penetrate. Persons wanted for 'crimes' of which the government has heard, and especially for crimes against Amhara and Galla or for large debts to them – these persons also try to move outside the government's reach.

On the other hand, there is probably an over-balancing trend nowadays to move to be nearer Galla and Amhara settlements. The reason is the attraction there of markets to sell honey and buy *wuri* (from Galla *hori*, 'cattle; wealth'): the manufactured items which the Majangir have grown greatly to appreciate and desire.

But these factors are of very limited importance, certainly compared with the effects of raiding in the past. The net effect of the extension of Ethiopian pacification to this region has been to quell some of the turbulence of the past, which often made 'moving' necessary for survival.

This turbulence, however, is by no means ended. Although intertribal warfare on a large scale has been discouraged, the Ethiopian government has not yet extended full enforcement of its laws into the area. Raiding for slaves has ended, but minor clashes between Majangir and members of neighbouring tribes occasionally occur, often resulting in the Majangir involved retreating or moving deeper into their own territory where the foreigners and government cannot reach them. No police posts or administrative centres exist inside Majangirland (see chapter 1), and the Majangir do not very much cooperate with the posts and centres nearest them. Violence between individuals and small groups, inter-tribal and intra-tribal, continues to occur and the government, even if it hears, can usually do little about such trouble, except to send an expedition of police which is unlikely to apprehend the persons wanted. Statements are taken, but the wanted men can easily move out of the range of the police.

Disputes among Majangir therefore continue to be treated for the most part in their traditional ways. These ways cannot be fully discussed here, but in relation to the subject of this chapter, the important point is that serious trouble between Majangir, particularly when it involves violence, often leads one or more of the persons involved to move residence.

When someone is killed, for instance, the killer and normally many of his relatives are liable to retribution. Nor are the relatives of the killed man necessarily safe. In effect, a state of war arises between two groups of persons. If the aggrieved side retaliates, the score is not evened and the feud is not ended, but is instead intensified. There exist practically no means of compensation or reconciliation. The only way the matter can be settled, short of extinction of one of the parties involved, is through distance. One or both of the parties must move so they both do not remain within the same community, and so are unlikely to encounter each other. Generally, the persons who feel in the weaker position will move away. The object is not only to avoid one's enemies but to join one's brothers or other kin so as to be protected by allies from attack.

Killings are not infrequent among the Majangir, and most killings are between persons living at least near enough to belong to the same community. And since many persons are implicated in a killing through principles of collective responsibility, it is not surprising to find in many men's life histories the fact that they moved residence at some time in the past owing to a state of feud.

Other acts besides killing may also make moving necessary. For instance, if one man steals the wife of another, the pair must abscond to a different area altogether to avoid a murderous encounter with the former husband and his relatives. Any sort of dispute which leads to fighting, even if not fatal, may eventually be 'settled' as in a feud: the parties separate by moving away, rather than risking encountering each other and fighting again. Even disputes which do not lead to fighting may, by raising the possibility of fighting and feud, encourage persons to move apart.

The nearer persons live to each other, the more intolerable is a dispute between them: neighbours will move apart because of a minor trouble, while only very serious disputes can make persons of different settlements feel the need to move.

If no one has been killed, disputes may be settled by some sort of reconciliation or adjustment between the disputants. But in many cases, and necessarily when a feud develops, moving apart is the most efficacious way of adjusting the parties' relations. In a society relatively lacking in institutional means of 'settling' disputes, Majang mobility serves to keep a modicum of peace by allowing Majangir to avoid each other if necessary, and so to let their disputes 'settle' and be gradually forgotten.

Moving to avoid conflict is also necessary in those cases (see chapter 7) where marriage is intended within the neighbourhood. The prospective groom and possibly his family must then move out of the neighbourhood to avoid the prospective bride's family. This avoidance is necessary not only because of certain prohibitions on contact which would embarrass neighbours, but also because the bride's male relatives are expected to use aggression against the groom and his brothers in order to extract bride-wealth. Male affines must avoid each other until after the marriage is well established and bridewealth payments have been satisfactorily made. Only then may they live as neighbours if they desire.

Thus far I have outlined only the major factors which frequently compel Majangir to move: the unavailability of new land in a particular spot, natural death or misfortune, intertribal and local conflicts including raids, feuds, disputes, arguments, marriages. But often Majangir move not because they are compelled for any of these reasons, but rather because they are positively attracted to some other neighbourhood. Often men give as their reason for moving, 'to be with X (Y, Z, my brother, my cousin, etc.)'. Sometimes this proves to be partly a rationalization of more compelling reasons for moving such as fighting with one's former neighbours, being involved in a feud, running short of *gedi*, etc. Often, however, no other motive can be found.

What happens in these cases is that a kinsman or friend from another neighbourhood, settlement or community persuades a person to leave his present location and immigrate to that of the kinsman or friend. Majangir want to live near persons whom they like (*porer*) and whom they can live with in the demanding close relationship of neighbourhood/kinship described in chapter 7. Just as Majangir seek to part from neighbours, by moving or gradually shifting away, when their relations with these neighbours become antipathetic or indifferent, so the Majangir are always seeking to recruit as new neighbours persons with whom they have warm and strong ties. They seek always to adjust geographical distance to accord with social distance. Their easy mobility makes it feasible to do this.

'Social distance' here should be understood more in terms of simple friendliness than of genealogy or descent. As I showed in chapter 7, Majang neighbours are more often non-kin than kin. Majangir do not need or want to live near unfriendly kin any more than near other unfriendly persons. Nor do Majangir seek to live near kin who are neither unfriendly nor very friendly – except when necessary, as when they must group together to protect themselves in a feud. In such circumstances Majangir fall back on ties of kinship. But normally kinship in itself means little; what counts is friendship.

'Friendship' among Majangir is not well defined – they have many terms for different sorts of 'friends' – but the content of friendship is roughly similar to the ideal behaviour I have described as obtaining between neighbours in such matters as sharing, helping, mourning, marrying, assuming kinship, etc. Friends need not be neighbours. But they tend to become neighbours.

Friends or friendly kin thus try to persuade each other to come live with them as neighbours. Members of small young settlements with much available land especially try to recruit others. Their rationale is 'the more people, the more drink'. Whether this is true or not, Majangir generally think it better to have at least a 'full' neighbourhood of five or six families rather than to live in settlements of only one or two or three domestic groups. Of course, as I pointed out in chapter 8, the larger a settlement is, the more likely it is for ecological reasons to disintegrate sooner, with its population dispersing to seek new homes.

Before this time, and barring the fighting or falling out of neighbours, they apply diffuse pressures on each other to remain in the neighbourhood rather than emigrate. These pressures are those of friendship and neighbourhood; if neighbours think one of them is contemplating leaving, and they do not want him to leave, they try to persuade him to stay, professing their friendship and kinship, telling him that if he leaves they will be very sad and angry, etc. When a neighbour moves away, unless he has a good reason such as unavailability of new land, the neighbours he leaves behind will more or less resent his action as unfriendly.

Therefore persons who plan to move often do not tell their neighbours their plans. They say they are going visiting and they do not come back. If one is moving far, there is little to take away: a few tools and a small bundle of beads and herbs, perhaps one's chickens and some seed. It is simple to move, and easy, as it were, to sneak away. Huts, fields and larger cooking equipment are left behind. Later, when a person's move has been confirmed, others may take over these things, though the original owner of them retains nominal ownership unless he gives them over by word.

Mobility

Except when required by emergency, such as in a raid or feud, a domestic group will not move while it has a crop growing or a large crop in storage. Most moving therefore takes place in the dry season, with some moving between the first and second crops. There are two ways to move. The more planned and orderly way is for the males of the group to prepare a field beforehand in the new location, and for the females and children to follow when the field is growing. The other way is simply for the whole group to move first and prepare fields afterwards.

Most Majang moves, and particularly the second kind, presuppose that the persons moving find some source of food at the new location during the transition period before their first crop matures. An exception is whenever a group moves a short enough distance so that the men making the new fields may return home to eat, or so that sufficient supplies of food may be carried to the new site. Majang food is too bulky, however, to be easily and regularly transported more than a few hours' walk; at least Majangir would be reluctant to make such an effort.

The usual arrangement for moves further than an hour's walk is to depend temporarily for sustenance on future neighbours. When a group has been persuaded by a friend or kinsman to join his neighbourhood, they also join and live off his homestead for the few months before their own fields and huts are ready (see case histories, chapter 6). Their status is as 'guests' (*konan*). Recruiting neighbours is therefore not without some personal material sacrifice for the host.

But even if a group is compelled, rather than invited, to move to another neighbourhood, the same arrangement of hospitality is usually made. I have mentioned that persons forced to flee from a raid or seek protection from a feud will go to where they can find refuge – usually at the home of a close kinsman (or kinswoman). There the refugees become guests while they make fields for their new homestead. Persons who must move for other reasons – whether from agricultural considerations or to escape a death or misfortune, or because of bad relations with others which have not resulted in killing – these persons have time to find a willing host to whose neighbourhood they may move, where they may be guests until their new homestead makes them self-providing. They let themselves be persuaded by friends or relatives to join them, similarly to what I have already described.

Almost all Majang domestic groups when they move to a new neighbourhood are therefore already on close terms with at least one of the other groups there, even if this is not indeed the reason why they have moved.

Before going on to discuss one other final factor affecting mobility, I think it useful to present an example of some of the things I have described. This example consists of information about the movings of a man named Lapita who was my neighbour in 1964–5. His history is not untypical of Majangir.

Lapita was born in the area of the Mi'i River in northern Majangirland. Until he was in his thirties he lived in the same area, moving and shifting residence when necessary. Many of his kin, especially patrilineal kin, lived in the same area. In 1957, however, his wife died and at the same time Majangir on the lower Mi'i were fighting with Anuak settlements downstream. This area was not even superficially under government control.

For these reasons Lapita said he decided to leave Mi'i and move further north to the settlement Jimti where he had other patrilineal relatives. He married another woman and settled in Jimti for three years before moving again. According to others, Lapita left Jimti because 'he was always fighting with his kinsmen while drinking'. A member of a nearby settlement, Til-Emyekai on the Shiri River, persuaded him to move there 'where he had no kin and so there would be no fighting'. Lapita's daughter subsequently was married by a man living within this settlement, but at the other end from Lapita, so no residential adjustments were necessary. After one year at one site, Lapita shifted his homestead across the river (within the same settlement) because of difficult relations with a neighbour. In 1964 when I arrived in Emyekai Lapita was living in neighbourhood with a friend who was a fellow descent group member, and with several unrelated men.

In April 1965 Lapita's brother was killed in Mi'i by a distant patrilineal relative. The circumstances of the killing were obscure. Lapita and a group of relatives from the Shiri and Jimti went to Mi'i and captured the killer whom they handed over to the government. Lapita was grieved by the killing and his grief was exacerbated by the subsequent interference and extortions of police expeditions sent to investigate the murder.

In May at a drunken dance Lapita inexplicably tried to attack a woman with a knife. Although they stopped him at the time, his friends and kinsmen later shook their heads and dissociated themselves from what they considered his crazy behaviour. In the same month he tried to shoot his son for the trivial offence of taking a bit of Lapita's honey to give to a girl relative. To me, Lapita accused his remaining brother of stealing from his hives; and he was critical of his brother and some other relatives for failing to help him in the affair of the killing. Lapita told me he didn't consider he had any kinsmen left, he didn't want any. Finally, he made plain he suspected his wife of adultery.

Suddenly he left. His move was apparently precipitated by his sister and her son. They had arrived and stayed at Lapita's for several days. They persuaded him and his wife to come with them to their settlement in Sholan, several days' walk away. One morning all of them left. They took what possessions they could easily carry, including their few chickens. They left behind their pots, jars, dogs, huts, fields and hives, but Lapita's teenage son Yanggan remained to care for them (see case history in chapter 6).

Few persons knew Lapita was leaving, and he told no one that he was moving, though his neighbours suspected as much. He told me, his son, his son-in-law and his two closest neighbours that he would return in a few months, but his taking his chickens seemed to indicate he was moving residence (*waitake*, from *wai*, 'homestead') rather than merely visiting (*jodake*, from *jop*, 'people'). At least this was what persons reasoned afterwards. When he left only a couple of neighbour women were on hand to say goodbye; one cried. She told me that with him gone, 'there will be no honeywine to drink'.

Most persons I talked to were not sad he had left. One of his friends was angry with him for moving, but most thought it was wise. Some persons said he had been acting crazily and would have fought if he had stayed. Others thought that it was better for him to leave because of the bad feelings between him and the relatives of his brother's killer at Mi'i: though they had disavowed the killing and refused to defend the killer, Lapita if drunk might yet attack them, or vice versa. Others thought Lapita was 'fed up' (*nyeeko*) with his life on the Shiri, and because he was grieving (*ngadeng*) his brother's death he was right to follow his impulse (*peni ngodoung*, 'affair of the throat') to move to other parts.

These reactions indicate typical Majang attitudes towards moving. Some persons – those who liked Lapita – were optimistic he might return when he was tired of life in Sholan. They said his wife's mother would want them to return for she would not want her daughter to be living so far away – especially when bridewealth payments were unfinished. Others did not think Lapita would abandon his many hives in the Shiri and Jimti areas.

Lapita did not return shortly, as he had promised. News came that he had made fields and huts in Sholan. Later in 1966 when I was living in southern Majangirland I heard that Lapita, after a year away, had returned to the Shiri; but I could not learn more about this.

Another factor affecting Majang settlement and mobility is the influence of a limited number of *tapa* (sing. *tapat*). The *tapat* is a ritual expert, with characteristics of both shaman and priest and with some variable quasi-political, 'chiefly' attributes. Although there are many *tapa* in Majangirland, only a dozen or so at any time are recognized as 'powerful' (*bangkauk*), and what I describe here applies only to these. Only powerful *tapa* influence settlement by the use of their powers. They attract other Majangir to settle near them, in their neighbourhood, settlement, or community, by offering a measure of security from both human and superhuman enemies.

A powerful *tapat* is feared and respected to the point where it is strongly felt that violence should not take place in his presence or even within his 'territory' (see chapter 11). Those who fight near him are certain to earn his strong censure, which, because of his moral influence in the community, may lead to widespread social censure of offenders. Practically, a *tapat* can refuse his ritual services and his largesse of beer and honeywine to offenders against his peace. In the last decade, some *tapa* have also been able to threaten to take offenders to the Ethiopian government authorities who have in some cases appointed *tapa* as responsible for public order in their territories. Usually, however, Majang *tapa* do not in fact have the power or inclination to carry out these threats.

The *tapat* relies for his power mainly on the threat of mystical sanctions. Those who commit violence near him are strongly felt to be liable to punishment through various afflictions – through misfortune, injury, sickness, or death – caused by the spirit, called a *wakayo* (cf. Galla *Wakayo*, 'God') which resides in a *tapat* and his territory. This spirit, as well as the *tapat* who represents it, resents human violence as an offence against itself. Therefore Majangir hesitate before committing violence within the territory of a powerful *wakayo/tapat*.

The result is that persons who feel vulnerable in fighting or a feud will often apply to a powerful *tapat* to accept them as 'followers' (*nyukwiyir*) and to let them live near him. If the *tapat* accepts them, they come under his aegis, and feel safer from violent retaliation by their enemies who cannot attack them in the *tapat*'s settlement without risking the mystical sanctions operating in the area. Powerful *tapa* may thus collect around them numbers of refugees from violence.

Refugees from superhuman violence also may come to live near *tapa*. Afflicted by sickness or misfortune, they seek the intervention of a *tapat* to identify the spirits causing their troubles, and to divine and perform the means of placating the spirits. A *tapat* will sometimes recommend that they come to live near him. Or persons will come on their own because they feel that in a powerful *tapat*'s territory they are less vulnerable to affliction owing to the *tapat*'s privileged relations with mystical agencies.

Majangir wanting peace with men and gods therefore often attach themselves to the neighbourhood, settlement or community of a powerful *tapat*. They live within his territory and call themselves his 'followers' (*nyukwiyir*). They serve him in various ways in return for his protection. Powerful *tapa* often collect such followers numbering into hundreds.

Not only do powerful *tapa* attract persons to move near them, but they can also prevent persons from moving away. Unless they gain the *tapat*'s permission to leave, they are afraid of offending his *wakayo*, who will pursue them with some affliction. Despite this threat of mystical sanctions, Majangir will not always stay near a *tapat* if they feel for some reason that they must move elsewhere. But the threat of retribution is sufficient to induce many who would otherwise leave to remain under a powerful *tapat*.

By several means, therefore, the dozen or so powerful *tapa* alive at any one time in Majangirland manage to attract and retain large numbers of 'followers' and settlers around them. Doing so of course creates ecological problems for the *tapat*'s settlement. Often its members must accept long walks to water, or must re-use old land to exhaustion for lack of appropriate *gedi*. Inconvenience and extra work are accepted for the sake of the *tapat*. But unlike other settlements, the *tapat*'s settlement finds a focus in him, and so it will follow him to other places within his territory if land is exhausted in one place. He can keep it together.

But even a *tapat*'s settlement is temporary. It is contingent on him, and when he dies the population will scatter. The neighbourhood of his burial will be abandoned and persons who want to leave his territory will move, no longer dependent on his permission to do so. Eventually a son of his may succeed to his position, but this requires a gradual process of the *tapat*'s successor attracting followers of his own to settle with him.

At this point I would like to introduce another case-history: that of a man named Bilawan and his three sons, whom I knew in Gabwi-Gilishi in 1965–6.

Bilawan was born and lived his early life in the Dawar River area. The Majangir of that area were dispersed by Shakko and Amhara raids in the 1920s, and Bilawan fled north to the Godare River area (see Map 1, p. 3). He married there and his wife bore him his oldest son. He then returned with his family to settle in the area where he had grown up and where there was now peace. For over twenty years he lived in a succession of different settlements in the area, and two more sons were born to him. His oldest son Leukek eventually married and left to live in the Gurrafarda Mountains area further south, where Leukek's wife's people were.

In 1962, according to Bilawan, fighting broke out between members of Bilawan's clan, and members of another clan in the area. As a result Bilawan and his sons, including Leukek, all moved north-east to join the settlement of the very powerful *tapat* Yodn. Yodn guaranteed their safety, and their enemies did not dare to follow them. Not only was Yodn's *wakayo* spirit much feared, but his settlement at Gilishi was near Galla and Amhara settlements and a police post. Majangir in the area claimed that the nearness of the police as well as Yodn inhibited them from fighting: they feared the intervention of the police if a killing took place there. During the time I was there, these inhibitions were not strong enough to prevent a Majang youth from killing a Galla trader at the latter's home an hour from Gilishi. But there was no bloodshed in anger in Yodn's territory itself during the ten months I lived there.

In any case, Bilawan and his sons settled twenty minutes' walk from Yodn's home. Bilawan's youngest son Melashin married and set up his homestead by his father's and his brother Leukek's. Bilawan, who was advanced in age, depended on his middle son Jengarshu to support him, together with Bilawan's wife, who could still work. (See their case history, chapter 6.)

Three years after they had arrived, Bilawan and his group did not have very close relations with most of their neighbours, and they even had disagreements with their only relatives in the neighbourhood, the family of Bilawan's wife's sister. The threat of the feud from which they had moved now seemed distant to them. In May 1965 Jengarshu indicated to me that he wanted to return to his old home where he had left hives. He said he did not like living in Gilishi, a heavily populated area due to the *tapat*, because there was little game near at hand. A week later he brought up the subject again and said that his father and brothers and he were going to move back to their old home. The new reason he gave was that the Amhara near to Gilishi beat people for taxes, and took away Majang land. (Though Majangir had suffered this in the past, there seemed no immediate danger of this treatment at the time.) I asked Jengarshu if he was not afraid of Yodn, who did not want people to move away. Jengarshu said that they were living now in Yodn's territory, but where they wanted to move was their 'own' land (i.e. they had 'owners'' rights to live there – see chapter 9), so they would go anyway.

In July Leukek and his brothers went off ostensibly to trap game at Waye, their *jang* hive site about four hours' walk from Gilishi-Gabwi in the direction of the Dawar. They were gone for longer than usual, and reports came back that they were clearing fields there near the homestead of Gompwi, a fellow clan member who had the year before begun a new settlement in that area. Their neighbours in Gilishi-Gabwi assumed Bilawan's sons were preparing to move in the dry season. Conversation turned to dividing up the homestead's fields and adjacent *gedi* claims – because of the concentration of 'followers' around the *tapat*, land was unusually scarce in the few miles around him.

When I asked the wives of Bilawan's group whether they were moving, they insisted they were not: that they were afraid of Yodn's *wakayo*. When

I told this to their neighbours the neighbours said that the wives insisted as they did because they were afraid of Yodn hearing of their move and forbidding them with a curse to leave, for then they would have to stay. But barring this, the neighbours thought Bilawan and his sons were not afraid to move because they had only recently immigrated here, so their leaving would not offend Yodn and his *wakayo* as much as if an older resident were trying to leave. Yodn would not hate their 'path' (*gopan*), i.e. their going.

When the men returned from Waye they insisted to everyone, incuding Yodn, that they were not moving. Their story was that they would clear two sets of fields, one at their present homesteads and one at their *jang* in Waye; the latter fields would need no watching because the monkeys there had not yet learned to steal and eat crops. This story sounded implausible to everyone. Yodn refused to say anything about it, a sign that he was displeased. Melashin told me later that the group might move in the further future (*kwi*) if Yodn did not forbid them – but they would not move in the next season.

By September, however, it was obvious that Bilawan and his sons and families were going to move, for they had made no fields in Yodn's settlement. They admitted to me that they would leave Gilishi-Gabwi as soon as they finished eating up their first (*banggi* season) crop. But to others they still claimed to be staying – at least part time. Yodn told Leukek's wife that they should not leave without asking his permission, and she said she would not dare. But Yodn himself had already appropriated, with Melashin's consent, some of Melashin's land for his (Yodn's) new wife. It was apparent that the move was inevitable, as Bilawan and his sons were presenting Yodn with a *fait accompli*: they had no fields so could not remain. The only question was whether, before they moved, they would tell Yodn the truth and ask his permission. Unfortunately I left Majangirland before the matter was finished.

I had asked Yodn whether he disliked people leaving his territory to emigrate to another. He said that if they were people who had immigrated previously (*kusher ba gopan*), then it was all right if they came and told him they wanted to move back to live in their 'fathers' land' (*dok babek*, see next chapter). But persons who belonged to Yodn's land 'originally' (*gore*), Yodn would tell not to move because his *wakayo* would resent it and would follow to kill them.

Despite this clear rule, Majangir in Yodn's land were unsure as to how dangerous it might be to move away from a *tapat* in any circumstances. They felt one could only know by testing: for instance if Bilawan's family was visited by a serious misfortune soon after moving, they might ascribe it to Yodn's *wakayo* even if Yodn had given them permission to leave. In that case they might choose, as had others in similar circumstances, to return to the *tapat*'s settlement.

Except in discussing the effect of the powerful *tapat* on settlement patterns, this section has been concerned more with residential mobility from the point of view of the individual person and domestic group, than with the patterns created by the totality of individual moves. In chapter 1, however, I sketched some of the general shifts and drifts of settlement in Majangirland resulting from foreign pressures and the availability of forest land for agricultural expansion. In chapter 8 I discussed the consequences on settlement patterns of other ecological factors.

The moves caused by death, misfortune, etc., do not add up significantly to any pattern. The moves caused by internal warfare (feuds) can however alter settlement patterns in the short run. Whole districts have been depopulated after an outbreak of killing spread to involve most of the population. Other results of feuds have been, as I described, (1) to add to the concentrations of 'followers' around powerful *tapa*, and (2) to group kin together. But even these changes are not permanent. Depopulated areas are eventually repopulated by others; kin break apart; and the agglomerations of settlement around *tapa* break up on the death of *tapa*. However, as powerful *tapa* tend to be the sons of powerful *tapa*, and live within the same territories, these areas tend to be the sites of recurrent build-ups of population. In some cases such cycles of concentration and dispersion of population are necessary in any case for ecological reasons, to allow enough land to regenerate in an area during depopulation to allow a future concentration of population. Unfortunately, lack of adequate historical information made it impossible to study this phenomenon, although one case is partially investigated in the next chapter.

Finally, we come to the question of the effect of various social ties, especially kin ties, in recruiting persons for neighbourhoods and settlements. In chapter 7 and earlier in this chapter we looked at the result in terms of neighbourhood composition. The results indicated that in the communities sampled, large groups of kin were not settled together. This was my general impression of settlement throughout Majangirland. Although Majangir are often moving, so they say, to join kin of various sorts, at the same time in moving they are usually leaving other kin. That is, their constant mobility does not result in concentrations of kin: it leads more to their dispersal. This process begins with the family. Most married brothers do not remain neighbours through life.

In Table 11 figures are presented on the dispersal of families after the maturity of their children. Samples of married and previously married

TABLE 11. *Residential dispersal of the elementary family: distances of persons' residences from the residences of their living and married primary relatives. 'Married' here includes those previously married but divorced or widowed.*

A. *Married males, Gilishi (sample of 45 men)*

	Bro	Sis	Fa	Mo	Son	Dau
Co-resident	—	2	1	5	1	—
Neighbours	22	6	4	6	5	2
10–60 min. walk	—	14	—	3	—	3
1–6 hours' walk	4	11	5	4	—	2
6–11 hours' walk	3	—	—	—	—	2
Over 1 day's walk	3	1	—	1	—	—

B. *Married females, Gilishi (sample of 73 women)*

	Bro	Sis	Fa	Mo	Son	Dau
Co-resident	1	2	—	3	6	3
Neighbours	5	12	3	2	6	2
10–60 min. walk	16	9	2	7	3	8
1–6 hours' walk	10	9	3	4	—	3
6–11 hours' walk	4	3	1	—	—	1
Over 1 day's walk	7	16	2	6	1	4

C. *Married males, Shiri (sample of 18 men)*

	Bro	Sis	Fa	Mo	Son	Dau
Co-resident	—	1	1	—	1	1
Neighbours	2	—	1	—	1	—
10–60 min. walk	—	—	—	—	—	—
1–6 hours' walk	4	2	—	—	—	—
6–11 hours' walk	1	4	—	—	2	1
Over 1 day's walk	4	8	1	2	—	3

D. *Married females, Shiri (sample of 22 women)*

	Bro	Sis	Fa	Mo	Son	Dau
Co-resident	1	—	1	—	—	—
Neighbours	—	—	—	—	—	—
10–60 min. walk	—	—	—	—	—	—
1–6 hours' walk	5	2	1	—	—	1
6–11 hours' walk	1	4	2	—	—	1
Over 1 day's walk	5	6	6	4	1	2

males and females from two communities were taken to establish at what distances these persons were living from any married or previously married siblings, parents, and children they might have.

We would expect brothers and married sisters, and fathers and married daughters, to be living apart, according to the virilocal rule of residence at marriage, and the necessity for affines, at least during the first years of marriage, to live apart. According to the patrilocal ideal of the Majangir, we would expect married brothers, and fathers and married sons, to be living in the same neighbourhoods. The figures in Table 11 seem to bear out these tendencies. Brothers tend to live closer together than do sisters, or brothers and sisters. Fathers and sons tend to live closer together than do fathers and daughters. The differences however are not as great as might ideally be expected.

The variance between the figures from the two communities, Gilishi and Shiri, may be explained by the natures of these communities. Gilishi is the home of the *tapat* Yodn, described above, and the number of brothers who are neighbours in Gilishi derives from the fact that most of them have immigrated there fleeing from feuds. Their feuds have banded them together as brothers as well as causing them to seek refuge in this settlement with Yodn: both actions were to defend themselves.

Many of the brothers living together in Gilishi were not neighbours immediately before fighting brought them together. It is possible to say that most brothers do not stay together through life – though when in trouble they may rejoin each other.

Gilishi is a less typical community than Shiri which has no *tapat* and is no refuge from feuding. In Shiri there are few married primary relatives of any kind living in the same neighbourhood. But even Shiri men tend to live nearer to their male than to their female married primary relatives.

Unfortunately the sample was not large enough to break down by ages. Presumably the younger a man, the more likely he is to be living next to his parents and brothers. But if, due to the special circumstances of Gilishi, we partly discount the high number of brothers living together there, the figures confirm my impression that Majang mobility rapidly disperses most families after their children reach maturity. Except in special conditions such as feud or famine, there are no compelling reasons for adult brothers or other kin to live together. They may and usually do disperse. Majangir are mobile in respect to their relatives, as well as in respect to places.

11

TERRITORY

The preceding chapters have emphasized the relative instability and form-lessness of settlement among the Majangir. The settlement and the neigh-bourhood are transient in location and composition; the community and usually the neighbourhood are not definable as discrete units. Majangir are very mobile, shifting or moving residence every few years; and such shifts and moves are often made by single households not acting in concert with others.

This flux of population, however, takes place over and within a terri-torial framework which is relatively fixed and persistent through time. Majangirland is parcelled into an indeterminate number of spatial units with socially defined boundaries and continuity of identity. These units I call 'territories'; the Majangir call them *do* or *dok*, a word which may also mean 'soil', 'earth', or 'land'. Some 'territories' are only a few dozen square miles in area; others include hundreds of square miles. Some contain few or even no inhabitants at present; others have populations of more than a thousand.

Three types of territory exist among the Majangir, each type with a different significance. I call these types 'traditional', 'governmental' and 'ritual'. For analytical reasons, each of these types may be presented as a separate territorial system. Three sets of often incongruent territories may be seen as overlaying each other on the same map, the same land. On the other hand the three systems are related: they conjoin in many places, in the same persons and in the same territorial boundaries.

In addition to the complexity of these three systems – in conjunction at places and in disjunction at others – is the complication that territories of the 'traditional' type are not necessarily exclusive; they often overlap or enclose each other. Furthermore, some territories are recognized by some people and not by others. Yet recognition or not of a territorial claim seems never to be a source of active conflict between Majangir. No one fights or dies for territory; no one overtly competes for it or, except rarely, even argues about it. Yet the concept of territory is not unimportant to Majangir.

Territory

To understand the phenomenon of territory among the Majangir, it is necessary first to describe how they define rights to natural resources, especially to land. I have repeatedly mentioned how Majangir possess a general abundance of land suitable for their mode of livelihood. There is no need to compete for land to farm. Yet Majangir recognize certain rights to it.

A domestic group which clears the forest from a piece of land are the 'owners' (duma: see below) of that land in the sense that they have exclusive and discretionary rights over its use until the land has re-grown to forest. In other words, a domestic group owns not only the current fields of its homestead but also its former fields which have been abandoned but have not yet returned to duk to complete the swidden cycle (see chapter 3). Once land has returned to forest, however, the ownership rights of its former cultivators lapse completely.

Ownership of land is therefore based on recognition of the labour needed to cut down the forest. Labour rather than land is the critical agricultural resource in Majang society. Theoretically, a domestic group can sell its former fields for the price of one axe, an axe being a suitable token to exchange for the labour of felling trees. In practice, land is rarely sold in this way. Instead, formerly cultivated land is sometimes lent, or given outright, by one domestic group to another. Land covered with aime, shompai or other immature growth, even if it has been abandoned by its former cultivators, should not be used by another domestic group until it has secured the permission of the persons who last cleared the land for gedi. Failure to obtain this permission, say Majangir, may result in either of two consequences: the original owner may return to quarrel with the person who 'took' (bonge) his land; or, the land may be cursed, resulting in a failure of crops.

In fact there is little demand for used land among Majangir. A domestic group which has recently moved into a new community, and has cleared only one year's gedi, will usually borrow from their neighbours an old field covered with shompai, to clear to make a kate field (see chapter 3). But otherwise, a homestead normally will have at hand its own old fields so that it does not have to borrow the old fields of another homestead.

A domestic group also has a recognized right to the uncleared forest land directly adjacent to its homestead: the land that it plans to clear for its next gedi. Where homesteads are adjacent to each other, they adjust their future gedi boundaries by mutual consultation. Only rarely is it difficult for them to arrive at an agreement. Where suitable land is limited at a particular location, one or more of the domestic groups involved will simply move away to a new location, as they recognize the inevitability of moving soon in any case. Usually, however, a domestic group will border more forest than it alone needs for its next *gedi*. A group will then allow, or often invite, another group to move its homestead into that spot. Each group will then claim a section of the adjacent forest for its next *gedi*.

Rights of ownership of land are therefore clear-cut while the land is being used for cultivation; or while it still bears the marks of that cultivation; or while it is being planned for imminent cultivation. The greatest part of Majangirland, however, at any given time does not fall into these categories. It is uncultivated, unoccupied 'bush' or 'wilderness', called '*jang*' by Majangir. Some *jang* is uncultivable: hilly, rocky, grassy, etc. But cultivable *jang* consists in effect of the agricultural reserves of the Majangir: the land they will be using two, five, ten or more years in the future, while their former cultivations return in the swidden cycle to *jang* and forest.

Because they live by shifting field cultivation, Majangir depend on constant access to *jang*. *Jang* is never 'owned' in the sense that any person or group of persons has anything approaching discretionary or exclusive rights over it. Access to *jang* is regulated, however, at least ideally, by customs which have to do with the Majang concept of 'territory'. Before entering into a discussion of this concept, however, two other kinds of rights to natural resources must be described: rights to hive sites and rights to wild food products.

Rights to the latter exclude considerations of land ownership or territory. In hunting, for instance, any man may hunt any animal freely anywhere. The largest share of the kill belongs, theoretically at least, to the owner of the spear or bullet or trap, if he should be a different person from the man who throws the spear, shoots the bullet, or finds the animal in the trap. However, the latter also has rights to a share of the kill. In the case of the rifle belonging to yet another man, he too has a right to a share. The actual distribution of the meat is determined by a complex of factors, such as who is present when it is killed, how far from settlement it is killed, the kin relations and ages of the men involved, etc. In relation to territory, however, it is significant that whoever claims rights of whatever kind to the land or territory on which an animal is killed, even if it is killed within a homestead, derives on that account absolutely no claim to any share in the game.

Before it is killed, game belongs of course to no one. Fish are also a free product, belonging to the person who catches them and to the person whose hook or trap is used to catch them (if the latter is different from the former) as in hunting – irrespective of where they are caught.

Wild vegetable products also belong to no one before they are collected. Wild coffee, mushrooms, wood and vines, and any other things not planted by man, belong exclusively to the persons who find and take them, irrespective of on whose land or territory they are found, even if they are found within a homestead. For instance, any woman may pick wild greens such as *jongge* (see chapter 2) from the fields of another woman's homestead, without asking permission. The same rule applies even to fire-wood, whether it comes or not from trees felled by the owner of the field: anyone may take wood without permission. Only the planted crops belong to the owners of a homestead: wild products belong to anyone who takes them.

In certain cases persons may attempt to reserve some wild products for future use. If a man, for instance, finds a wild bees' nest, or a log suitable for making a hive, he can try to claim either of these for future use by leaving some mark on them and publicizing his claim. His rights to the item will then be recognized in principle, though it is not unlikely that they will be violated in practice. But such rights of reservation do not apply to other edible wild products, such as greens, mushrooms, coffee, etc.

Rights to wild products generally parallel rights to farmland in Majang society: ownership is primarily created through the investment of labour.

The same principle applies to Majang apiculture. Hives are owned by the men who make them; any honey produced in a man's hive belongs exclusively to him. Swarms of bees, on the other hand, are not owned, even in the rare instances when Majangir keep track of their movements. Hive sites are 'owned' in the sense that a man who puts a hive in a tree will claim not only that tree but an area around it as *jang nak*, 'my wilderness', meaning in this context 'my hive area'. He will have the right to put up hives within his *jang* area, and no one else should do so without his explicit or implicit permission.

The area of a man's *jang* may vary, and its boundaries will be only vaguely fixed. Near settlement, men put up their hives very near to each other's. But far from settlement, a man will establish his *jang* sites well separate from those of other men – at least a quarter of a mile, often further. The reason for such separation is not scarcity of hive sites, bees, or nectar resources. As in agriculture, Majangir do not conceive of themselves as being involved in competition for the raw materials of apiculture. The final product of apiculture, however, is regarded as a scarce good. Honey is very valuable (see chapter 2), and hives far from settlement tempt, and are vulnerable to, easy theft of honey. Majangir do steal honey from each other, but when one man's hive sites are isolated from others' sites, his honey is safer from theft. It is more dangerous for a man to steal from hives in an area apart from his own: he risks being seen going or coming from a place where it is known he has no business.

Therefore, to be safe, men who do not quite trust each other do not put their hives near to each other's, but claim and exploit separate *jang* areas. On the other hand, men who do trust each other often share the same *jang* area. A man invites or allows others – especially his brothers and sons, but also other kin or friends or neighbours – to put up their hives near to his, perhaps even in the same tree. They in turn jointly 'own' the same *jang* area, use the same overnight shelter (*kal*), and usually accompany each other on honey-collecting expeditions.

Much of Majangirland, apart from settled areas, is therefore claimed by individuals and by small groups as 'theirs'. Men have rights to *jang* as well as in homesteads. But while homesteads shift, and rights to fields lapse as the land returns to forest, *jang* rights are relatively permanent: as long as a man keeps up his hives in an area, his 'ownership' of it is recognized. And in effect his children, or anyone else he chooses, may inherit his *jang* rights if he allows them to put up hives in the same area. But men who move too far away to keep up their hives will lose their *jang* rights, and others may take them over; in fact, men who must abandon their *jang* may assign persons to take their hives and hive area. Hives may be sold, though this is rare; *jang* rights, however, are never sold.

Many, probably most, hives are located in areas which are never used for agriculture, usually because the areas are too far from water, or are grass-land, or rocky or steep, etc. Some *jang* is suitable for farming, however, and the presence of hives in a *jang* area does not exclude the land from being taken for cultivation. In fact, a man's *jang* rights do not include the right to prevent another man from converting its forest to fields. A man who clears a *gedi* which includes another man's hives must only be careful not to cut down the particular trees containing those hives, or in any other way to destroy the hives. If he should do so, he may have to quarrel with the hive owner, and pay compensation. Usually a man who wishes to clear the forest will consult with the owners of hives in that forest, to arrange how the hives may be protected, and to offer to watch and care for the hives. In this way men avoid quarrels over the matter. But rights to land and rights to hive sites are clearly distinguished by Majangir, as I have described. *Jang* ownership gives a man only apicultural rights over an area.

Individuals or, more often, small groups of Majangir therefore own small areas in that they have full rights to these plots for agricultural or apicultural use. Taken together these owned areas constitute a large portion but not all of Majangirland. There remain many areas which are owned by no one in the sense hive sites and homesteads are owned. These residual areas, however, are claimed by persons and groups as part of their 'territories', which include also land which is used for hives and homesteads.

Ordinary claims of 'ownership' are established basically through the investment of labour. Territorial claims of 'ownership', however, are established differently, and constitute a very different kind of 'ownership'.

2 THE TRADITIONAL TERRITORY

The type of territory which involves rights to natural resources is the 'traditional' territory. I call it this because its identity and boundaries are defined by tradition: that is, by convention justified through reference to history or myth.

Territorial boundaries are usually fixed by definitive geographical features: ridges, stream-beds, hills, rocks. On a trail there will usually be some natural feature which conventionally marks the boundary between two territories. Occasionally an arch will be erected as an artificial boundary marker. In some areas off the trails there may be no continuous features such as ridges or streams to mark a boundary exactly. But the ambiguity will be limited wherever Majangir have hives, as hive sites are reckoned to be in either one territory or another.

Traditional territories are of various sizes. Most of them are smaller than a Majang 'community' (see chapter 9), and therefore all the persons living within a particular territory will usually be acquainted. A territory usually includes more than one settlement (see chapter 8) but the populations of different territories vary widely.

It should be stressed that the traditional territory is not a social unit in any meaningful sense: its population does not form an exclusive group for any social purpose, nor does it conceive of itself as a group in opposition to like groups. The people of one territory are united only by the fact that they live within the recognized boundaries of a geographical area that conceptually is a unity in that it is known usually by one name – though even conceptually, as I will later explain, ambiguities and discrepancies may exist among different points of view.

The name of the area, however, will not be an autonomous or 'geographical' name. A territory is named after a group of persons, who will form only a part, often a small part, of the territory's population, but who nevertheless are identified with the territory. Their relationship to it may be expressed by Majangir in several ways. The persons related to the traditional territory may be said to be *duma doka*, translatable as 'owners of the land', using the same word (*dumat*) which means personal, exclusive ownership of any property. The territory is 'their land' (*do nengk*); they use possessive pronouns in relating themselves to it. Not only do Majangir speak of these persons and groups as 'owning' certain territories, but as also being preeminent within them. A senior 'owner' may call himself *epen doka*, 'father of the land', and claim to be *ubi*, 'big', within it.

Such preeminence and 'ownership' is derived traditionally, or rather historically. The 'owners' of any particular territory claim this title by virtue of the territory being *dok babek*, 'land of our forefathers' (literally, 'fathers' land'). That is, they are patrilineal descendants of Majangir who settled the territory in the past. Majangir do not usually remember the personal names of the earliest settlers in an area, but they know their clans (*komwoyir*), and they recognize the patrilineal descendants of the first settlers as 'owners' of the areas their 'forefathers' pioneered.

Because the original settlers of an area are remembered as belonging to a certain clan, and because their patrilineal descendants and present-day territorial 'owners' belong to the same clan, the territory will be identified with that clan. Where in a few cases more than one clan have traditionally the status of first settlers in the same area, a territory may be identified with both.

Majangirland is therefore parcelled into territories known by clan names. Areas are referred to as *dok Oborirung*, 'territory of the Oborir (clan)'; *dok Kushirung*, 'territory of the Kushir (clan)'; etc. It is important to note, however, that a territory is rarely 'owned' by an entire clan, but usually only by a clan segment: the patrilineal descendants of those members of the clan who were the early settlers of the area. It is the clan name of this clan segment which identifies the territory: but other members of the clan do not claim 'ownership'. Also, different territories may be known by the same clan name, but belong to different clan segments.

Nor are these usually 'clan territories' in the sense that most members of a clan are settled, or once were settled, in the territories known by its name. Clans are very dispersed, and, indeed, members of the clan segment which 'owns' a territory may have left the territory to live elsewhere. In a few territories no members of the 'owning' clan segment remain. If the 'owners' of a territory leave it for a long period of time, their 'ownership' of it seems to lapse gradually and be forgotten. If all 'owners' leave, the territory will eventually become identified with another group of early settlers. Many Majangir claim 'ownership' of some territory, but many cannot. And only a small minority of Majangir reside within territory they 'own'.

Nevertheless, the evidence I have indicates that 'owners' of territories are less mobile than other Majangir in that 'owners' tend more to remain settled within their territories. Like all Majangir, they are constantly shifting and moving residence. But most territories are large and under-populated enough to allow 'owners' to confine their moves within territorial boundaries. Other Majangir may also, of course, confine their settlement within a given territory, but non-'owners' appear much more ready to move from one territory to another than do 'owners', who usually prefer if possible to remain in their 'own' *dok* if they are living there. If forced to leave, for instance by a raid, they will be more likely to return than non-'owners'.

The attachment of 'owners' to their territories is therefore a real phenomenon, and different from the normal attachment – weak as it is – of all Majangir to neighbours and community. The attachment of 'owners' seems partly sentimental, partly habitual. Majangir say they feel more at home in land that is *dok babek*, as it is land with which they are familiar through growing up there. Their territory is their home, where they feel they belong. A settlement, being transient, cannot serve as the object of such attachment; a territory can.

But the attachment of 'owners' to their territories is also rooted in the concept of territorial 'ownership'. Above all, 'owners' enjoy emphasizing that they have a right to live in 'their' territory which is not derived from anyone except their 'fathers' (*babek*). Also, 'owners' enjoy the preeminence they obtain from a related fact: that others living in 'their' territory have derived the right to live there either from them, the present-day 'owners', or from the 'owners'' forefathers.

The right to live in a territory is different from property rights or agricultural rights over a homestead. A domestic group which occupies a homestead in a territory necessarily has the right to live there. If, however, the domestic group wishes to move to another territory having other traditional 'owners', it should either have a prior right to live there, or it should obtain the right through the 'owners'' explicit or implicit permission to move there.

Prior rights to settle in a territory one does not 'own' may be derived from one's own former settlement there or past settlement there by one's father or other ancestor in any line. In the latter cases one can claim the area as *dok babek*. One can even claim it as *do nak*, 'my land' or 'my territory', but this claim is recognized as different from that of the original settlers in the area, the traditional territorial 'owners'. The territory is referred to by the clan name of the 'owners', and their historical precedence is admitted. In fact, Majangir reason, the forefathers of non-'owners' living in a territory must have obtained permission to settle there from the forefathers of the owning clan segment. So, in this sense, the right of a non-'owner' to settle in a territory because it is *dok babek* may be assumed to have been ultimately derived from the 'owning' clan segment. One does not need permission to live in the territory, because one's ancestors received such permission.

Rights to settle in a territory without permission may also be claimed by persons who are related by close cognatic kinship or by marriage to members of the 'owning' clan segment.

The 'owners' of a territory therefore share their rights of settlement in the territory with three other categories of persons: (1) their kin and affines, (2) former settlers, and (3) the descendants of former settlers in the territory. Only the 'owners', however, have the right to permit others not belonging to these categories to settle in the territory. Would-be immigrants without rights to settle should ask permission of the senior men of the 'owning' clan segment.

As I have described it, the system of rights over traditional territory, and of rights to settle, is fairly clear-cut. It is based on an ideal model I extracted from knowledgeable Majangir, mostly older men, many who were territorial 'owners' themselves and intent on emphasizing the proper, formal aspects of 'ownership'.

In practice, however, the 'rights' I have described are often treated as irrelevant. Many Majangir are confused by any attempt to discuss settlement in legalistic terms, in terms of rights. They simply state that one can settle anywhere one has friends or kin or affines. Essentially this formulation is correct. For despite the convention that 'owners' permit others to settle in 'their' territories, 'owners' in fact seem never to refuse permission, and it is highly improbable that a situation could arise in which an 'owner' would refuse.

This improbability stems from the following considerations:

(1) A man normally moves only to an area where he has a friend or friendly kinsman who has invited him or accepted him as a neighbour, and the territorial 'owners' would probably never consider offending an established settler by trying to exclude his friends or kin, even if they had the force to do so.

(2) A man would not seek to move into an area where he had a personal enemy, whether or not the 'enemy' was an 'owner' of the territory.

(3) Except for personal enmity, no motive would exist for excluding anyone, as land in most territories is generally plentiful, and even if it were scarce in a particular area Majangir do not normally think of natural resources as objects of competition.

(4) 'Owners' place little value on empty land, but much value on the numerical strength of their community: like all Majangir, they believe that the more people who live in an area, the happier life is because there is more

drinking and social life, and everyone is safer because there are more men to resist attack.

If 'owners' apparently never refuse to allow new settlers into their territories, then necessarily their 'right' to permit them to settle is a very nominal right. Nor is the actual asking of permission a formal or ritualized act. A prospective settler simply informs an 'owner' that he wants to move to the territory, and this information is given and received in the same manner as if the immigrant were informing someone not an 'owner'. And in many cases, I believe, the prospective settler does not even declare his intentions directly to the 'owners', who are informed instead by others in the course of gossip.

In no case do the members of the 'owning' clan segment gather as a group for any sort of deliberation on an immigrant's intention. In fact, in no matter does this clan segment act as a group: it is a corporate entity only in concept, as related to the territory it traditionally, nominally 'owns'. According to Majangir, any 'owner' may grant permission to an immigrant to settle, but the latter would normally ask or inform the 'owners' nearest to where he wanted to live.

The same conditions, of almost purely nominal 'ownership' rights with little practical exercise, apply to *jang* rights as well as settlement rights. Ideally, the basic 'rule' is that a non-'owner' wanting to establish a new *jang* hive site in a territory should apply to the territorial 'owners' for permission. However, there are many exceptions. Anyone with the prior right to settle in a territory, whether or not he is actually settled there, may establish a new hive site there without permission from an 'owner', though ideally he should consult one first about its location. Also, anyone settling in a territory has the right, without asking permission, to put up hives in the vicinity of his homestead, and the right, after consultation with an 'owner', to put hives up at a new site elsewhere in the territory.

These exceptions leave only one category of persons who should ask permission of the 'owners' to establish a new *jang* site. These are persons living outside a territory and having no rights to settle there. Yet persons living outside a territory, unless they lived near its borders, would rarely establish a new *jang* site there. They would almost invariably prefer to put up hives at a previously established site belonging to friends or kinsmen who could watch after their hives for them.

A man not establishing a new *jang* site but putting up new hives at a previously established site of a kinsman, friend or neighbour – the normal practice – does not have to ask permission of, or consult with, the territorial 'owners'. He is sharing an old claim, not establishing a new one.

Therefore very few persons ask a territorial 'owner' for permission to take an unused area for a new hive site. I heard of several cases of such asking, and none were refused: again, as there is an abundance of possible hive sites available, there would be no reason for an 'owner' to refuse.

Others who established new sites, but who had the right to do so without asking, did not always tell the territorial 'owners' of their plans beforehand, much less let the 'owners' decide for them where they should locate their hives. They were more concerned to consult about their proposed new site with the persons who had other hive sites or homesteads nearby. These were the persons they must trust to watch out for their hives and not to rob them.

In practice, therefore, territorial 'owners' exercise next to none of their nominal 'ownership' rights, over either *jang* or settlement. Their 'ownership' of territory bears little practical resemblance to the ownership by Majangir of other things in their culture. Normally, things are owned in the sense that individuals or domestic groups have exclusive rights over them – as against other persons – and exercise these rights. But territorial 'ownership' involves what amounts to a principle of non-exclusion.

It is necessary, therefore, to analyse more closely the idiom of 'ownership' which the Majangir use in talking of territory. Territorial 'ownership' does not give 'owners' any practical power to regulate settlement, nor does it give 'owners' more influence than other Majangir in community activities. 'Owners' take no special indigenous 'political' roles different from those taken by other Majangir.

The practical content of 'ownership' seems to lie instead in the attachment of 'owners' to their territories. As I have said, they tend to remain settled within 'their' territories. They like to emphasize their special, historical relationship to 'their' territory known by their clan name. On this basis they claim a certain preeminence or prestige for themselves, which others will verbally acknowledge. Their special relationship of intimate attachment to 'their' territory is also recognized by others.

It is this attachment which is represented as 'ownership' by the Majang concept of *dumat doka*. This concept, however, includes another notion which is not adequately translated by our term 'ownership'. The opposite of *dumat* in many contexts, including settlement, is the Majang term *konat*, which usually translates as 'guest' or 'visitor'. A person who is visiting another area from his home has the status of *konat* where he is visiting, whether the visit lasts several hours or days or even months. To be a *konat* implies dependence on the hospitality of others, of one's hosts. Ideally, in Majang society a guest should be treated well by his hosts, and not be excluded from food, shelter and drink. A host is obliged to provide for his guest. Majangir have no other word for 'host' than *dumat*. A host is necessarily an owner: he owns the homestead at which a guest stays, and owns the food, shelter and drink which a guest shares. A visitor, however, owns none of these where he is visiting, which is why he must be a guest.

In speaking of settlement or territory, the term *konat* has a somewhat different meaning. A man living in an area may be called a *konat* there if he has not lived there many years. Even a man who has been living for ten or more years in a locality will refer to himself as a *konat* there if he feels he does not belong there, if he feels his primary attachment is to another territory where he plans ultimately to return.

Konat therefore implies temporary as opposed to more permanent residence, and non-'ownership' as opposed to 'ownership'. *Konat* is the opposite here of *dumat*. The two terms imply more than visitor/resident, non-'owner'/'owner': they also imply a relationship of guest/host. In fact, the Majang concept of 'territory' may be understood in terms of 'hospitality', as well as in legalistic terms of 'rights' and 'ownership'. I have mentioned how territorial 'ownership' is a non-exclusive kind of ownership. In this it does not fit the Majang concept of ownership of other things, but it does parallel the Majang concept of hospitality. A guest depends on his host for food, etc.; the host ideally provides for his guest, and does not try to exclude him; in return, the host receives recognition and prestige for being generous, for being a host. A consistently generous man who provides hospitality, frequently and for many people, will be considered *ubi*, 'big' or eminent.

Approximately the same formulation applies to territorial 'hospitality' (that is, 'ownership'). An immigrant without rights to settle is in the position of a 'guest', and is called a *konat*. He nominally depends on the territorial 'host' (that is, 'owner') for access to land; the 'host' ('owner') will always grant him such access, and not exclude him; in return, as it were, the 'host' ('owner') receives the recognition and prestige of such a status, as being *ubi*, 'eminent'. The status of *dumat doka* may therefore be translated 'host of the land' as well as its 'owner': for the status involves not the exclusion of 'guests' and non-'owners', but instead their inclusion, acceptance.

By adding the dimension of hospitality to the Majang concept of territory, we are able to understand territorial status in simpler terms than it was previously explained. In any territory there are both 'hosts' and 'guests'. The former claim their status as 'owners' of the territory by virtue of prior settlement there. They may thus be 'hosts' to immigrant 'guests' newly settling in the territory.

In addition to persons of these two statuses, there will be living in a territory a large proportion of persons of an intermediate category, combining elements of both *dumat* and *konat* status according to their attachment to the territory. If 'guests' remain long enough in the area, and come to regard it as where they belong, they gradually cease to be considered 'guests'; their descendants can claim an independent right to be settled in the territory while recognizing the historical claims of the first 'owners'. With their loss of the status of *konat* in a territory, settlers may eventually come to regard themselves as possessing a status approaching *dumat*, as minor 'owners' and 'hosts' of land within the lands claimed by the original and preeminent *duma doka*.

How this tendency works in practice will be seen in the examples I discuss below. Actual territorial arrangements in Majangirland are still more complex than I have so far presented.

The cross-section of Majangirland I can best describe is the area between the Baro and Shiri Rivers presented in Map 3. This area is generally recognized as being divided into five territories: an Anuak and a Galla territory (in both of which some Majangir live), and three Majang territories known after the clans of their first settlers – Deragir territory, Kelayir territory and Kushir territory. The boundaries of these territories are recognized by all involved, with one exception. There is disagreement about the claims and boundaries between the Deragir and the Anuak.

The Deragir claim to be descended originally from Anuak, though they retain no Anuak customs or language. They claim to have come from the south a number of generations ago. When they reached the Shiri River (Chiru in Anuak) some of them preferred to settle downstream: they remained Anuak. Others settled upriver and became Majangir, preferring, it is said, to cut forest rather than hoe grass.

Such is the tradition. Today both the Majang Deragir and several Anuak clans recognize and maintain a special, rather tenuous, relationship similar to clanship. One of these related Anuak clans, the Okuna, still live on the lower Shiri in the area nearest to Majang settlement (number 1 on map). The Deragir like to say this area is 'theirs' by reason of prior settlement. But in fact the Anuak-settled portions of the Shiri are regarded by the Anuak as 'Okuna' Anuak land, having nothing to do with Majangir. As Majang claims of territorial 'ownership' mean so little in terms of practical control over land, there is no conflict between Okuna and Deragir over these claims. Deragir do not attempt to settle in 'Okuna' land, but when in the past Anuak from other areas raided Majang settlements, Deragir sought refuge with the Okuna Anuak on the basis of their traditional clan relationship. The Okuna protected them from other Anuak. Later the Deragir returned to the upper Shiri.

The Deragir are a small clan, and male Deragir are almost all living

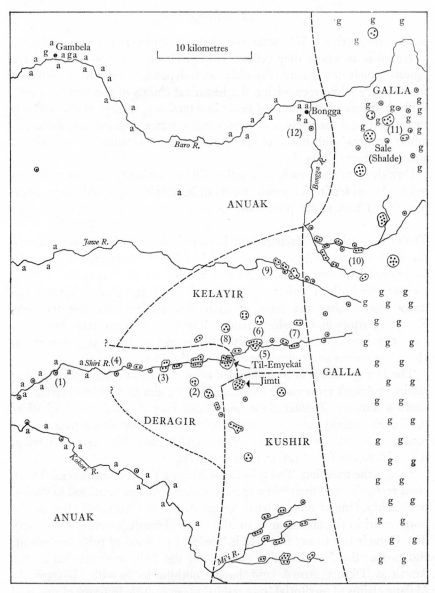

Map 3. Territory and settlement in the Baro–Shiri–Mi'i region, 1965.

Key and notes: Dots within rings indicate Majang settlement. Each dot should represent two homesteads, or an average of about eleven persons. The representation is fairly accurate as regards the settlements in the vicinity of Til-Emyekai. The further from this point, the less accurate the representation pretends to be, particularly as regards the Shalde and Mi'i areas. The populations of these further areas have been grossly estimated on the basis of short visits and general questioning of informants.

Locations of settlements, in the absence of any aerial or ground surveys or within their own territory. They intermarried in the past with the Kushir to the south and with members of other Majang clans. Members of other clans came to live with them, and the Deragir are now a small minority within their own territory. They are divided into two subclans, the Ukunayir (after those related to the Okuna) and the Umwulir (related to other Anuak clans). Deragir territory is subdivided between these two groups. The Umwulir are 'owners' of the area (number 2 on Map 3) south of the Shiri River. The Ukunayir are 'owners' of the Shiri River valley.

Whether these two 'subclans' (Majangir call them *komwoyir*, the same word as for 'clans') are the result of some sort of lineal segmentation, or rather simply a separation into clan segments according to the localities they settled, is impossible to say, as Majangir do not recall the relevant genealogical or historical information. The two groups do not claim the same rights of 'ownership' in the territories of each other as they claim in their own. On the other hand, non-Deragir do not pay much attention to this segmentation: 'Ukunayir' and 'Umwulir' are rarely heard as terms, and the entire territory is commonly known as *dok Deragirung*, as land of the whole clan.

Today there are only four male Deragir Ukunayir, out of about 150 male Majangir living in their territory. These four are a man named Pajau, his two sons and his deceased cousin's son. Pajau's eminence, as the only 'owner' of his territory belonging to the elder generation, is recognized by everyone. They acknowledge him as one who is 'big' (*ubi*). He himself is very serious, even emotional, about his 'ownership'. Speaking to foreigners, he insists they recognize his status. Once when drinking with some visiting Galla traders, he burst out passionately: *Wot epen dokeshe? Et, et, et, et, et, et, et!* – 'Who is father of this land? I am, I, I, I, I, I, I!'

Perhaps because he is the only senior 'owner' of his territory, Pajau's role seemed to me to be more pronounced than that of 'owners' I observed elsewhere. Pajau insisted that he should control settlement in his territory. Others agreed that no one without rights would settle there without asking

---

accurate maps of the area, are also meant to be approximate, dependent on my gross impressions and on information from Majangir. For the same reasons, the boundary lines drawn on this map are only approximate, which does not mean that boundaries may not be fairly exact in native eyes (see text).

This sketch-map is meant to convey informed estimates only of the distribution of Majang settlement, and should not be interpreted as demographically exact. 'a' indicates estimated extent (not density or exact location) of Anuak settlement. 'g' indicates estimated extent (not density or exact location) of Galla settlement.

Water: there exist springs and many more water-courses other than those indicated on the map. Therefore Majang settlement is possible in many areas not shown as settled in 1965. For example, the area just north of the Mi'i River was settled until recent years, when it was abandoned.

his permission. Some told how they had come to ask him. On closer inquiry, however, such asking permission appeared to be a matter more of courtesy than anything else. There was no recollection of Pajau having ever refused anyone permission to settle. He himself was proud to say that he let anyone settle in his territory: *Kwe boye jop*, 'I don't dislike people.'

Thus, as I explained earlier, such a claimed but untested right as Pajau's to refuse others permission to settle in 'his' territory seems at best a nominal right. And his boast of not disliking people is that appropriate to a host in Majang society. In fact, Pajau actively encouraged persons he liked to settle near him.

Some men living within Pajau's territory claimed their right to reside there was not derived from Pajau but from past Deragir who were their ancestors in a non-patrilineal line; or from non-Deragir ancestors who had settled in the area in the past. They claimed *dok Deragirung* as *dok babek* though they were not Deragir themselves. On the other hand, they admitted that their rights ultimately in the past were derived from Deragir, that they were once 'guests' and the Deragir their 'hosts'. They granted Pajau his status as senior Deragir *dumat* of the territory; but in practice they did not feel dependent on him or subject to him.

For instance, within Pajau's territory, the lower south side of the Shiri (number 3, Map 3) was claimed by a segment of another *komwoi*, the Jorayir subclan of the Kushir clan. They said this area was 'theirs' because their *babek*, 'forefathers', had settled there in the past. I asked them whether the same area was not claimed by the Deragir. The Jorayir admitted it was part of Pajau's territory, but said it was their territory too, as both the Deragir and Jorayir were early settlers.

There was no conflict between the two groups – who in any case had intermarried and were related – because nothing material was at stake which could have divided their interests. The Kushir Jorayir followed public opinion and deferred verbally to the Deragir, especially in Pajau's presence, acknowledging that the Deragir were the original settlers. Their claim to be 'owners' and 'hosts' of a territory within his territory did not substantially detract from his status, nor did his from theirs. Only titles were involved, and public opinion was the judge of relative precedence.

The same kind of situation, of territories within territories and occasionally also of overlapping territories, appears elsewhere in Majangirland. This situation complicates the drawing of traditional territorial boundaries on a map. A further complication is that the territorial lay-out is often differently conceived by different persons. There is no necessary consensus of Majangir, especially of those living apart, about which lands are whose, or whose claim has precedence. Any version of territorial arrangements, to be entirely consistent, must take the point of view of one informant, or of informants who agree with each other. Persons who live together will tend to agree: 'territorial' claims are apparently not important enough to quarrel over or contest. Map 3 is largely based on the views of the settlers of Til-Emyekai and nearby settlements. The boundaries might have looked somewhat different if I had composed the map from the point of view of another community.

For instance, although the Jorayir recognize Pajau's claims, no doubt because they are related to him and live nearby, the few Majangir living further downstream on the Shiri (number 4, Map 3) do not regard Pajau or the Deragir as 'owners' of their land, or their 'hosts'. Pajau regards himself as such, but since he rarely visits their area, the difference of opinion is not resolved, nor is it important.

These Majangir on the lower Shiri, who have not been settled there long, think of their territory as 'owned' by Anuak, possibly because Anuak headmen have been empowered by the government to collect taxes from these Majangir. This practical criterion sometimes has more weight in defining 'territory' nowadays than have traditions of first settlement. Later in this chapter I will return to this subject.

The territory of the Deragir is bounded on the east by the territory of the Kushir – actually of segments of its Nemeyir and Dawarir subclans only, and not the Jorayir subclan. Kushir territory covers a very large area extending further south than Map 3, beyond the Mi'i River. Within it live a great number of Kushir – probably most of the male members of the clan. The relation of the Kushir to their territory is different, therefore, from Pajau's relation to his. Many men can claim to be *dumat doka*, 'owner', and most of the population of their territory are related to Kushir by consanguineal or affinal ties which they can use to justify their rights to settle in Kushir territory. 'Ownership' does not focus on one man, as on Pajau in Deragir territory. Therefore the eminence or prestige of individual Kushir is in practice very much diluted.

Pajau, for instance, partly succeeded in assuming a role of leadership in his territory – or at least that part of it upstream where he lived. He insisted on being consulted about all important events. And specifically, he tried to control the direction of settlement in his territory, telling others where to shift their homesteads, where not to move, etc. He said that if his settlement, Til-Emyekai, had to move because of grass or shortage of land, he would 'lead' (*yange*) people to a new spot in the territory – just as he had in fact led a party of settlers back to his territory after the Anuak raids.

Other Majangir verbally acknowledged Pajau's leadership in matters of settlement. The major factor was perhaps that he had a forceful personality.

But people were not compelled, against their convenience, to obey him. There was no idea that Pajau could expel anyone from 'his' territory, or force them to do as he wanted. Consequently, in several instances during the year I lived near him, persons went against his wishes and settled where he had advised them not to settle.

The influence Pajau did exert in his territory – or rather, only that half of his territory where he lived – derived essentially from the facts that he was an older man, yet still vigorous; and that he had close relations of kinship and friendship with others living near him. It is difficult to judge the practical importance of Pajau's role as *dumat doka*, for his influence was not different from that generally exerted by older, respected men, whether 'owners' or not. The difference, rather, was in Pajau's attitude: he felt more responsible than others did for the future shape of settlement in his territory. He was concerned that people he liked remained in his territory and that they used land so as to keep together and near him. He was committed to continue living in his territory as 'guests' and non-'owners' were not.

The Kushir had the same attitudes towards their territory, which they claimed to have inhabited since time before memory. But as they were so many, none of them individually assumed particular responsibility or tried in any special way to manage settlement. Neither did they, as a clan segment, cooperate as a group in joint action. They dominated their territory in terms of population, but not in terms of any corporate control over what happened there.

Yet, as a concept, no one ever questioned the identification of 'their' territory with them, as *dok Kushirung*. Groups of various other clans had not established recognized sub-claims to parts of Kushir territory as the Jorayir had done within Deragir territory. Many non-Kushir could claim that areas of Kushir territory were *dok babek* because their 'fathers' or ancestors had lived there, but these non-Kushir were always settled near to or interspersed with Kushir. Therefore their claims did not isolate some particular areas as less exclusively 'owned' by Kushir than others, as had happened in parts of Deragir territory through the absence of Deragir.

North of Kushir and Deragir lands is Kelayir territory. The situation here in 1964–5 was similar to that in Deragir territory. The Kelayir are a large clan, but not many of them were living, or had ever lived, in this territory. The few Kelayir of the 'owning' segment all lived in one corner of the territory (number 8, Map 3). Although their forefathers had been the original settlers of the whole territory, and Kelayir 'ownership' of it was traditionally recognized, the inhabitants of the greater part of the territory nowadays use land and invite in immigrants without consulting the 'owners' and 'hosts'. As in the Deragir situation, lack of numbers, or of any real control over 'their' territory, has resulted in Kelayir claims being paralleled by other claims in certain areas.

For instance, the south bank of the Shiri (number 5 on Map 3) above Deragir territory is claimed by several Kushir Dawarir as 'theirs'. It is not *dok babek* because their fathers did not occupy it, but they themselves settled it many years ago, when no one else was living there. They are aware of the Kelayir claim to it, but when no Kelayir are present, they freely assert their status as 'hosts' and 'owners' of the land. Their children will regard the land as *dok babek*, and be confirmed in their status. The two claims, Kelayir and Kushir, co-exist; people in the vicinity recognize both, and admit either depending on whom they are talking to or what they are saying. Immigrants to the area where the Kushir Dawarir live would regard them, and not the Kelayir, as their 'hosts'. They would verbally pay homage to the Dawarir claim, and not to the historically older claim of the Kelayir.

Practically the same situation occurs on the north bank of the river (number 6, Map 3) where the Shewiyir and several other early settlers claim the territory as 'theirs' while admitting, if asked, the prior and wider Kelayir claim.

Land further up the river (number 7, Map 3) a group of Melanir Jibiyir claim as 'their' territory, in the same manner. Their senior member, a minor *tapat* named Dobun, is verbally accorded the preeminence of being *ubi*, 'big', and *dumat doka*. As Kelayir do not live here either, Dobun's preeminence in this sphere does not conflict with their own.

Other numbers appear on Map 3, but descriptions of the situations in these areas are left until after I have explained the two other types of territory recognized by Majangir: 'ritual' and 'governmental'.

3 THE RITUAL TERRITORY

In chapter 10 I discussed the importance of the ritual experts Majangir call *tapa*, especially in influencing patterns of settlement. Influential *tapa* often claim the areas around where they live as their 'territories', and these are recognized by other Majangir. For instance, the area on Godare River known as *wai Baltekaung*, 'home of Baltekan', or *dok Baltekaung*, 'land of Baltekan', is the territory (*dok*) claimed by the *tapat* Baltekan. Similarly, *dok Darbogidaung* is the territory claimed by the *tapat* Darbogidan, and so on.

Large portions of Majangirland, particularly southern Majangirland, are claimed by various influential *tapa* as their territories. In other areas, however, there are no such *tapa* to claim territory: an example is the area in Map 3 discussed in the last section. *Tapa* may live in these areas, but they are not sufficiently powerful or respected to induce the populace to recognize their claims, if they make any, to specific territories. Majangir do not identify geographical areas by the names of such weak and minor *tapa* living in them.

A *tapat*'s territory, which I will call a 'ritual territory', is distinct from the 'traditional territories' which it usually includes. A *tapat* does not claim territory on the basis of prior settlement. He does not call himself 'owner of the land' (*dumat doka*), although he claims it as 'my territory' (*do nak*). His claim is based on his ritual activities within the territory, and its inhabitants' recognition of his ritual power. They acknowledge this claim by calling him 'our *tapat*' (*tapat nangk*) and by calling themselves his 'followers' (*nyukwiyir*, sing. -*in*).

A 'follower', when threatened by an affliction, should seek the ritual services of 'his' *tapat*. A 'follower' should also pay homage to 'his' *tapat* in various ways. For instance, on every occasion he hosts a drinking party he should send the *tapat* a pot of beer or wine. He should give his *tapat* a portion of any large game he kills. He should do special work for the *tapat* and run errands whenever the *tapat* asks him. He should discuss important affairs with the *tapat*, and inform the *tapat* before moving or leaving on a long journey. He should ask the *tapat*'s blessing in matters of hunting, marriage, childbirth, death, etc. He should attend rituals designed by the *tapat* to protect all the inhabitants of the territory. He should respect the *tapat*'s exhortations and advice about various matters. It is a *tapat*'s duty, on the other hand, to help and protect his followers in any way he can – usually by ritual, but also occasionally in material and 'political' ways. All the elements involved in the relationship of *tapat* and *nyukwiyin* are too many to be detailed here, where I am interested only in the territorial aspect of the relationship.

A *tapat* may perform ritual services for 'pilgrims' who come from outside his territory to ask his help. They are often sent by their own local *tapat* as part of a sort of informal system of reciprocity among *tapa*. *Tapa* on trips outside their territories may also perform ritual for persons in the areas they visit. *Tapa* serve, and are honoured by, Majangir other than those they claim as *nyukwiyir*.

It is only the people living within his territory, however, who will regularly seek help from a *tapat* and do him homage. Indeed, it is on this basis that a *tapat* claims and defines his 'territory', and on which his claims are popularly accepted. Each *tapat* creates his own territory by attracting a congregation of 'followers', that is, regular supporters and suppliants: he may claim the areas in which they live as 'his' ritual territory. Only persons living within a few hours' walking distance from a *tapat* can become his regular supporters and suppliants. Therefore a *tapat*'s territory will tend to be no larger than his 'community' (see chapter 9), the persons living within five to ten miles of his home. Most ritual territories are in fact smaller, depending on the influence of the *tapat*, or on the nearness of different *tapa*.

Virtually everyone living within a *tapat*'s territory will claim to be his *nyukwiyir*, and most will act like such. The term *nyukwiyir* may be loosely used, however, and often men will claim to be *nyukwiyir* of a *tapat* when in his presence, even though they live too far away to help and be helped by him regularly. Also, some men may claim to be *nyukwiyir* of more than one *tapat*: for instance, of the *tapat* in whose territory they presently live, in addition to the one in whose territory they formerly lived. In practice, however, men are able to be active *nyukwiyir* only of *tapa* living near them – and primarily of the *tapat* in whose territory they reside. But in any case, most Majangir claim to be followers of only one *tapat*: the one nearest them and within whose recognized 'territory' they live.

The boundaries of a *tapat*'s territory are fairly definite, even through areas where no people live, because a *tapat* will tend to claim any land, *jang* or settlement, claimed by his followers. The boundary of 'ritual' territories therefore tend to be congruent with the boundaries of 'traditional' territories. Most 'ritual' territories subsume one or more of these territories. The two types of territory have a definite relationship, corresponding to the relationship of *tapa* with traditional 'owners'.

Majangir tell a myth explaining the origin of the Melanir clan from which most *tapa* come. The myth varies greatly according to the teller, but all agree that the first of the Melanir (on whose name they do not agree) was taken as a baby out of a rock cut open by men of the Bormayir clan. The baby then rapidly grew to be a man (some say in one day) and proved to possess the great ritual powers of a *tapat*.

The Bormayir had previously been ritual experts as well as 'owners' of the territory south of the Akobo, where the first of the Melanir was found. Now they acknowledged his superior ritual powers. He could sacrifice (*budage*) and foresee events (*laganye*) while they were 'stupid' (*gagai*) and could not. So they became *nyukwiyir* of the new (some say first) *tapat*. He superseded them as a ritual expert, leaving them only *dok*, the 'ownership' of their traditional territory. As members of other clans also became his followers, and followers of his descendants, the same relationship applied: these clans 'owned' their lands but recognized Melanir *tapa* to be superior to them.

The myth in fact describes the present-day relationship of *tapa doka* and *duma doka*. When the 'owners' of a traditional territory become, along with the others living in their territory, 'followers' of a particular *tapat* living among them or near them, they accept his superiority to them not only ritually but socially.

A *tapat*'s preeminence over ordinary Majangir is recognized in various customs. In terms of territory, the identification of the traditional territory with its 'owning' clan segment is at least temporarily submerged. Instead of being generally known by its clan name (e.g. *dok Kewetirung*) it is known by the name of the *tapat* who claims it as part of his ritual territory (e.g. *dok Baltekaung*). The conceptual map of Majangirland is affected, inasmuch as areas with influential *tapa* are associated with them and not with the traditional 'owners' of the areas.

Where a *tapat*'s claims are popularly accepted, more than the people's conceptual map changes. A change also occurs in theoretical rights to regulate settlement. Immigrants into an area who do not have a prior right to settle there ideally should apply to the area's *tapat*, and not to the traditional 'owners', for permission to settle. The same change occurs in the applying for permission to establish a new *jang* hive site. In fact immigrants usually do apply directly and almost formally to *tapa*, who have power, which traditional 'owners' do not, over the future health and welfare of people. They must mediate settlers' relations with the local god(s). The powers of *tapa*, however, to grant immigrants permission to settle and to establish new hive sites, are as nominal as traditional 'owners'' powers to do the same. Again, there is no evidence of a *tapat* ever refusing anyone permission. The *tapat* Yodn told me he would accept any settler provided they had not '*bokute meno*', 'killed a friend', because then Yodn would incur trouble from the Ethiopian government.

But in fact Yodn had accepted as settlers in his territory many killers, refugees from feuds who had sought his protection, as I described in chapter 10. In that chapter I also discussed how powerful *tapa* were able to retain the many settlers they attracted to their territories. Though they apparently never refuse permission to settle, they may and do sometimes refuse permission to leave, and their refusals carry the weight of possible supernatural sanctions against those who ignore them.

Though the traditional 'owners' of a territory lose to *tapa* both their social preeminence and their nominal right to regulate immigration, they retain the notion of 'ownership' of their territory, at least to the degree that they know they have an independent right to live where they do. Their territory, identified as it is with a continuing clan segment, is relatively permanent compared to the territory of a *tapat*, which may change or even disappear as an entity after his death.

A dead *tapat*'s name cannot be uttered for many years. Majangir may then revert to thinking of the area that was his territory in terms of the traditional territories that composed it. The 'owners' of these lands may reassert their social preeminence and their claim to regulate settlement. Traditional territories may reemerge from the dissolution of the ritual territory.

In most cases, however, a dead *tapat*'s influence is inherited eventually by a brother or half-brother, a son or sons, or infrequently a daughter. The succession of one *tapat* to the place of another is gradual, and the ritual territory which emerges may assume a different shape from before, depending on the influence gained by the new *tapat* or *tapa* involved. More than one successor may divide the territory depending on their relative powers to attract adherents. Or settlers in an area may shift their allegiance to a neighbouring *tapat*. Or, conversely, after many years a *tapat* might succeed in extending the boundaries of his predecessor's territory by gaining followers in neighbouring areas. Only in cases where no successor arises with the will and other qualities necessary to reassert his predecessor's territorial claims will the ritual territory disappear altogether.

On the other hand, in certain areas where a series of strong *tapa* have succeeded each other over several generations, the boundaries of the 'owners'' territories tend to be forgotten as irrelevant, and only vague traditions remain of who were the first settlers within the larger area of the ritual territory. An example of this situation is presented below (p. 183).

Traditional 'owners' living in a ritual territory do not resist or apparently even resent the *tapat*'s claims. In fact, 'owners' and all old settlers in a *tapat*'s territory will still claim prestige and eminence, as against more recent immigrants and 'guests'; but their claims will be based less on traditions of first settlement, than on the correspondingly long history of their loyalty, and perhaps their fathers' and grandfathers' loyalty, as followers of the *tapat* and his predecessors. The terms of settlers' attachment to an area shift from direct identification with it through claims of 'ownership', to identification with the *tapat*, or line of *tapa*, who are identified with the area.

While over territorial claims there exists no real competition or conflict between *tapat* and 'owner', or indeed between 'owner' and 'owner', a situation of real competition does exist between *tapat* and *tapat*. Traditional 'ownership' involves some prestige, but no power or material privileges. Ritual leadership, however, involves a relatively great amount of prestige, many social and material privileges, and quasi-political power. With this at stake, neighbouring *tapa* may be regarded as competing for the allegiance of settlements and territory situated between them. And *tapa* may also be regarded as competing for followers, though not territory, when they attract immigrants away from the territories of other *tapa*. This competition is muffled, covert, and perhaps not fully conscious. No open conflict appears. *Tapa* behave as a professional guild: they are circumspect in never saying bad of one another, and in maintaining polite and at least superficially cordial relations. They exchange gifts and visits as tokens of respect, and send their followers to each other on pilgrimages. Only the formality of these relations, a formality unusual in Majang society, indicates possible tension between *tapa*.

Majangir evaluate, and are attracted to, a particular *tapat* for a number of reasons: whether he seems wise, fair, 'strong', generous, etc., as well as whether his ritual seems efficacious. A *tapat* can only fill his cultural role as best he knows, and be lucky in his curing and predicting. He cannot campaign directly for followers. Majangir may decide to follow a particular *tapat* or not, presumably according to what advantages or disadvantages they believe this will entail for them. But the processes of personal or collective evaluation of *tapa* are too subtle, gradual and complex to be described, at least here.

The prestige and fame of *tapa* tend to correlate with the sizes of their territories and followings. However, a positive correlation is not necessary, and major exceptions occur. For instance, the two *tapa* most widely acknowledged in 1966 to be the 'biggest' (*ubi*) and most powerful were Burji (or Joati) of south of the Gurrafarda, and Marget (a woman) of the Sale or Shalde region of north Majangirland (see next section). Both of these *tapa* discouraged many Majangir from living near them, and in any case they both lived in areas where other tribes had taken much of the land. Their territories and numbers of regular followers were relatively small. But their prestige could be measured by the constant flow of pilgrims who came, often from great distances, to visit their shrines and ask for ritual.

Powerful and renowned *tapa* collect enough wealth and command enough labour to be able to marry and support many wives – in some cases, up to five or six wives at the same time. They tend therefore to have many children. Most of an eminent *tapat*'s children will not themselves become strong *tapa* with territories; they will instead be minor *tapa*, performing ritual occasionally but not claiming or receiving any special social or political standing. The role of a minor *tapat* is usually all they want. A major tapat's oldest son, if he is ambitious and capable, will often succeed to his father's influence, though perhaps only after a number of years. Other children may go to live in other areas where they may gain followings and territories. Otherwise, they may remain in the territory of their older brother as minor *tapa*, until perhaps after his death one of them will succeed to his influence, emerging as a major *tapat*. Who succeeds a major *tapat* depends on several factors: age and generational seniority are important, but also important are the personalities and reputations of the dead *tapat*'s siblings and children. Public opinion, as always, decides the issue: who people 'follow' determines the person who is regarded as 'powerful' and is identified with a ritual territory.

Major *tapa* usually have a number of minor *tapa* living in their territories. These minor *tapa*, some relatives and some not of the major *tapat* in whose lands they live, will necessarily follow public opinion in recognizing the ritual superiority and social preeminence of the major *tapat*. Again, they will not openly compete for power or oppose each other. It is possible for a minor *tapat*, who aspires to more power, to accept a few 'followers' (usually neighbours) who are simultaneously 'followers' of the major *tapat*; but such a minor 'following' does not result in a territory being claimed by, or identified with, the minor *tapat*. Only major *tapa* have recognized territories.

I could go much more into detail about the phenomena I have mentioned above, and about the role of the *tapat* in Majang society. But for the purposes of this chapter, it suffices to have indicated the salient features of the relationship of the *tapat* to territory.

To clarify my general description, I have added to this section the case-history of the 'ritual territory' in which I lived in 1965–6, '*Dok Yodntung*' at the confluence of the Facha'a and Bakko Rivers in southern Majangirland.

Dok Yodntung, the territory of the *tapat* Yodn, is shown in Map 4, p. 182, as it was in 1966. About seventy-five years previously, before Yodn was born, his father and his father's clan segment of Kermeyir occupied their traditional territory, co-'owned' by some Shewiyir, in the area of the hill called Gokwi on the south bank of the Bakko (M. 'Yobi') River.

It was there that Yodn's father, Kwekn, was possessed (*game*) by a *wakayo* spirit and became a *tapat*. His *wakayo* was powerful and Kwekn eventually gained a following from the people of his own and the neighbouring traditional territories shown on Map 4 (the capitalized clan names). This area became his ritual territory.

For a decade or so Kwekn and his followers were forced to take refuge from Galla raids. They settled to the north (off the map) in the Godare River area. They eventually returned to their own territories, however, and except for this interlude Kwekn lived all his life in the neighbourhood of Gokwi. When he died, this area was completely abandoned by settlement. Majangir think this necessary when an eminent *tapat* dies, to protect

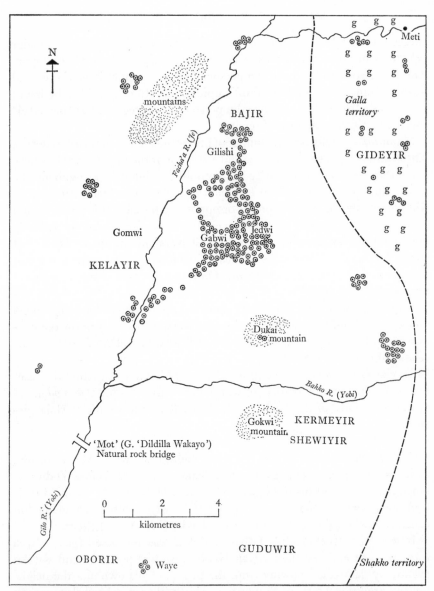

Map 4. *Dok Yodntung*: settlement in the ritual territory of the *tapat* Yodn, 1966.

Key: Dots within rings indicate Majang settlement. Each dot represents *one* homestead, or an average of five to six persons. Capitalized names indicate general locations of former clan territories. For an explanation of significance of other names, see text. The letter 'g' indicates areas settled by Galla, interspersed with some Majangir.

Notes: Much of '*dok Yodntung*' is not shown on this map, as it extends a little further to the north and south and much further to the west, where it consists mainly of savannah and grassland *jang*. All settlement in Yodn's territory is included themselves from death and misfortune. The population of the Gokwi area moved from the south bank to the north bank of the Bakko, mainly to around the hill called Dukai.

It was on Dukai that Kwekn's oldest surviving son, Deshok, established his home and *shalo*, shrine. Deshok eventually inherited the allegiance of Kwekn's followers, and maintained Kwekn's ritual territory. It was composed of the traditional territories of the Kermeyir, Shewiyir, Guduwir, Gideyir, Kelayir and Bajir clan segments, as well as part of the large Oborir territory stretching southwest (largely off Map 4) towards the Dawar River. (Other old settlers in the area were the Bongir and Namwiyir clan segments, but today no one recalls the exact locations of their traditional territories, if any.) The total territory of Kwekn and Deshok was immense, including great areas of forest *jang* to the northeast, and savannah *jang* to the west, where no one was settled. However, the population, or 'congregation', of Kwekn's and Deshok's ritual territory was by all accounts small and concentrated in settlements near to Dukai.

Deshok's settlement at Dukai was several times attacked by Galla and Shakko, causing him to move to a new settlement at Gomwi across the Facha'a (M. 'Je') River. After several years, however, he moved back to Dukai where he died in the early 1950s. After his death, of course, Dukai was totally abandoned, and also Gomwi, because he had lived there.

During Deshok's eminence, his younger half-brother Yodn had lived at the settlement called Gilishi. Yodn had maintained his own shrine, and had been followed by a neighbourhood of *nyukwiyir*. But he and his followers had also served Deshok, and had recognized Deshok's preeminence. After Deshok's death, Yodn succeeded him in his territory. The succession was accomplished easily because Yodn was already past middle age, and had already acquired a considerable reputation for ritual power.

Both his ritual power and the nearness of government 'law' and police encouraged many refugees from feuds to join Yodn's settlement at Gilishi, and later Jedwi. The nearness of *dok Yodntung* to the Galla and Amhara honey markets also encouraged immigration. These factors, which I discussed in chapter 10, greatly swelled the population living in Yodn's lands. In 1966 the immediate area around Gilishi (see Map 4) was probably the most densely settled in Majangirland, with upwards of 1,000 persons

---

in this map, however, as well as practically all of the territory which is fit for cultivation and settlement.

This is a sketch-map drawn from my own experience and crude surveying of the terrain, and it should not be regarded as precisely geographically accurate. Boundary lines are approximate, as are locations of homesteads and settlements. Numbers and gross distribution of homesteads should, however, be fairly accurate.

within about twenty-five square miles. This density was leading inevitably to land shortage and other pressures (see chapter 8) which were becoming critical at the time I left the area, and which would ineluctably cause the disintegration of Yodn's particular settlement. Yodn and his followers around Jedwi soon would have to move to another part of his territory.

By Yodn's time the 'owners' of the traditional territories had largely forgotten the exact boundaries of these territories. Nor did they retain any nominal rights to regulate settlement. They did not even refer to themselves as 'owners' (*duma*). And when asked on whose land they lived, they would say '*dok Yodntung*'. And all *dok Yodntung*, and not any special part of it, they claimed as 'their' land in the sense of it being their home. And they claimed prestige on the basis that they and their fathers had been loyal followers of Yodn, Deshok and Kwekn.

Yodn claimed territory beyond that shown on the map, but this was land without settlement, used only for bee-keeping and hunting. Directly to the north were Majangir living in a series of smaller territories of lesser *tapa* than Yodn. These *tapa*, some informants said, resented Yodn for taking away people from them; and it is true that they paid no courtesy visits to Yodn during the months I was there.

To the west of Yodn were grasslands without any inhabitants until Anuak settlements many miles down the Gilo River. The Majangir had no relations with these Anuak. To the southwest was Oborir traditional territory, one settlement (Waye: see map) of which counted itself as part of Yodn's ritual territory. The rest of the large Oborir territory, to the Dawar and beyond (off Map 4; see Map 1), belonged partly to another *tapat*'s ritual territory, and partly to an area outside any ritual territory.

Except for Waye, no Majang settlement existed south of the Bakko within Yodn's territory. The traditional territory of the Guduwir had been abandoned by even the 'owners'. Gokwi was still felt to be too dangerous to settle, though Yodn and others maintained hives there and Yodn went there once a year to sacrifice a goat to his and his father's god.

Yodn or his successor would perhaps someday approve resettlement of the Gokwi area (or Dukai area) and would probably lead the resettlement. In 1966, however, Yodn felt his home at Jedwi was still a good place to live, because there people were close to the honey markets. Yodn also had relations with the government at Meti which would probably oppose him moving south of the Bakko outside their jurisdiction. The Bakko–Gilo River is the provincial boundary between Illubabor (north) and Kaffa (south).

To the southeast of *dok Yodntung* was Shakko territory and sparse settlement. To the east was Galla and Amhara territory, at least since recent times. Highland Ethiopians had heavily immigrated into this region during the last fifteen years, with the opening of air service from Teppi nearby and the attendant markets for coffee. The highland immigrants grew this crop for cash, and other crops for subsistence. Majangir remained settled among them in many areas, but gradually land was becoming too scarce for their shifting agriculture and they had been leaving, displaced by the immigrants. Generally, Majangir did not resent or fear this trend, as they still saw plenty of land for them to go to. The spread of highland Ethiopians was also limited by tse-tse fly (see chapter 1).

Galla settlement in 1966 had penetrated into Yodn's ritual territory, the traditional territory of the Gideyir (see Map 4). The government had appointed over the Majang population in this area a *shumi* ('chief') of the 'owning' Gideyir clan segment. The government appointed another *shumi* over the Galla. Yodn therefore did not claim this area any more as 'his' (*do nak*) because he exercised no political influence there, and collected no taxes there for the government. He accepted the boundary set to his territory by the government (see dotted line, Map 4).

However, for ritual purposes Yodn was still the *tapat* of this Gideyir area, and most of the Majangir there were his *nyukwiyir* in the traditional sense, so this area could still be counted as part of his ritual territory. Why Yodn did not think of it as 'his', however, is explained by considerations I will introduce in the next section.

4 THE GOVERNMENTAL TERRITORY

Since World War II the Ethiopian government has attempted to extend its law and administration and control into Majangirland, without actually stationing administrators or police there, through the appointment of native leaders as officials responsible to the government. (This system also applies elsewhere in Ethiopia.) The title given to these native officials is, in Amharic, *bal-abbat*; or, in Galla, *shumi*. Both terms can be translated as 'chief' or 'headman'. Majangir sometimes translate these titles as *tapat*, which is the nearest equivalent in their society to the Amhara and Galla concept of 'chief'. But Majangir also distinguish between their traditional *tapat*, or *tapat wakayotung* ('*tapat* of god'), who may or may not be a government appointee, and a *tapat manggiftiung* ('*tapat* of the government', from Amh. *mangisti*, 'government'), who is not a ritual expert and traditional *tapat*. Majangir may simply call the latter a *shumi*. I shall use the term *shumi* to mean the government appointee whether he is a traditional *tapat* or not.

The government appointed many *shumi* among the Majangir, and gave to each man or pair of men a defined territory within which he or they were responsible to the government for:

(1) helping to collect an annual head-tax;

(2) maintaining order by apprehending perpetrators of serious crimes (killing or wounding a person, hunting elephant, stealing something very valuable, refusing to pay back a large debt, etc.) and taking them to the police; or, alternatively, calling the police to come;

(3) transmitting special government orders to the population;

(4) raising the supplies and labour requisitioned by government officials, including police, travelling through Majang territory.

In practice the system works unevenly. Generally, government interference in Majang life is greater, the nearer the Majang community is to government police posts and administrative centres. The more government interference, the more the man appointed as *shumi* must fill that role. Many but not all parts of Majangirland are visited once a year by a tax-gathering police expedition. The parts not reached by these expeditions are in effect not governed and have no *shumi*: these parts include the areas between the Godare and Shiri Rivers, and between the Dawar (Amh. Alanga) and Bakko–Gilo Rivers, as well as other small pockets of Majangirland. There are no 'governmental territories' in these areas.

Where the tax-gathering expeditions do go, the *shumi* takes on an important role in mediating between government forces and the Majang community. His sympathies and interests necessarily lie with the latter. A *shumi* should receive an annual small salary from the government, in proportion to the taxes collected in his territories, but in fact he receives such money irregularly, if at all. In any case, the money does not interfere with his natural loyalties.

Most Majangir in taxed areas have more or less accepted the inevitability of paying the small sum involved (Eth. \$3 to \$5). They accept also what seems worse to them: the legal requisition and illegal extortion practised by the police to obtain free food, drink and personal profit out of the expedition. A *shumi* who is a strong *tapat* is able to muster the supplies and labour requested by the police, but other *shumi* usually cannot, and the police must seize what they want.

No *shumi*, even if he wants, has the power normally to apprehend law-breakers. The Majang reaction to the various acts regarded by the government as serious crimes takes little account of government wishes. Unless they live very near to the government, Majangir handle these cases in a traditional manner: killing leads to feud, not apprehension of the initial culprit; theft leads to fighting; elephant hunting leads to nothing, etc. Only when it is convenient for them, or when they very much fear government intervention, might Majangir hand anyone over to the police – if it is possible to apprehend him and tie him up. What Majangir try to avoid most of all is a police expedition through their territory: therefore they do not usually call the police or relay information which might cause the police to come.

The *shumi* cooperates with the community in their non-cooperation with the police. The Majangir expect him to do so. From their point of view the *shumi* is their ambassador to generally hostile powers: he is the man who should find out what these powers intend, and try to ameliorate or deflect their intentions to protect his community. He cannot make other Majangir comply against their will with government wishes; nor does he want to. But in his role as representative of Majang wishes – usually the simple wish to be let alone – the *shumi* assumes a sort of political leadership in devising suitable strategies to achieve what Majangir want. Majangir tend to trust and follow him as long as they believe he is acting in their interests.

The government, on its side, can threaten or punish a *shumi* if they think he is derelict in his duties, but threats and punishments are ultimately ineffective: they simply make the Majangir afraid to deal at all with the government. Nor can the government succeed by threatening to depose the *shumi*: the office is not so desirable to Majangir that this threat is effective. And in fact the government usually would not know whom to appoint in his place, except by consulting the persons who had supported the deposed man.

Shumi appointments have apparently been made in the past by picking the man in an area whom the Majangir cite as the most important or eminent among them. Thus major *tapa* are usually *shumi* for the territories they claim. In other areas the *shumi* are usually either (1) a senior traditional territorial 'owner'; or (2) a man who understands Galla language and customs better than other Majangir. The latter may be a young man, with little actual influence in community affairs except in his role as go-between to the government. The former usually also has little real authority apart from his seniority. Only a powerful *tapat* can really mobilize and direct his people in a way satisfactory to the government. But also such a *tapat* can mobilize his people the better to resist or evade government interference.

The territories assigned to *shumi* are usually but not always congruent with the boundaries of ritual and/or traditional territories. It is unclear whether the government has actually fixed these boundaries on a map, or whether the government merely relies on its *shumi* to act within whatever areas they define for themselves. The government has little information, except from odd Galla honey-traders, as to the changing patterns of Majang settlement. Small settlements are often missed by tax-gathering expeditions which are unaware of their existence.

On the other hand, the *shumi* themselves take seriously the boundaries of their territories, partly because these are often the boundaries of ritual and traditional territories, but also because a *shumi* does not want to be held responsible for tax-paying or killing outside of his territory. Thus *shumi* are careful to delimit their territories in speaking to the police.

Majangir are in cases uncertain how the territorial principle should apply. A youth named Tigre assaulted an Anuak at a beer party. The Anuak demanded compensation, and threatened to bring the police. The beer party had been in one governmental and traditional territory, but Tigre's home was in another. As Majang disputes are settled not through territorial groups, but instead through other groups including kin, the dispute was taken to Tigre's father, who happened to be *shumi* where Tigre lived. The Anuak was dissatisfied with the small compensation given, and he later returned with the police (who were on another mission) to the area. The police took the matter to the *shumi* of the territory where the assault occurred, and accused him of being derelict in not handling the case. This procedure somewhat surprised the Majangir, who had not thought jurisdiction necessarily belonged within the territory a 'crime' was committed.

In some cases ritual and traditional territorial boundaries have tended to adjust to fit the boundaries drawn for tax-paying, as well as vice versa, possibly because tax-paying is a more concrete act than vague acknowledgements of traditional or ritual primacy. Men who pay their taxes through a *tapat* or traditional 'owner' tend to regard themselves as resident in the ritual or traditional territories of these *shumi*, simply because they confuse these territories with the governmental ones.

In the previous section I mentioned how the *tapat* Yodn no longer counted Gideyir lands (see Map 4) as 'his' territory even though most Majangir from there still acted as his ritual followers. Yodn excluded this area perhaps because he took seriously the boundaries given him by the government, who assigned a man of the Gideyir 'owning' clan segment to be *shumi* for Majangir in that area. But it is more likely that Yodn wanted to exclude the area because of the many Galla living there under the Galla *shumi*, whose political authority Yodn would not have liked to appear to challenge.

Yodn did claim as his territory lands south of the Bakko–Gilo River, which were in another Ethiopian province and therefore technically outside his 'governmental' jurisdiction. Yodn did not understand this situation when Galla traders told him. In any case, only a few families lived there, and were not bothered to pay taxes by Yodn or anyone else, so the question never arose. But Yodn claimed he was *shumi* of this area, for he equated this office with his position of *tapat*.

The interrelations of ritual, traditional and governmental territories frequently show such complications. To illustrate these interrelations, I will return to the analysis I began in section 2 of the territorial framework of the Baro–Shiri region shown in Map 3 (p. 170).

The Kushir traditional territory shown on this map is identified by Majangir with a governmental territory. Two Kushir men of 'Jimti' settlement are appointed as co-*shumi* of the area by the government. However, government forces never venture further than Jimti, which is the settlement in Kushir territory nearest the Shiri. Therefore only the populace of Jimti pays taxes, and Majangir to the south in Kushir territory do not. 'Governmental' territory is therefore actually limited to the Jimti region.

In Deragir territory Pajau (see above, section 2) is *shumi* of the upper Shiri, and a man of the Deragir Umwulir subclan is *shumi* of the area south of the Shiri, corresponding to their traditional claims. Majangir of the lower Shiri River area (numbers 1 and 4, Map 3) pay taxes to an Anuak *shumi* and regard themselves as belonging to the traditional territory of this man's Anuak clan – in contradiction to Pajau's unenforceable claims.

In Kelayir territory the *shumi* are the eminent men of various localities within the whole territory. An 'owner' is regarded as *shumi* for the small area in which Kelayir are actually living (number 8). A man of the Shewiyir clan segment is *shumi* for the areas (5) and (6); and Dobun of the Melanir for area (7). (Cf. description above, section 2, of their other claims.)

On the Jawe River (number 9) a man named Opungke is *shumi*. He is a very minor *tapat*, son of another minor *tapat*, now old and blind, living in Til-Emyekai in 1965. Neither Opungke nor his father, however, ever claimed a ritual territory: their supernatural powers are thought to be weak (*balang*). Opungke, however, makes immense claims to leadership on the basis of his unique experience of serving with the Allied troops who occupied Gambela and Gore during World War II. Opungke is more world-wise than other Majangir, speaks Galla fluently, and is well known to local government officials and to Galla in general.

These facts give Opungke much more influence than he could claim on the basis of traditional position, ritual power or seniority. The other *shumi* of the Shiri region often let Opungke represent them in governmental affairs, which he enjoys but they do not. Officials and police also prefer to deal with him, as he is familiar to them and speaks their language. Therefore Opungke often acts as he claims to be – a sort of super-*shumi* of the whole Shiri–Jawe region. But the government also recognizes the other men, noted above, as *shumi* of the several localities of this region. In fact the latter have more influence with the Majangir of their territories than does Opungke, whose contacts with Galla and claims to authority Majangir regard with some distrust. Despite Opungke's ambitions, which are perhaps nurtured by his close observation of Anuak and Galla chiefship, Majangir let him lead them only in matters involving foreigners or foreign concepts with which they cannot cope.

West of Kelayir territory is territory traditionally owned by the Galla. Majangir have settled there only within the last generation. None of them claims 'ownership' of the land they live in, but say they have the permission of the Galla to settle there. Majangir settled in the Bongga River Basin (10) are independent of much interference by Galla as this area is too low and tse-tse fly infested for the latter to settle. There is no major *tapat* in this area, so there are neither ritual nor traditional Majang territories. The area is instead parcelled into several small governmental areas, each with a *shumi* who speaks Galla. These men are responsible to Galla *shumi* living up the mountains from them.

North of the Bongga, on top of the Plateau, is the region known to Galla as Sale and to Majangir as Shalde (number 11). Many Galla inhabit this area, and Majangir are late-comers dependent on the Galla for their rights to settle there. The two populations live in separate but nearby settlements.

In Shalde, therefore, no 'traditional' Majang territories exist. However, several important *tapa* live in the area, each claiming a small territory both in a ritual and a governmental sense. They collect taxes, etc., from their ritual followers. They claim to be *shumi* as well as *tapa*.

The most renowned and powerful *tapat* of the Shalde region is the woman Marget who does not claim to be a *shumi*. She lives among the Galla, who reportedly respect her ritual powers as much as Majangir do. Marget has few followers living near her, but she derives tribute and service from the many Majangir who journey to her on pilgrimages.

West of Shalde on the lowlands live mainly Anuak, a few Galla and Koma, and a few Majangir (number 12). This territory is regarded as traditionally Anuak, and the Majangir living there are under Anuak chiefs in all matters.

North of the Baro (off Map 3), in the foothills of the Anfillo and 'Sholan' areas and towards Dembidollo in Wallaga province, are other large settlements of Majangir grouped into ritual and governmental territories. As in Shalde, there are no Majang traditional territories, for Majangir have only recently moved into these areas 'owned' by other tribes, Mao, Galla and Koma.

Although I have not had the space to describe fully the relations of Majangir to the Ethiopian government, or to their *tapa*, I have tried to outline the territorial systems which arise from these relations. The significance of the governmental territory, as well as of the ritual territory, has been relatively easy to assess; less so, the significance of the traditional territory.

In addition to my earlier analysis of the significance of the different types of territory in Majang society, I should like to stress one other point. Territory is important to Majangir in its conceptual use by them. By identifying particular geographical areas (territories) with particular social groups (clan segments) or persons (*tapa, shumi*), Majangir are able to conceive some order within the drastically changing patterns of Majang settlement, the constant shifting and moving of people described in earlier chapters.

The territorial framework remains relatively unchanged by this flux: territories possess both definition and continuity – as settlements, neighbourhoods and communities do not. Of course this stability is only relative; there is change also in the territorial framework. I have described the changes which occur in ritual territories: their definition and continuity depend largely on the lives and personalities of individual *tapa*, although a dynastic element is also present.

Traditional territories seem more permanent, inasmuch as they are identified with self-perpetuating clan segments whose claims and relationships to their territories are theoretically also perpetual. It is difficult to imagine that the traditional territorial framework does not change over time, and that territorial claims are not gradually readjusted to reflect changing facts of settlement. Lacking deeper historical information, however, it is impossible to verify these suspicions.

But in any case such changes in traditional and even ritual territorial arrangements are largely irrelevant from the point of view of the individual Majang. Whatever changes occur, they must be too few and gradual to interfere seriously (except at the death of a major *tapat*) with this individual Majang's conception, illusory or not, of the geography around him and of all Majangirland, as ordered into defined, stable, named spatial units – that is, territories.

Territory involves not only a conceptual continuity, a tying of names to places, but also a real continuity of settlement. The men who are identified with the territories they 'own' may not exercise any significant control over 'their' lands, but their nominal 'ownership' reflects their long-term attachment to their territories, and in fact there exists a definite tendency for them to remain settled within their territories. Over generations, in many territories this tendency may give an actual continuity to settlement, as lines of 'owners'–'hosts' constitute stable cores of settlers about whom, and in relation to whom, more transient settlers come and go as their 'guests'. In ritual territories, lines of *tapa* may provide a similar continuity.

12

CONCLUSIONS

In the introductory chapter to this monograph, I stated that my subject was the social aspects of land use among the Majangir, or the spatial aspect of their society. In this closing chapter I would like to summarize the important points of my analysis on these lines.

The two key ecological factors, or conditions, in Majang land use and socio-spatial organization, I would isolate as:

(1) the abundance of land, and the absence of population pressures on vital natural resources;

(2) the particular system of shifting field agriculture practised by the Majangir.

These two conditions are of course interrelated, as a certain abundance of land is necessary to the agricultural system, but the system itself partly determines what may be called 'abundance'. Nevertheless, it is useful to state separately these two points, as land abundance is an exogenous factor to Majang culture, whereas of course the agricultural system is not.

In summation, I would like to relate the two above conditions to other features of Majang social and spatial organization.

The domestic organization of the Majangir is obviously tied into their system of cultivation. An important part of domestic organization is the organization of labour for agriculture. The small size and economic independence of the Majang domestic group is made possible by the nature of Majang shifting cultivation, which does not inherently require the co-operative labour of a larger group of persons. The Majang domestic group may consist, as it normally does, of the nuclear family.

The agricultural system may also be thought of as part of domestic organization to the extent that problems of agriculture are solved through domestic arrangements – as, for instance, through the spatial arrangement of huts. Huts are situated primarily to guard the fields as required in Majang agriculture. Eating, sleeping and other kinds of domestic intercourse are in turn arranged in a way which not only fits the arrangement of huts, but finds this arrangement useful for other than agricultural purposes. For instance, the separation of huts within the homestead is not only convenient for guarding the fields, but also convenient for observing the cultural avoidance of certain males and females eating and sleeping together.

Conclusions

The insubstantial nature of Majang housing can also be related to their shifting field system. And the nature of the housing again affects domestic and neighbourhood intercourse in many ways: for instance, in the difficulty of maintaining secrecy in eating, brewing drink, etc. This difficulty makes it practically inevitable that neighbours should be well-informed of each other's activities; and, given Majang attitudes towards sharing, that sharing should be such an important part of neighbour relations.

However, neighbour relations are more directly related to the Majang system of cultivation. As each domestic group maintains its residence within its fields to guard them, households are necessarily separated and 'villages' do not arise. Furthermore, as fields must shift and residences must shift with them, a 'neighbourhood' as a physical site is very temporary. As a set of spatial relations between domestic groups, it may be less temporary, for neighbours may shift residence more or less together in the same direction. But neighbourhood in this sense is contingent on the diverse wills of the domestic groups concerned. They are not bound in neighbourhood by necessities of fixed property, labour cooperation, etc.: they are neighbours by choice.

Their choice is guaranteed by the abundance of land in Majangirland. There exist, ecologically, a practically unlimited number of alternative sites to which a domestic group may move. Socially, the alternatives are more limited but still very wide. Rights to land are easily acquired, and there are few barriers of a jural or political kind to freedom of movement and settlement within Majangirland. The abundance of crucial natural resources for Majangir is coupled with their virtually free access to them.

The availability of land allows mobility, and other factors encourage it. Among these are ecological factors related again to the Majang system of shifting field cultivation. As a result, Majangir frequently move residence. Their mobility is an important condition in all their social relations.

By moving, Majangir may leave neighbours they do not like. In moving themselves, or inviting others to move near them, Majangir may largely choose for neighbours those they like. Friendship is translated into neighbourhood. Neighbour relations therefore tend to be close, 'like kinship' to Majangir, and are expressed in much sharing of things. Because much is expected of neighbours, however, when disaffection occurs neighbours are impelled to move or shift apart.

Spatial distance is continually adjusted to accord with 'social distance', or friendly relations. This is true also outside the sphere of neighbourhood in regard to very unfriendly relations. Serious disputes, especially those involving killing, often end in the distancing of the disputants, the greatness of the distance tending to reflect the gravity of the conflict. The possibility of 'settling' disputes by moving may be seen as probably related to the underdevelopment of other institutional means in Majang society for keeping the peace. Mobility suffices.

However, a state of feud is one of the few important factors which restricts the mobility of Majangir. Those involved must not only avoid settling near their enemies, but to feel safe they must also settle either under the protection of a feared *tapat* or together with their close kin, or both.

Kin tend to come together when in trouble. In the last resort, they recognize a moral obligation in kinship which is binding and permanent in a way neighbourhood and friendship are not. Kin should be friends and neighbours, but in fact under normal conditions of mobility they tend to drift apart. Outside of the domestic group and elementary family, they are not bound together by any corporate interest in property – which again may be seen as a concomitant of their modes of subsistence and of the absence of competition for natural resources.

Local groups are therefore not kin groups. Neighbourhoods contain friends and friendly kin, but neighbourhood composition shows no particular structure. A neighbourhood in fact is usually not a discrete unit but rather an ill-defined sphere within which certain forms of behaviour tend to operate. A settlement is an ecologically discrete aggregate of homesteads linked by adjacent fields. But socially or politically it has no significance, and may best be regarded, if small, as a neighbourhood, or, if larger, as a series of overlapping spheres of neighbourhood.

The social insignificance of the settlement in Majang society is related to its impermanence under the conditions of the Majang system of shifting cultivation. The Majang system in practice is incompatible with the stability or continuity, in form or composition, of any discrete local unit of population. Stability of settlement is further impaired by mobility from other causes.

The temporary and volatile nature of settlement among the Majangir renders impossible any allegiance or attachment to local groups, as groups. Instead, the long-term attachments of Majangir are to kin and clan, who are dispersed but at least ideally permanently related; or perhaps to individuals, such as *tapa*; or perhaps to territory. All of these provide foci of continuity in Majang society. In the present work I have dealt fully only with territory; I have dealt with kinship, clanship and *tapa* only in their spatial aspect, i.e. in regard to homestead, settlement and territory.

Territory in Majang society is only indirectly linked to indigenous political organization. Owing to the abundance of land, territorial claims do not involve aggression or competition for natural resources. The significance of territory is in settlement, but not in its restriction. The powerful *tapat* especially, and to a lesser degree the traditional territorial 'owner', attempt to attract population to 'share' their territories. Indeed, one can say that all Majangir try to attract persons to settle near them – persons they like. Only *tapa* and some *duma doka*, however, think in terms larger than neighbourhood, because the former are concerned with having large followings for prestige, while the latter are concerned (though less so) with the state of community in their territories, as they tend to feel committed to living there.

For various reasons, usually expressed in the idiom of drinking, Majangir generally value large communities: the settlement of many people within a limited radius. Powerful *tapa* may attract very large communities. Otherwise, as is apparent from Map 3 and from my descriptions, most Majangir actually live in fairly scattered settlements. Even the large communities around *tapa* are held together only temporarily, and partly by ritual sanctions.

This contradiction between what Majangir would like – larger community life – and what they achieve in their settlement is partly explicable in terms of their system of agriculture. By adhering to the need to shift fields yearly and to leave old fields to fallow many years, Majangir cannot achieve in an area a permanent density of population above a certain level. This level is further reduced by Majang preferences for being very close to water, game, forest products, etc.

Abundance of land offers Majangir many alternatives as to where they may settle. But their system of shifting field cultivation very much restricts the alternatives as to what forms their settlement may take.

These two factors, and the consequences which arise from them, have been the underlying theme of this study. By confining the analysis largely to this theme, I have neglected or merely touched on other aspects of Majang society. But in this work I have attempted to lay the necessary groundwork for further analysis of Majang society.

BIBLIOGRAPHY

A. REFERENCES CITED IN THE TEXT

Bohannon, P. 1963. '"Land", "Tenure" and Land-Tenure', pp. 101–11 in *African Agrarian Systems*, ed. D. Biebuyck (London)

Bryan, M. A.: see Tucker, A. N.

Cerulli, E. 1956. *Peoples of South-west Ethiopia and its Borderland*, Part III of *Ethnographic Survey of Africa, North-eastern Africa*, ed. D. Forde (London)

Cheshire, F. R. 1888. *Bees and Bee-keeping*, II (London)

Conklin, H. C. 1957a. *Hanunoo Agriculture* (Rome)

Conklin, H. C. 1957b. 'Population–Land Balance under Systems of Tropical Forest Agriculture', pp. 63 ff. in *Proceedings of the Ninth Pacific Science Congress of the Pacific Science Association*, VII (Bangkok)

Conklin, H. C. 1961. 'The Study of Shifting Cultivation', pp. 27–61 in *Current Anthropology*, II, no. 1

Corfield, F. D. 1938. 'The Koma', pp. 123–65 in *Sudan Notes and Records*, XXI

Evans-Pritchard, E. E. 1940. *The Nuer* (Oxford)

FAO. Food and Agricultural Organization of the United Nations. 1961. *Agriculture in Ethiopia* (Rome)

Fortes, M. 1949. *The Web of Kinship among the Tallensi* (London)

Fortes, M. 1958. Introduction to *The Developmental Cycle in Domestic Groups*, ed. Jack Goody (Cambridge)

Greenberg, J. H. 1963. 'The Languages of Africa', in Part II of the *International Journal of American Linguistics*, XXIX, no. 1

Jenyns, F. G. 1886. *A Book about Bees* (London)

Last, G. C. 1962. 'The Geography of Ethiopia', pp. 82–134 in *Ethiopian Observer*, VI, no. 2 (Addis Ababa)

Leach, E. R. 1961. *Pul Eliya* (Cambridge)

Lyth, R. E. 1947. 'The Suri Tribe', pp. 106–14 in *Sudan Notes and Records*, XXVIII

Montandon, G. 1913. *Au Pays Ghimirra* (Neuchâtel)

Pelzer, K. J. 1957. 'Land Utilization in the Humid Tropics: Agriculture', pp. 124–43 in *Proceedings of the Ninth Pacific Science Congress of the Pacific Science Association*, XX (Bangkok)

Radcliffe-Brown, A. R. 1950. Introduction to *African Systems of Kinship and Marriage*, ed. A. R. Radcliffe-Brown and Daryll Forde (London)

Schapera, I. 1956. *Government and Politics in Tribal Societies* (London)

Schlippe, P. de. 1956. *Shifting Cultivation in Africa: The Zande System of Agriculture* (London)

Tucker, A. N., and M. A. Bryan. 1956. *The Non-Bantu Languages of North-Eastern Africa*, Part III of *The Handbook of African Languages* by the same authors (London)

Watters, R. F. 1960. 'Some Forms of Shifting Cultivation in the Southwest Pacific', pp. 35–50 in *The Journal of Tropical Geography*, XIV

Bibliography

B. PREVIOUSLY PUBLISHED MATERIAL ON THE MAJANGIR

Very little material exists which deals with the Majangir, and the value of this material is very limited. The two most informative articles are:

Brotto, E. 1947. 'I Magianghir', pp. 86–96 in *Rassegna di Studi Etiopici*, VI, no. 1 (Rome)

Cerulli, E. 1948. 'Il linguaggio dei Masongo nell'Etiopia occidentale', pp. 131–66 in *Rassegna di Studi Etiopici*, VII, no. 2 (Rome)

Both of these articles, however, are misleading in part.

An item under the title 'The Ujang Tribe' appears on pp. 169–70 of *Sudan Notes and Records*, V, no. 3, taken from a government 'intelligence report' of March 1922. This intelligence consists apparently of Anuak misrepresentations of Majang customs, and is fairly useless.

Scattered references to the Majangir appear in writings on neighbouring tribes such as the Mekan, Suri, Gimirra, Anuak, etc. However, with the exception of the work by Montandon cited above under Part A, the amount of information these sources give is nominal and usually ill-founded, based on rumour rather than on observation.

For bibliographies dealing with other tribes in the region, I refer the reader to the *Ethnographic Survey* volume by Ernesta Cerulli cited under Part A; as well as the 'North-East Africa' section of the *African Bibliography Series* published by the International African Institute (London, 1959).

INDEX

affines, 6, 122, 155, 165; as members of same domestic group, 54–5, 65–7, 72, 73–5, 96–7, 103; eating avoidance, 92, 103, 114; and neighbours, 114, 117

aime, see shifting cultivation: field types

Amhara, 2, 4, 13, 19, 24, 143, 151, 152, 183, 184–5

Anuak, 1, 2, 3, 12, 13, 15, 17, 20, 31, 107, 142, 148, 169, 170, 171, 173, 184, 185, 187, 190

apiculture, 21–3, 135, 160–1; and mobility, 22–3, 141–2; *see also* honey, *jang*

beer, 19, 41–2, 47, 68; collective activity, 135–6; and community, 134–7; preparation, 49, 94; *see also* drinking, working parties

bori, see shifting cultivation: field types

bridewealth, 6, 20, 54–5, 72, 74, 86, 113–14, 145; amount of, 21

butan, see shifting cultivation: field types

chief, *see tapat*

children: adolescents, 69–70, 87–9, 91; in subsistence activities, 54, 62, 67–8, 71

clans (*komwoyir*), 6, 122, 194; subclans, 169–74, 189; and territory, 163–6, 169–75, 178, 191; of *tapat*, 177

coffee, *see kari*

community, 134–7, 142, 162, 165, 195; and sharing beer, 136–7; *tapat's*, 177, 195

cooking, 41, 43, 47, 48–9, 89–90, 91–2, 94; *see also* eating, gathering

corporate groups, 51, 61, 121, 163, 166

co-wives, *see* marriage

disputes: causes, 7; settlement, 7, 143–5, 193–4; *see also* feuds

divorce, *see* marriage

domestic group: composition of, 54–61, 62–75, 97, 100, 105–6; core and attached members, 60–1, 72; developmental cycle of, 53–4, 61–4, 67–75; and kinship, 97, 100, 106; and labour, 51, 64, 135–6, 158–61, 192; Majang model of, 53–4, 57, 59, 76–7; mobility as a unit, 122, 123–5, 147; and neighbourhood, 109, 116–17, 121, 122; and nuclear family, 51, 53–5, 57, 192–4; obligations within, 46–51, 55–6, 64–5, 68, 100, 105; and pooling of food, 47, 48; property of, 51, 71–5, 97, 158; rights to land, 158–9; and settlement,

122, 123; sharing between, 91, 93, 97–100, 102–3, 110, 111; and territory, 158; *see also* eating, homestead, sexual division of labour, sleeping

drinking, 7, 19, 134–6, 148–9; *see also* community, working parties

eating, 41–4, 48, 77, 83; avoidances in, 77, 90–1, 92, 103, 114–15; eating groups, 92, 102; etiquette, 93; sharing meals, 90; and sleeping groups, 92–3, 110; *see also* cooking

ecology, *see* apiculture, environment, fishing, hunting, mobility, settlement, shifting cultivation

environment, 10–12, 15, 17, 19, 22, 23, 27–9, 31, 36, 39, 162

Ethiopian government, 2, 5, 13, 19, 143–4, 151–2, 173, 185; and *shumi*, 185–90; and *tapat*, 178, 183, 184, 187, 188

family: extended, 72–5, 102–3; nuclear, 45, 51, 52, 53, 55, 57, 59, 61–3, 68, 77, 192, 194; parents and children, 55–6, 70–2; residential dispersal of, 154–6; *see also* domestic group, marriage

feud, 7, 148; and kinship, 115, 156, 194; and mobility, 7, 100, 144–5, 151, 154, 156, 193–4; and neighbourhood, 115; refugees from, 97, 150, 178, 183; and *tapat*, 150, 178, 183, 193

firewood, 30, 32, 84–5, 160

fishing, 17–18, 41–3, 47, 159

food, *see* cooking, eating

forest, 12, 15, 17; and *gedi* field, 27, 36–8, 40; *see also jang*, shifting cultivation

friendship, 71, 146; and mobility, 124, 145–7; and neighbourhood, 122, 146–7, 193; and settlement, 124

Galla, 1, 2, 3, 4, 13, 19, 20, 24, 31, 107, 142, 151, 152, 169, 170, 171, 181, 182, 183, 184–5, 187, 188, 189, 190

gathering, 24–5, 47, 160

gol, see shifting cultivation: field types

homestead: abandonment of huts, 82, 142; affiliation to, 82; definition, 53, 76–7; dispersal of huts, 31, 107, 123, 192; hut-types, 31, 52, 76–7, 80–6; number of huts, 82–3; plans of actual and ideal homesteads, 78, 95, 98, 99, 101, 104; rights in

198

Index